IMAGES
*of America*

# TRUMBULL

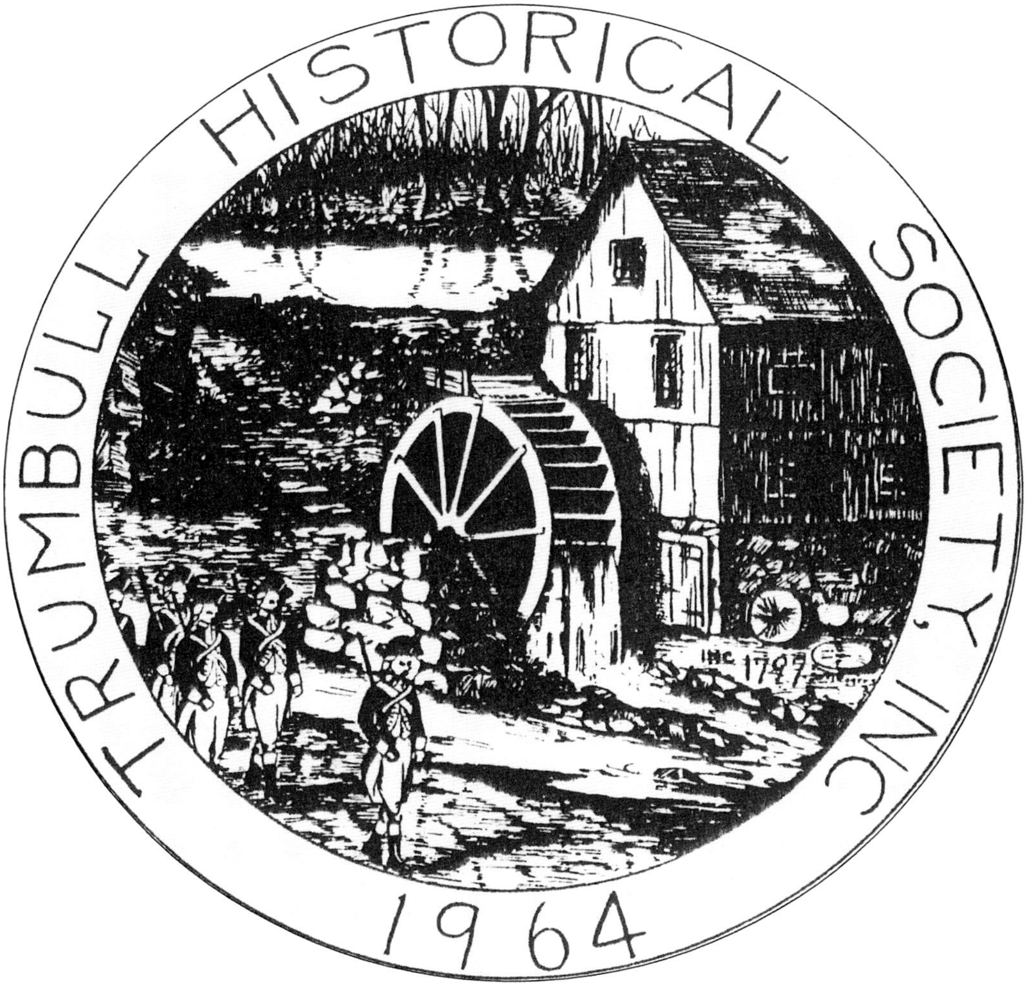


The Trumbull Historical Society has come a long way from a cold December night in 1963 when Trumbull's first selectman, at the urging of Town Historian E. Merrill Beach, called a meeting of interested townspeople with the express purpose of forming a local historical society. By March 1964 bylaws were written and officials elected, and the fledgling society got off to a good start with 225 charter members.

It maintains a museum and research center at the Society House located at 1856 Huntington Turnpike. The Society's members actively support its mission to preserve, document, and protect the educational and historical heritage of the town of Trumbull. The Society is an active part of the community, sponsoring an annual antiques show, student tours, an ice cream social, scholarships, and educational trips and programs.

The Trumbull Historical Society has come a long way in thirty-three years.

IMAGES
*of America*

# TRUMBULL

Trumbull Historical Society Book Committee:
Lois Levine, chairman
Paula Neumann, co-chairman
Paul Corban
Karen DiEmma
Dorothy Healy
Louise Jacques
Dorothy Koger
Gloria Murphy

ARCADIA
PUBLISHING

ISBN 978-0-7385-3458-9

Published by Arcadia Publishing
Charleston, South Carolina

Printed in the United States of America

Library of Congress Control Number: Applied for

For all general information contact Arcadia Publishing at:
Telephone 843-853-2070
Fax 843-853-0044
E-mail sales@arcadiapublishing.com
For customer service and orders:
Toll-Free 1-888-313-2665

Visit us on the Internet at www.arcadiapublishing.com

*To Trumbull's people past, present and future:*
*"It is a town to live in, a town to remember, a town to love."*

*—E. Merrill Beach, 1955*

# Contents

# Acknowledgments

This book would not have been possible without the cooperation and contributions of many individuals who shared their memories and recollections. Special thanks go to Raymond Beckwith, Raymond Cable, Katherine Shelton Curtis, Vera Eck, Millicent Lenhard, Barbara Linsley, Dan Neumann, Sara Neumann, Dale Radcliffe, Margaret Schneider, and the writings of E. Merrill Beach, Helen E. Plumb, Dorothy Seeley, Earle Sullivan, and Lora Freer Wachenheim.

# Introduction

The accuracy of a town's history is only as good as the effort that is made to preserve it for future generations. Through the years Trumbull has been lucky to have had town officials and residents willing to record its important moments as well as its everyday life.

In this century in particular, we have benefited from community-minded residents who photographed the town, researched Trumbull's history, and shared the stories they knew with enthusiasm and joy. Among these individuals are writer Dorothy Seeley, businessman and historian E. Merrill Beach, and longtime town clerk Helen Plumb. We also are indebted to the many residents who contributed family photographs and mementos to the Trumbull Historical Society, whose archives supplied the pictures in this book.

While we can only imagine what life was like for the town's earliest settlers some three hundred years ago, official records and early historians provide us with a "picture" of those early years. The area we now know as Trumbull was first settled in the late 1600s, as residents from the Society of Stratford, which had been established in 1639, sought a less "crowded" place to live. In 1725 they founded the Parish of Unity in the area that is now known as Nichols. The first church, Unity Congregational Church, was established in 1730. Expansion was continuing elsewhere also, with residents from other areas settling into what is now Trumbull Center around 1705, as well as Long Hill and then Tashua.

In 1744 the Parish of Unity joined with Long Hill to become North Stratford. All that time, North Stratford remained under the governmental control of Stratford, but by the late 1700s, local residents decided North Stratford had grown sufficiently and that trips to attend meetings in Stratford had become burdensome enough that they began petitioning the state to become incorporated as a separate town. After repeated requests, the General Assembly granted the petition, and the Town of Trumbull, named for the well-known family that included Revolutionary War Governor Jonathan Trumbull, was incorporated in October 1797.

Now Trumbull is celebrating its bicentennial year, having progressed to become a modern, suburban town of 32,000 residents. Growth has brought with it enormous changes, both positive and negative. Once a rural farming community at the turn of the century, Trumbull is now home to a combination of residential and corporate interests. While the town is nearly fully developed, local officials have taken care to preserve its open space through expansive parks and recreation areas.

Trumbull is a town that still treasures its past and appreciates the link that binds us to those who came before us. Maintaining that link gives us a better understanding of who we are and where we came from. As our contribution in this bicentennial year, we have compiled this pictorial history of Trumbull, for those who live here now, and for those yet to come.

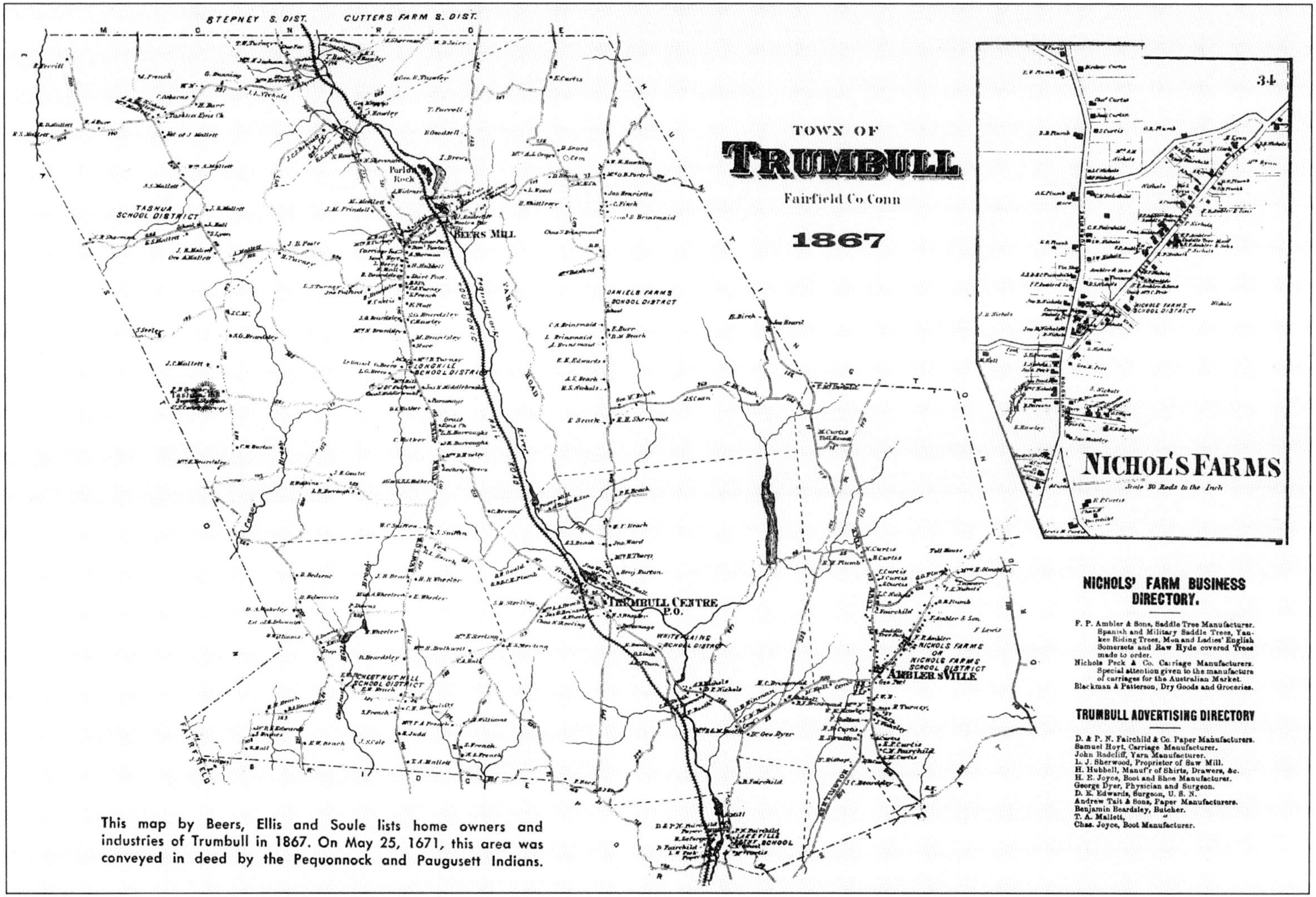


This map by Beers, Ellis and Soule lists home owners and industries of Trumbull in 1867. On May 25, 1671, this area was conveyed in deed by the Pequonnock and Paugusett Indians.

# *One*

# Glimpses of Yesterday

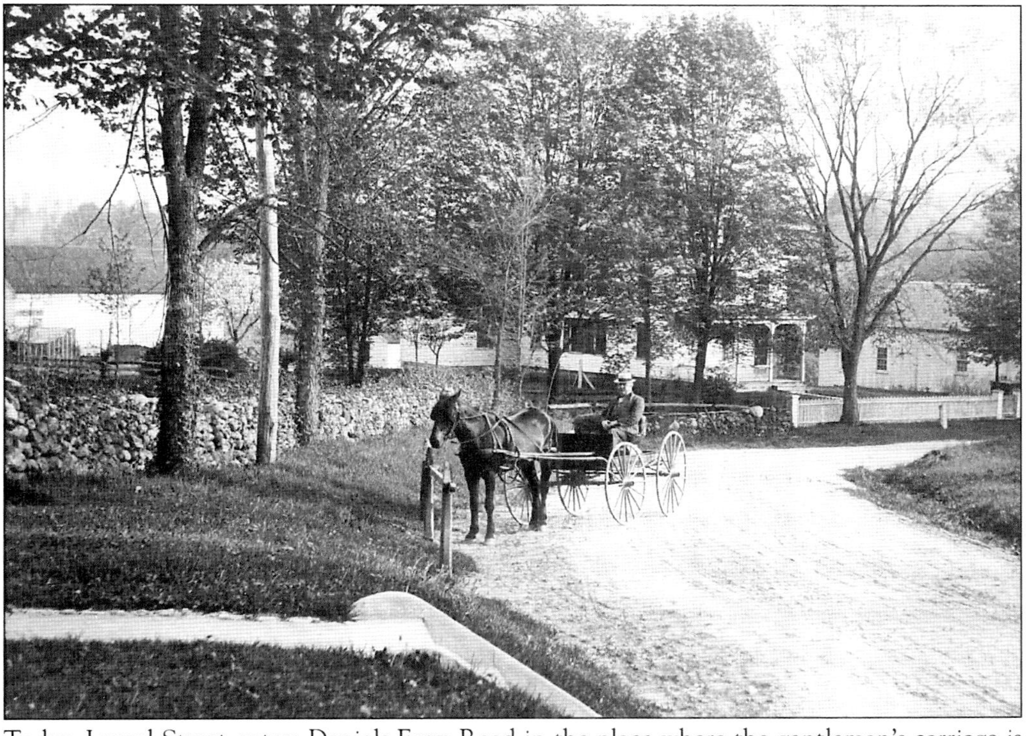

Today, Laurel Street enters Daniels Farm Road in the place where the gentleman's carriage is hitched in this photograph. The house in view belonged to the Laufer family. Their property extended to the Pequonnock River, where they operated a small mill.

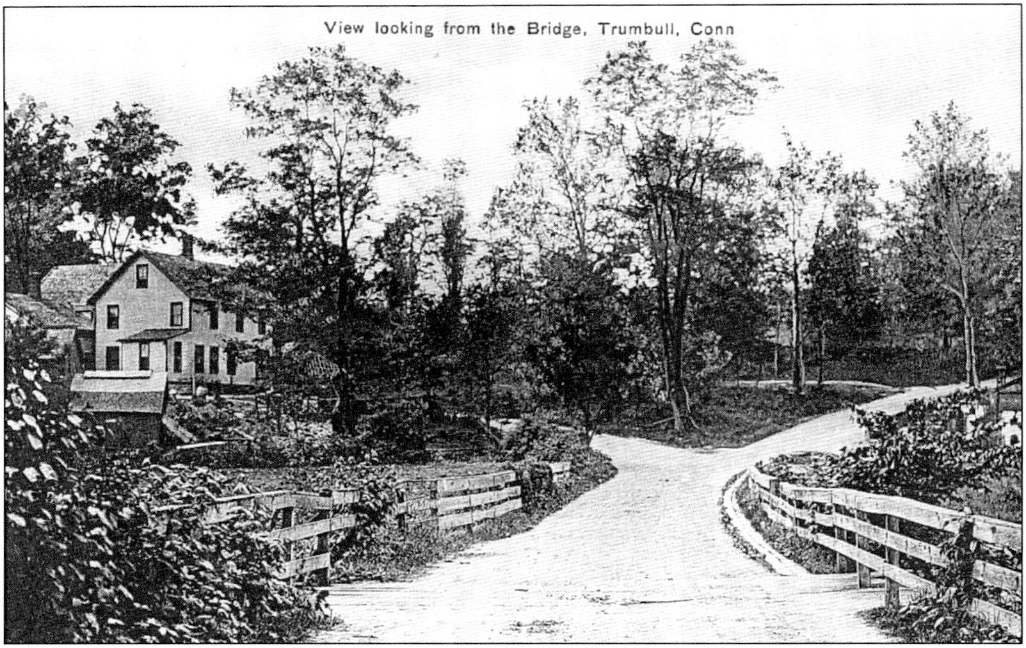


Looking toward White Plains Road from Daniels Farm Road, one certainly sees a very different view today. The green at the intersection is now just a shadow of its former self. What appears to be a house on the left is actually the rear of Parks' (later Kurtz's) Store, which is now a gas station.

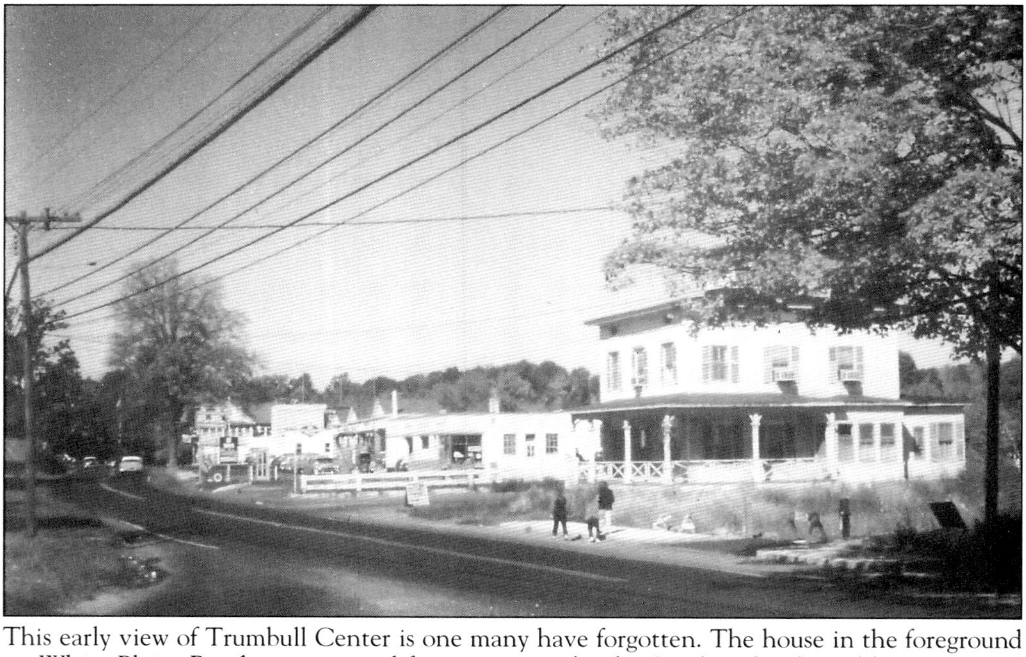

This early view of Trumbull Center is one many have forgotten. The house in the foreground on White Plains Road was occupied for many years by the Sperling family and later was used for medical offices (remember Dr. Corbett?). The house came down in 1958 when the shopping center expanded and Grand Union arrived.

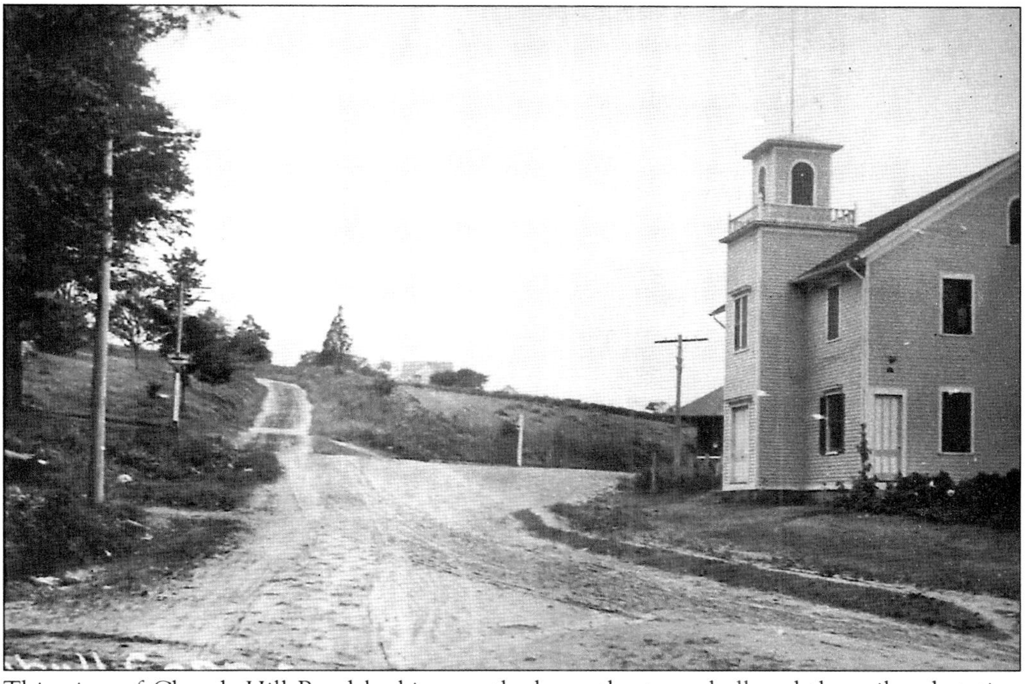

This view of Church Hill Road looking north shows the town hall and the railroad station beyond. At the top of the hill is the home of longtime town clerk Helen Plumb. The town hall building, constructed on land purchased from Birdsey B. Plumb, fulfilled its mission for the town from 1883 to 1957, when the present town hall building was opened. The building was renamed in honor of Miss Plumb in 1989.

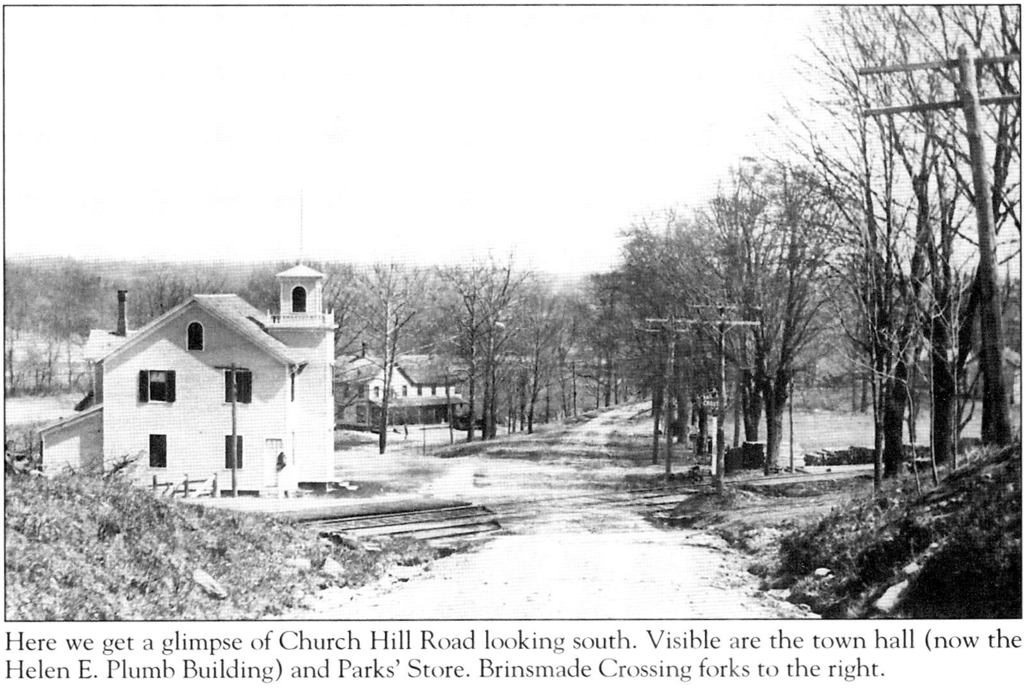

Here we get a glimpse of Church Hill Road looking south. Visible are the town hall (now the Helen E. Plumb Building) and Parks' Store. Brinsmade Crossing forks to the right.

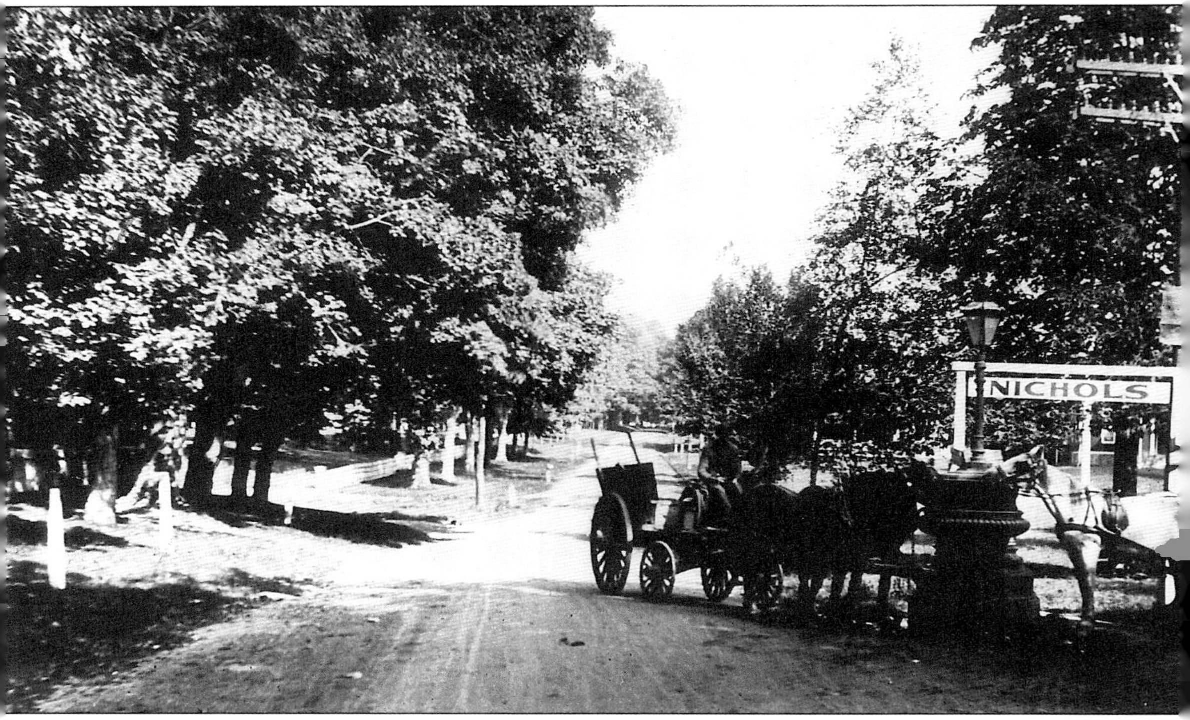


A refreshing drink of water in the summertime was an important travel requirement for animals and people in the age before the automobile. A fountain topped by a lamp was erected in 1895 at the junction of Huntington Turnpike and Wells Hollow Turnpike (now Shelton Road) by Mrs. Antoinette B. Peet in memory of her late husband, John B. Peet. Horses could drink at the upper bowl, people could drink from a tap. A small bowl at the base was designed for dogs. The fountain, no longer used as a source of drinking water, was moved a short distance in 1931 to an island at the junction of Huntington Turnpike and Unity Road. It was redesigned by Lewis D. Christie Sr. and was adorned at the top by plaster bunnies, an enlarged mushroom, and cattails. It became locally known as the "Bunny Fountain."

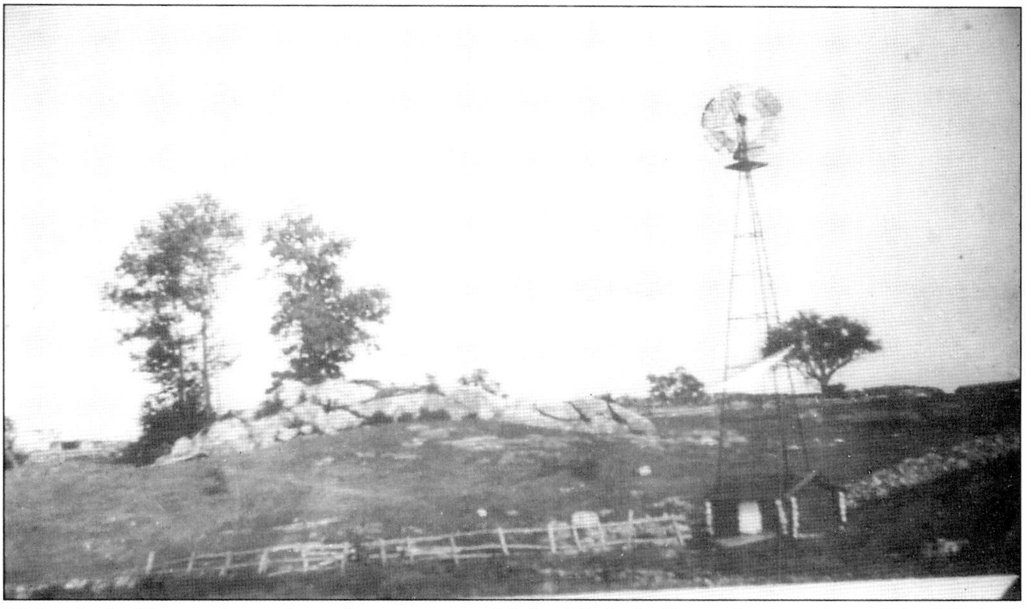

This windmill was situated on the property of John Nichols (later the location of the Nichols Improvement Association), north of Unity Road. It provided the power for supplying and pumping water for the Nichols Farm. As we approach the year 2000, it is interesting to note that although this area is now quite wooded, the rock outcropping in the photograph is still readily visible.

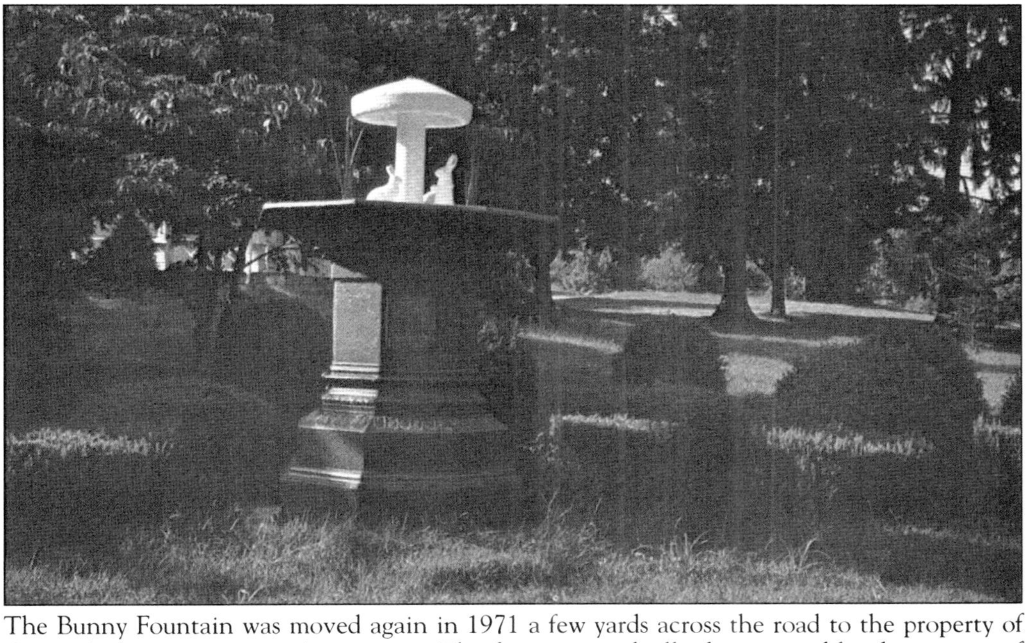

The Bunny Fountain was moved again in 1971 a few yards across the road to the property of the Nichols Improvement Association. The fountain gradually deteriorated by the actions of weather, pranksters, and outright vandalism. In 1995, the Nichols Improvement Association's very successful fund-raising campaign made a major restoration possible. The Bunny Fountain continues to be a prominent landmark with its original aura of quaintness and nostalgia.

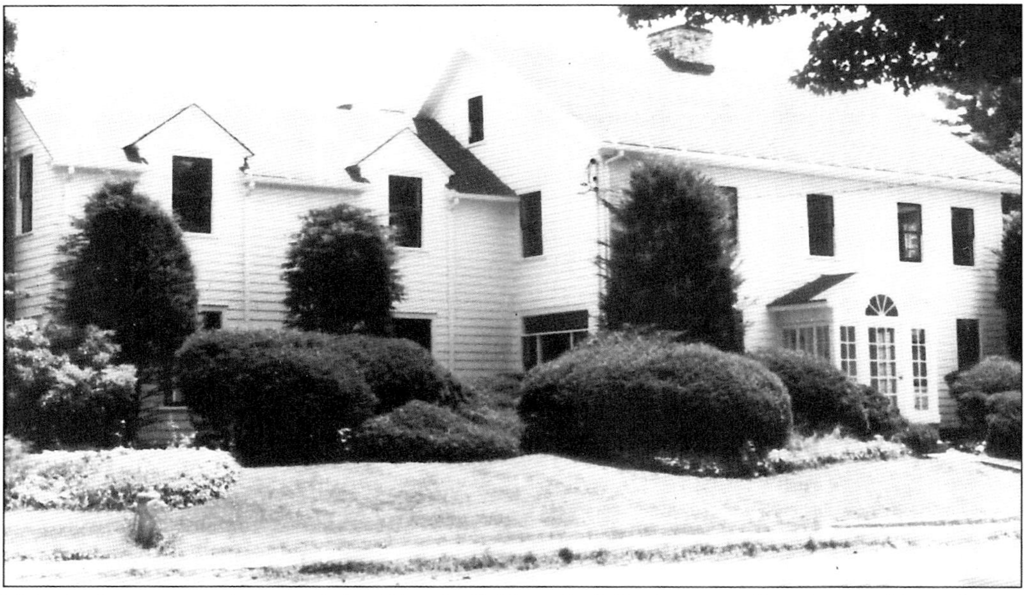

This is the present home of the Trumbull Historical Society on Huntington Turnpike in Nichols. It is the former home of George Woods and his wife, Florence Nichols Woods. The property was originally part of the lands owned by Abraham Nichols, one of the original settlers from Stratford. The main part of the home was built in 1820. Upon the deaths of Mr. and Mrs. Woods, the property was deeded to the Nichols Methodist Church. The town purchased it from the church through a federal grant in 1974. In 1978, the town leased the house and the immediate land around it to the Trumbull Historical Society for a period of ninety-nine years. The balance of the estate became the Abraham Nichols Park.

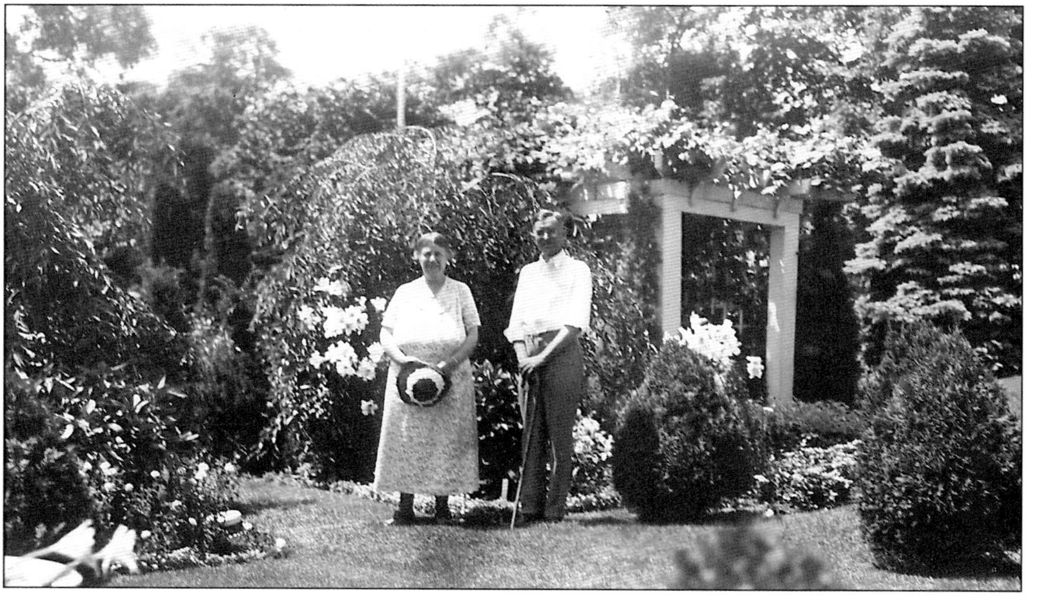

George and Florence Woods lavished interest and love on the gardens of their estate. From the extensive well-kept apple orchards on the upper level, to the beautiful flowers and exotic plantings nearer the house, the grounds were a joy to behold.

The gardens, tended by gardener Llewelyn Hughes, were known for their exotic plantings. Each spring, Mr. Woods, chairman of the board and former president of People's Bank in Bridgeport, would take massive bouquets of blooms to the bank for all to enjoy.

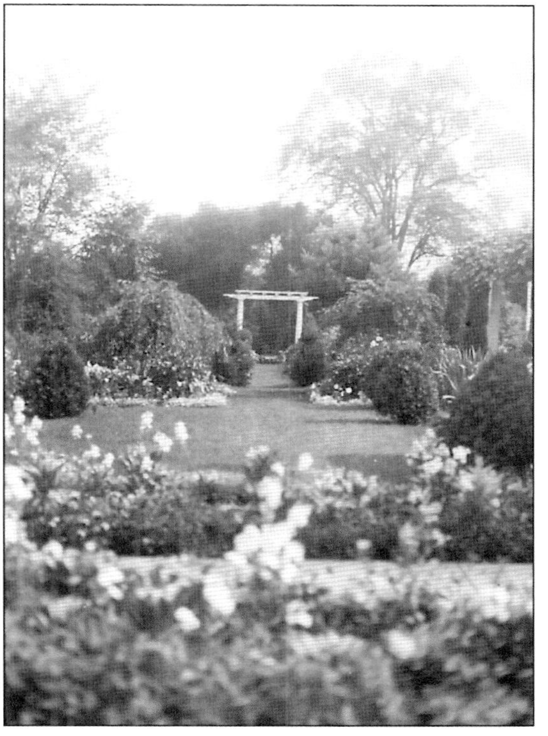

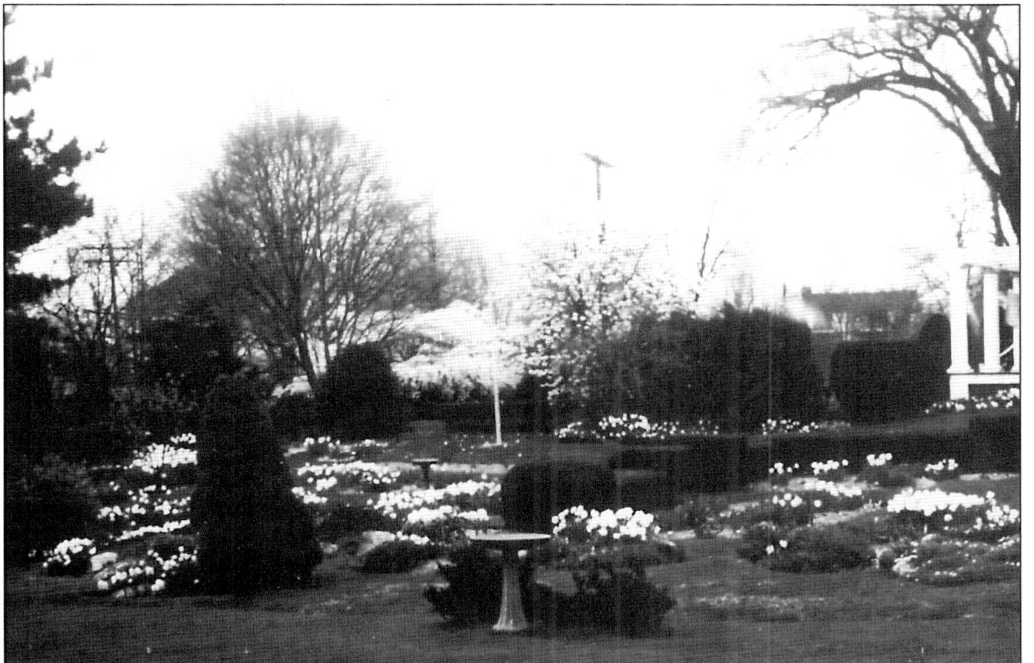

This image shows the formal gardens of the Woods Estate, looking toward Huntington Turnpike. The portico pictured on the right was removed and now is the location of the society's Helen Plumb Herb and Perennial Garden.

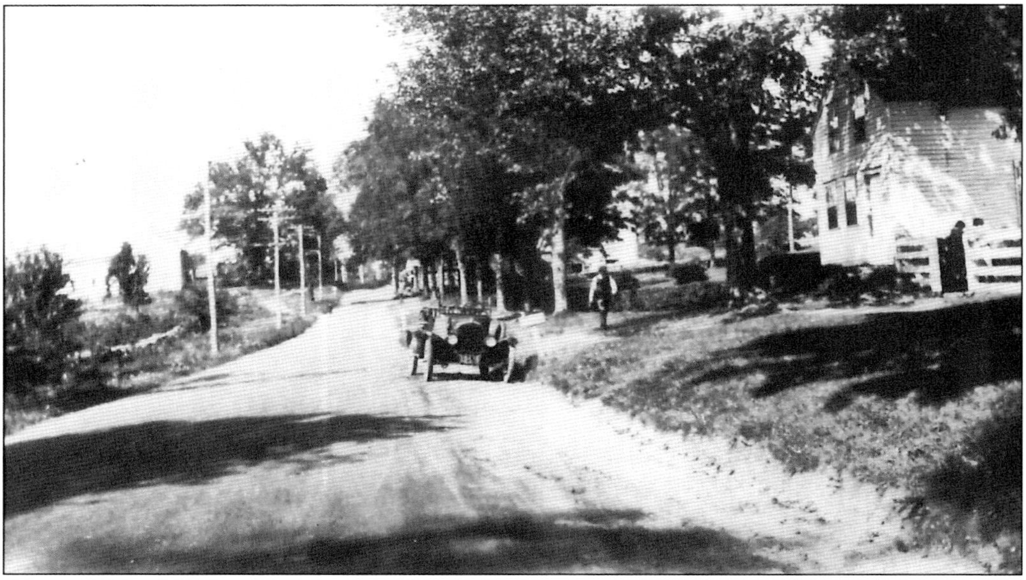

This old Nichols homestead was located where the present entrance to Abraham Nichols Park is on Huntington Turnpike. Although the construction date is unknown, it is said the Nichols family lived in this house while the larger house, now home to the Trumbull Historical Society, was being built. This building stood until 1926.

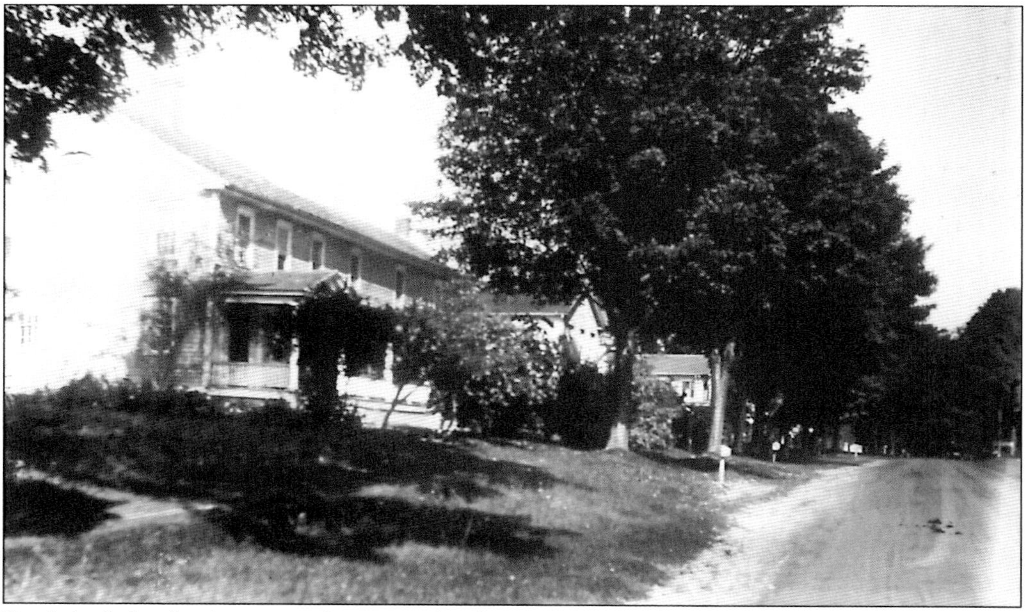

Don't look for this house on the west side of Huntington Turnpike. You won't find it. In 1920 it was cut in half and moved down to Priscilla Place (known then as Park Place) to serve as two separate residences. Recycling buildings was a common occurrence then.

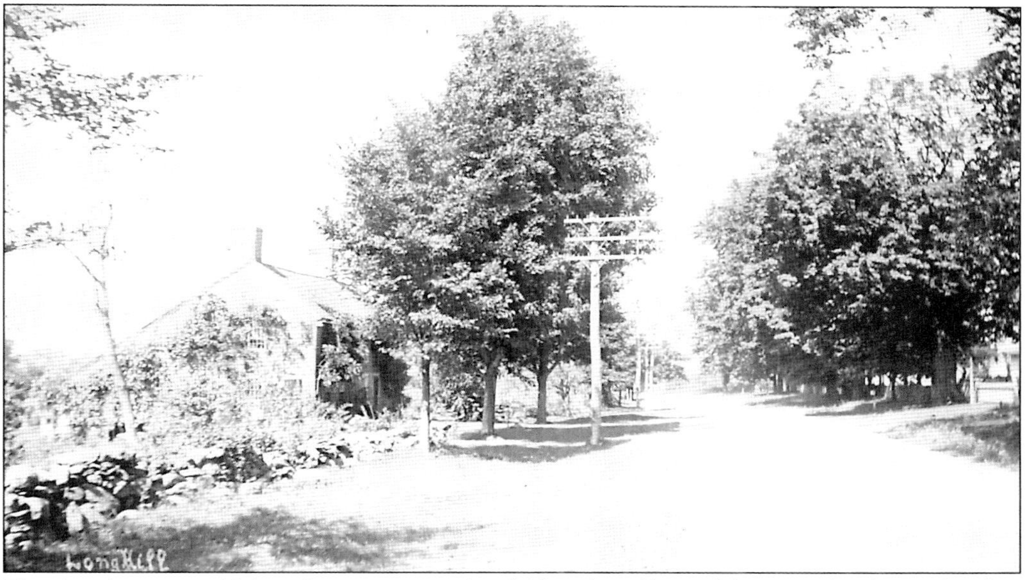


This lovely scene of Main Street just north of Church Hill Road has greatly changed today, due largely to the absence of roadside trees. The saltbox home on the left was built by John Wildman in 1745 and was home to members of the Walker family for many years.

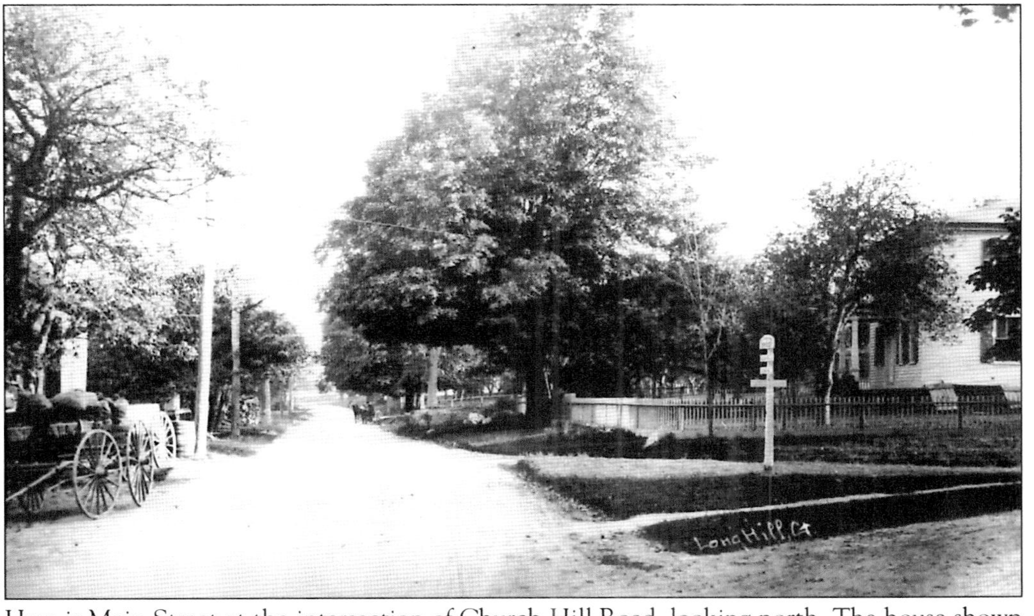


Here is Main Street at the intersection of Church Hill Road, looking north. The house shown on the right was demolished. The new Long Hill Village development is just beyond this view.

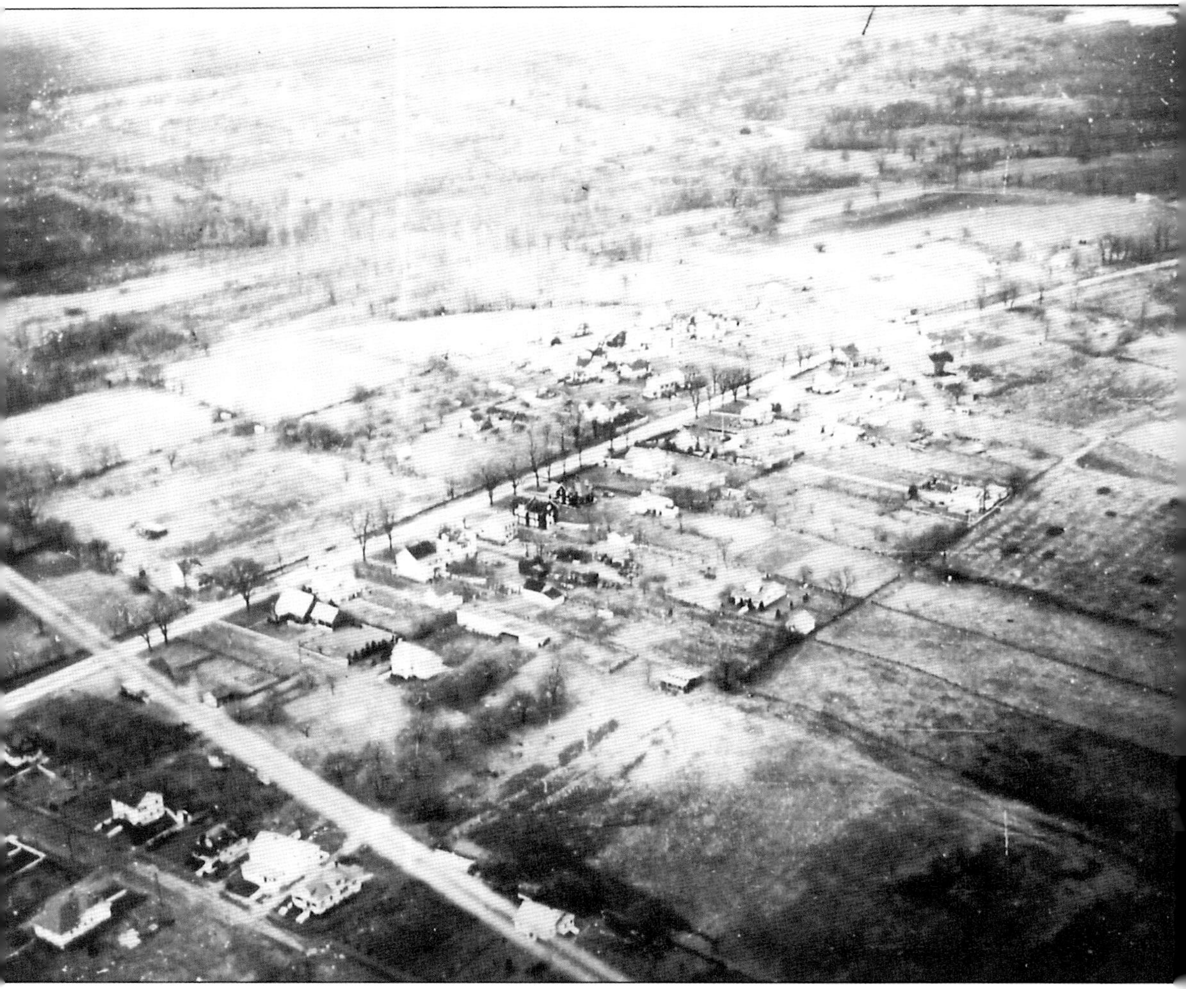

This is an aerial view of Main Street, south of Edison Road. The photograph was taken at an altitude of 800 feet in April 1934. The heavy line in the lower left is the plane's wing strut. The large open space area in the center of the photograph, called Stuart's Hill, was a favorite spot for sledding and ball playing. It is now the site of the Trumbull Shopping Park. Canoe Brook Lake is visible in the upper right. Mr. Gorham, who took this picture, was the owner of Gorham's Gas Station, which stood opposite the Main Street entrance to the shopping park.

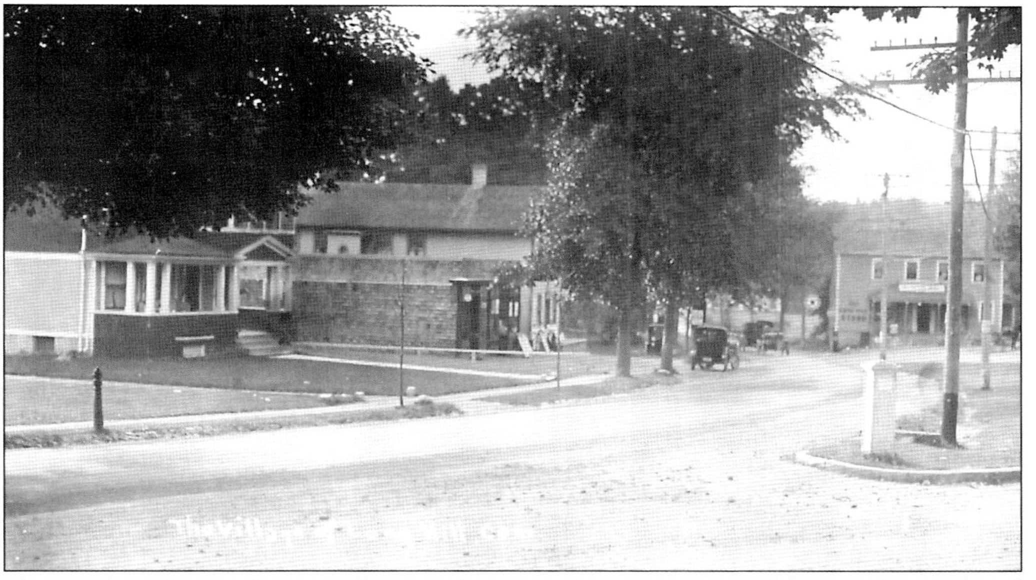

This northward view of Long Hill Green shows Hurd's Store and Post Office on the north and Lackman's Feed Store on the west side. Many stores have surrounded the green over the years in this long-standing commercial area.

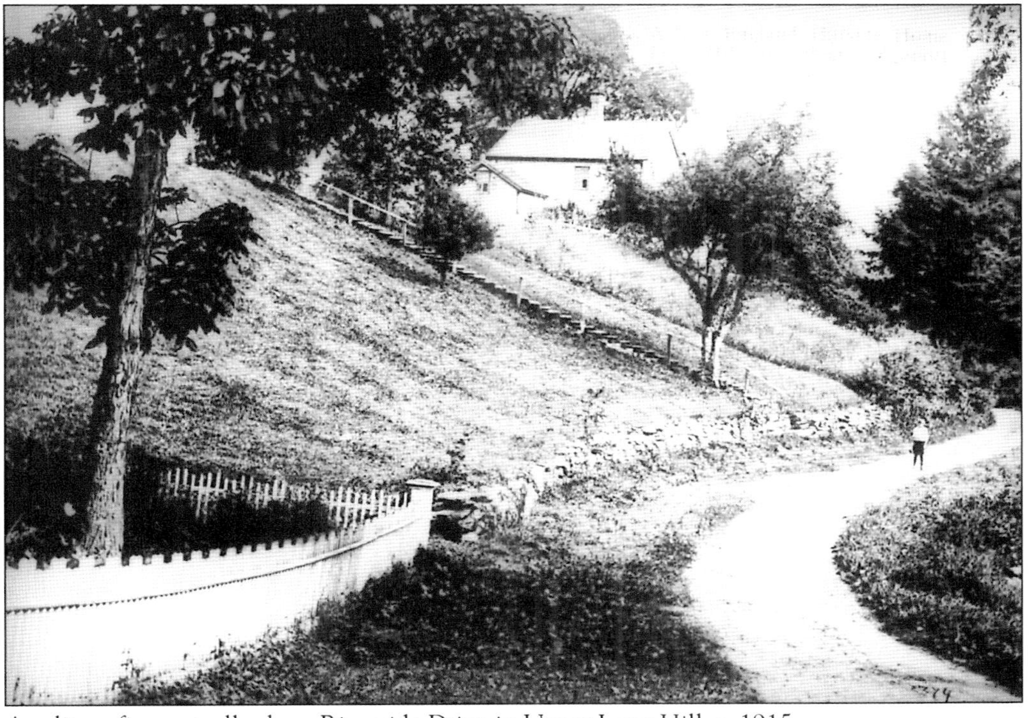

A solitary figure strolls along Riverside Drive in Upper Long Hill, c. 1915.

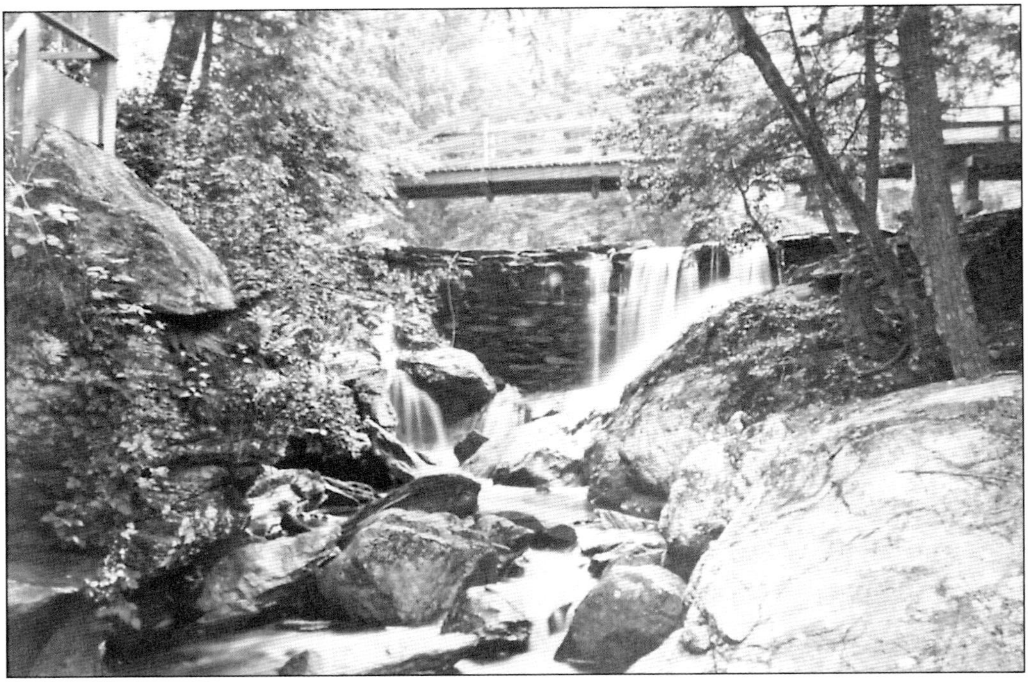

This bridge was located over the Pequonnock River and Dam in the Parlor Rock area c. 1878. It was a restful stop, beautiful in all seasons. On sunny days it became a special swimming hole, and fish were said to have jumped to the bait during the fishing season.

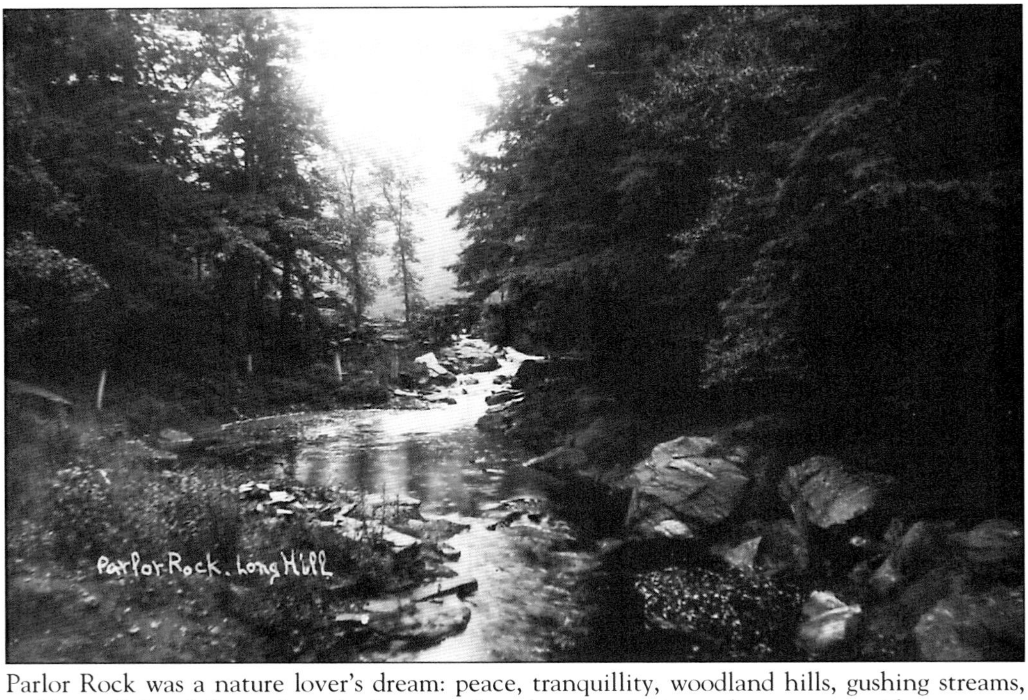


Parlor Rock was a nature lover's dream: peace, tranquillity, woodland hills, gushing streams, and beautiful rock formations. It also was a fun place for picnics and amusement rides.

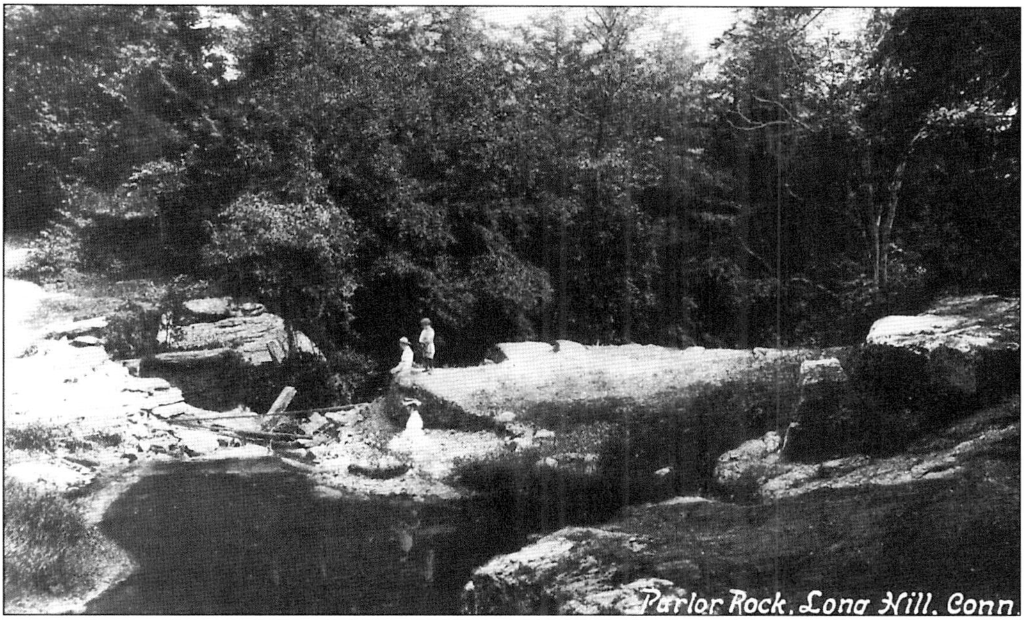


A very large oblong flat rock surface that had an odd, naturally formed circular recess gave the Parlor Rock area its name. For the pleasure of the visitors, long wooden stairs led down to the rock area.

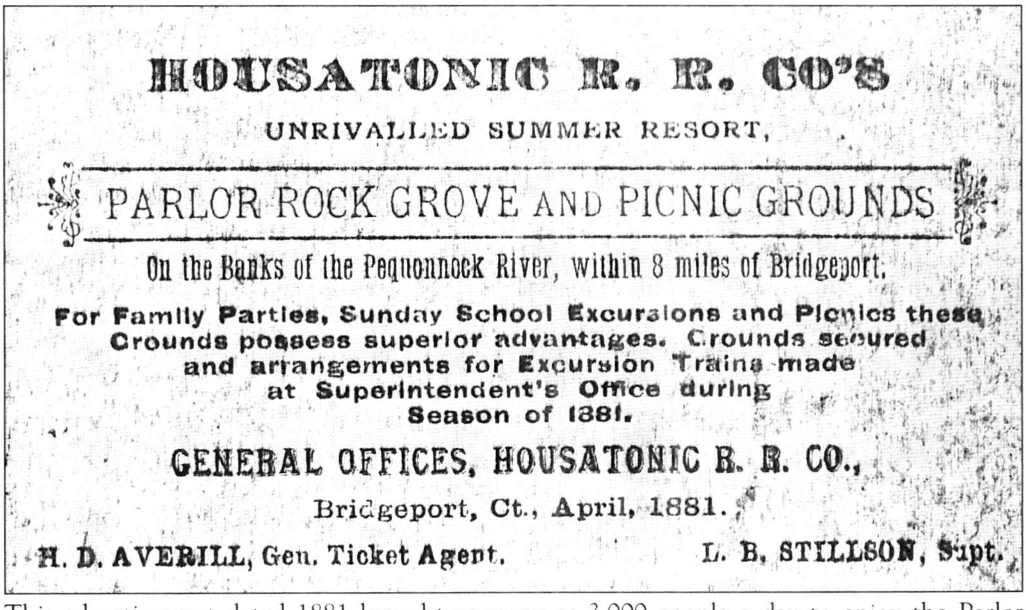

HOUSATONIC R. R. CO'S

UNRIVALLED SUMMER RESORT,

PARLOR ROCK GROVE AND PICNIC GROUNDS

On the Banks of the Pequonnock River, within 8 miles of Bridgeport.

For Family Parties, Sunday School Excursions and Picnics these Grounds possess superior advantages. Grounds secured and arrangements for Excursion Trains made at Superintendent's Office during Season of 1881.

GENERAL OFFICES, HOUSATONIC R. R. CO.,

Bridgeport, Ct., April, 1881.

H. D. AVERILL, Gen. Ticket Agent. L. B. STILLSON, Supt.

This advertisement dated 1881 brought as many as 3,000 people a day to enjoy the Parlor Rock area. The Housatonic Railroad owned Parlor Rock Grove and many crowds enjoyed this summer resort from 1878 through 1907.

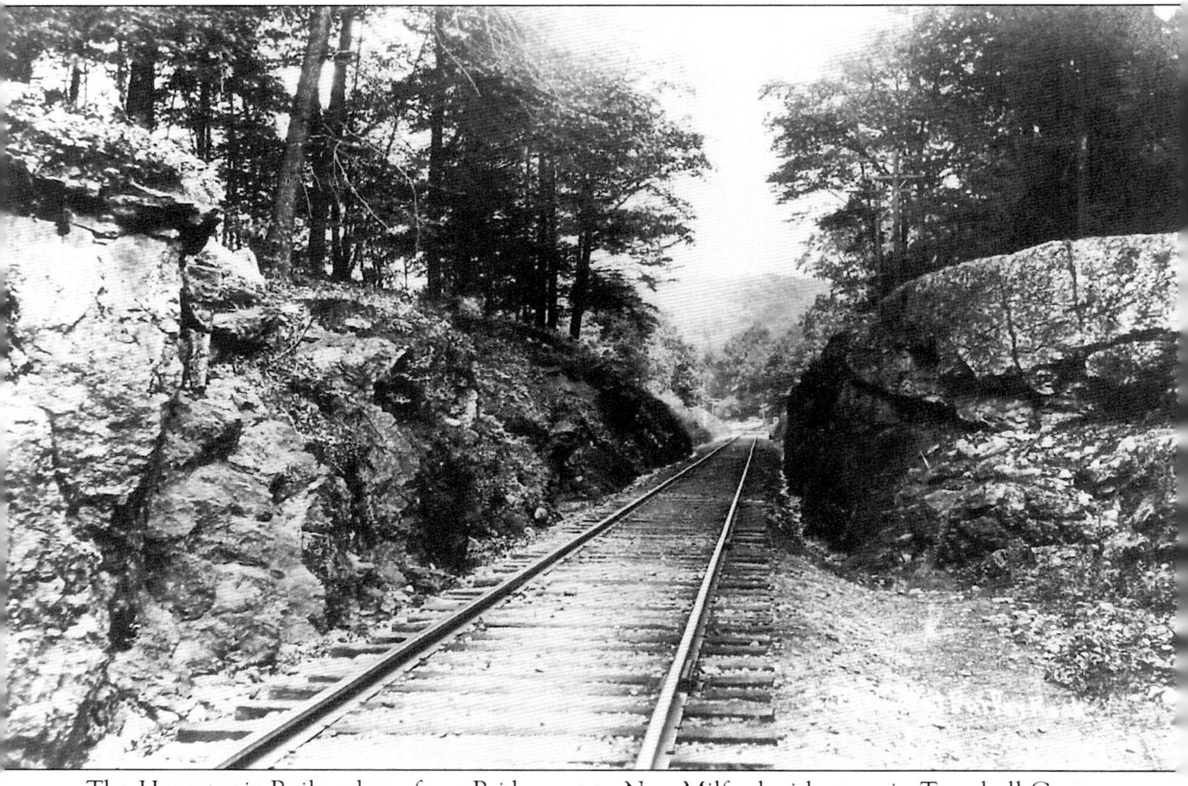

The Housatonic Railroad ran from Bridgeport to New Milford with stops in Trumbull Center and Long Hill in 1840, carrying coal, freight, livestock, and passengers. In the White Plains Road area, the tracks lay to the west of the road, and the friendly firemen on board were known to throw off shovelfuls of coal to some property owners along the route to help them keep warm during the winter. In 1878 the railroad had fifteen excursion trains that were shunted off the main line at Long Hill and continued on to Parlor Rock. The increasing popularity of the automobile brought the rail line to a close in 1932. This area of the old railway is now part of the Route 25 connector.

# *Two*

# Spiritual Ties

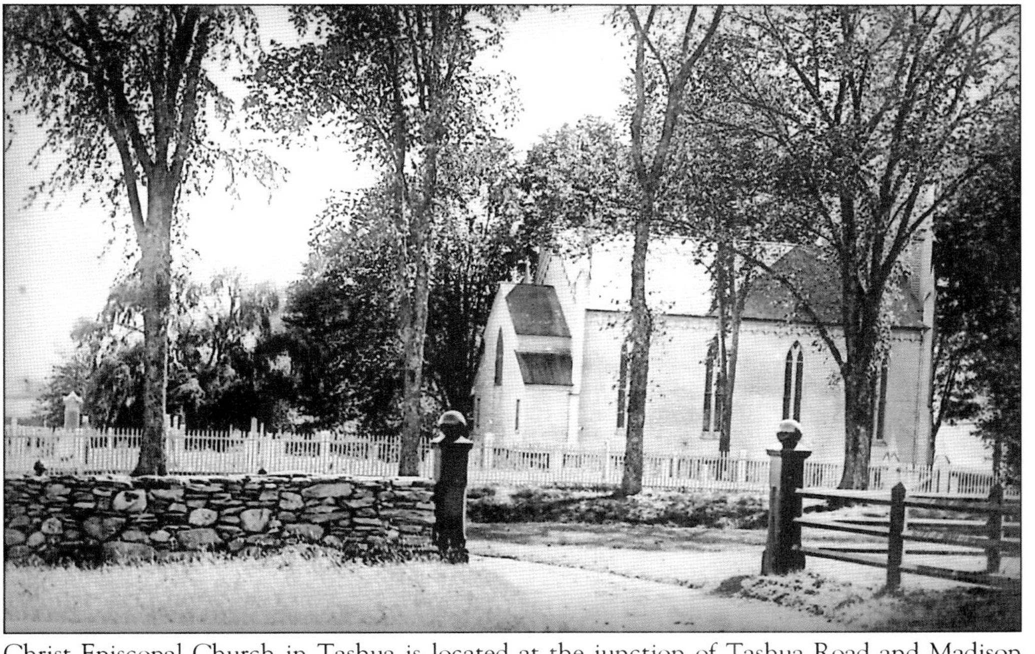

Christ Episcopal Church in Tashua is located at the junction of Tashua Road and Madison Avenue. The cornerstone was laid in 1826 and the building was consecrated in 1847. It was believed to be designed by Alexander Jackson Davis. This was the third church building for the parish of Christ Church. The church is seen from the north side of Tashua Road, the site of the second church. Note the burial ground located behind the church building.

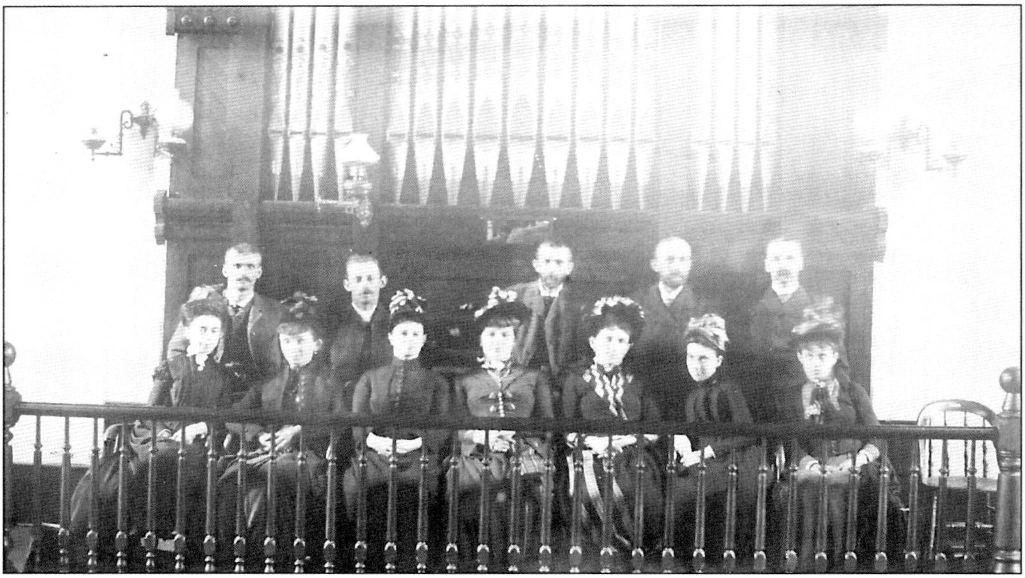

Dressed in their finest and poised for action are the members of the choir of the Congregational Church in 1888. The organ was purchased in 1884 at a cost of $1,300. Mr. Willard Plumb, the organist, was allowed the use of the organ to teach any students he may have had.

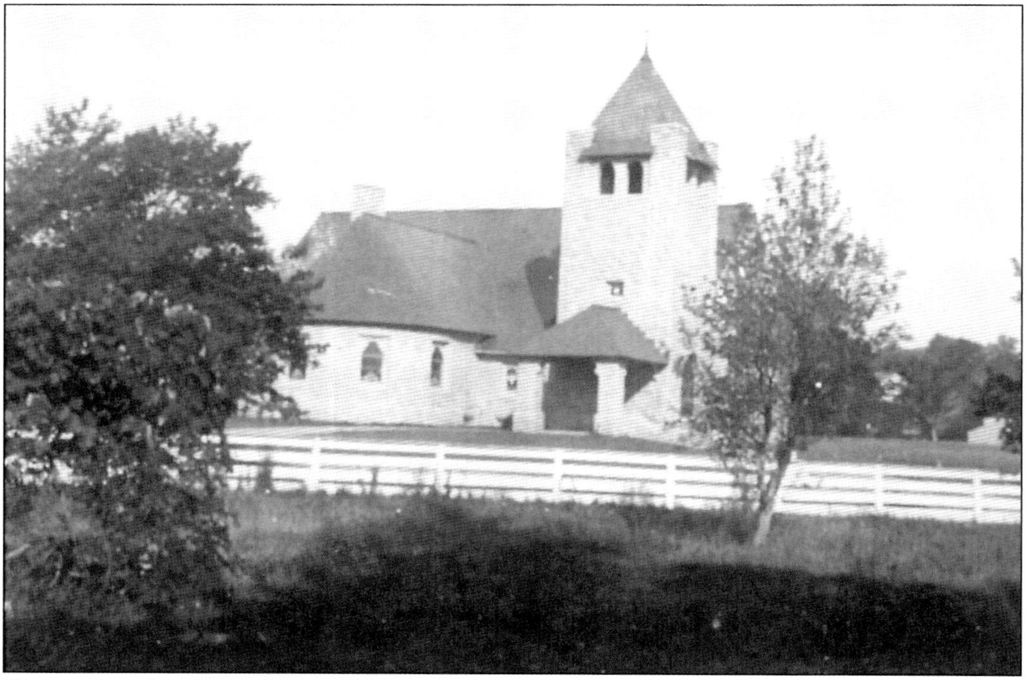

On a grassy knoll overlooking the center of town, the Trumbull Congregational Church now occupies its fourth building. Formerly located on Unity Road and then on Church Hill Road, this building is a departure from the other three, as it is made of stone quarried north of Beardsley Park.

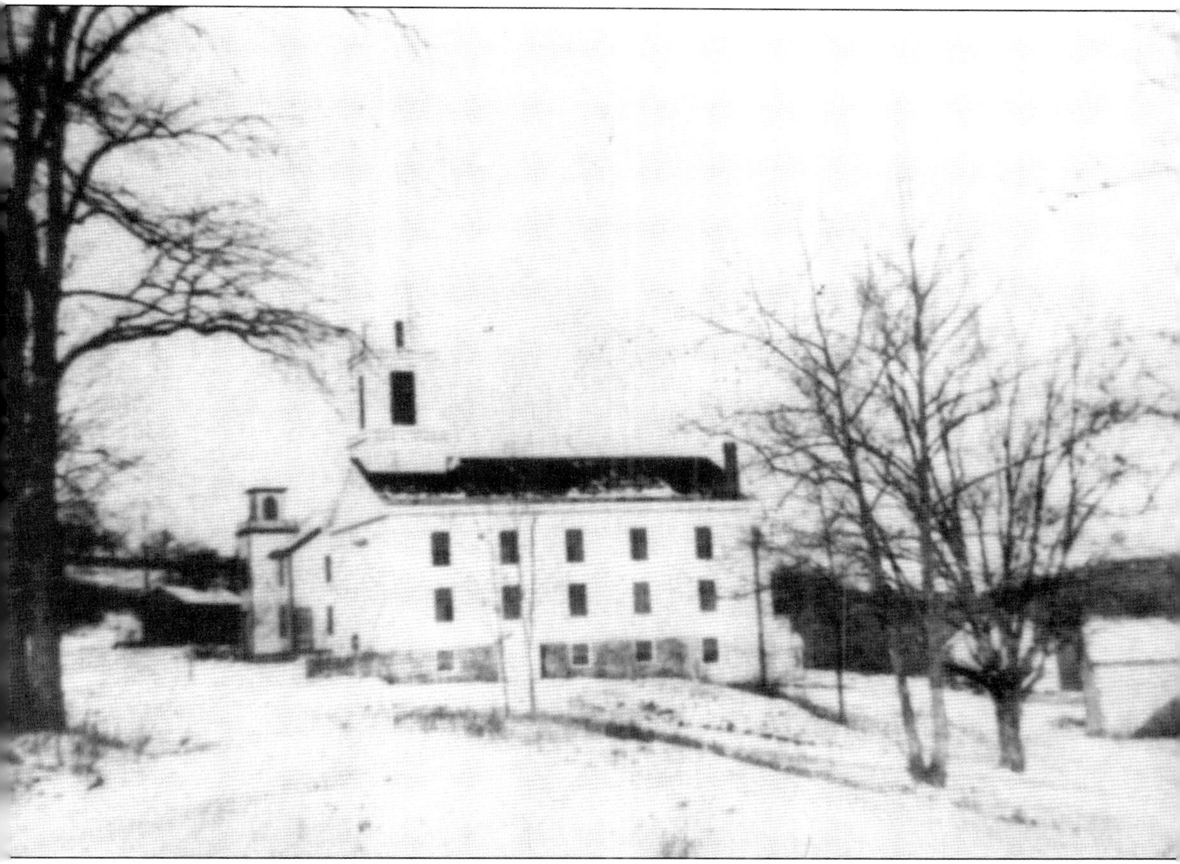

Church Hill Road in the late 1800s, when this picture was taken, was home to three important structures in town. The imposing building in the foreground is the Congregational church. The town hall can be seen behind the church and, beyond that, the railway station is visible. This section of Church Hill Road was often referred to as "Pudding Hill" because the dusty road took on the consistency of pudding during the spring rains. The church building pictured here, dedicated in 1842, is the third Congregational church and the second at this location. It burned to the ground on the night of April 20, 1898.

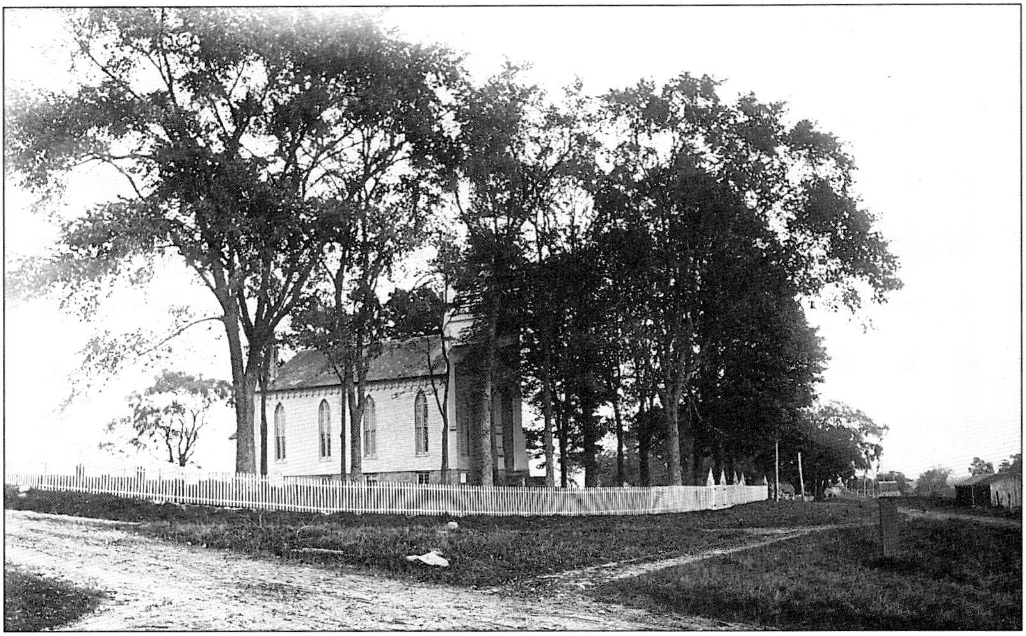

Christ Church in Tashua is part of the oldest diocese of the American Church, Christ Church Stratford, which was established in 1707. This third parish building was built next to the burial ground on land owned by Lucy Mallett. Built in 1846, the church is now the oldest church edifice in Trumbull. This picture shows a very rural Tashua Road, the footpath going past the church and Madison Avenue (right center).

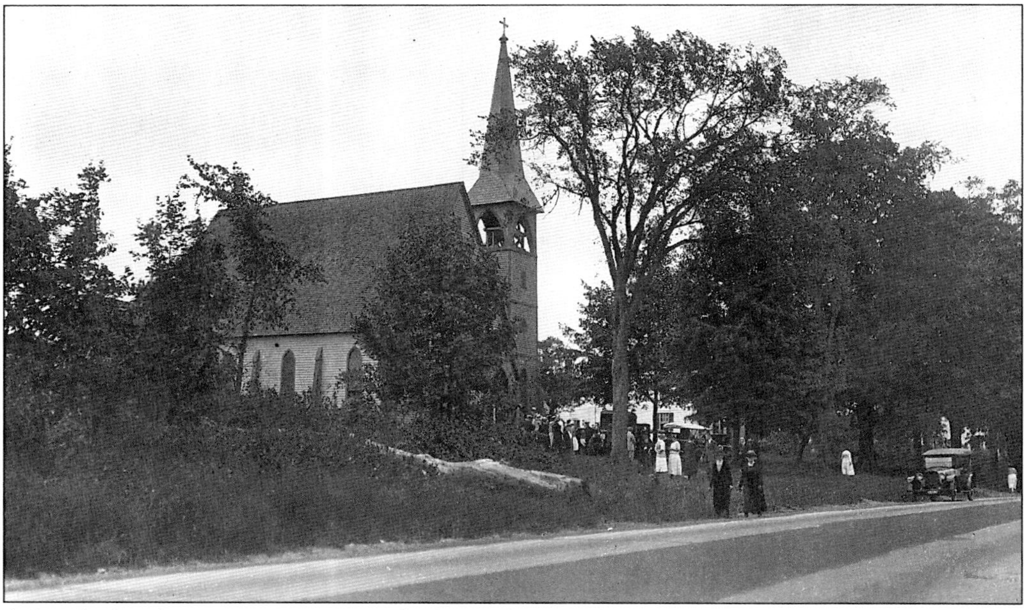

A lovely Sunday morning in 1906 finds parishioners leaving the "plain Gothic building" of Grace Episcopal Church on Main Street. Built in 1881 at a cost of $6,000 after the previous chapel was destroyed by a fire, this building paid for in subscriptions, and the church was debt-free when the first sermon was preached on Easter Sunday 1882.

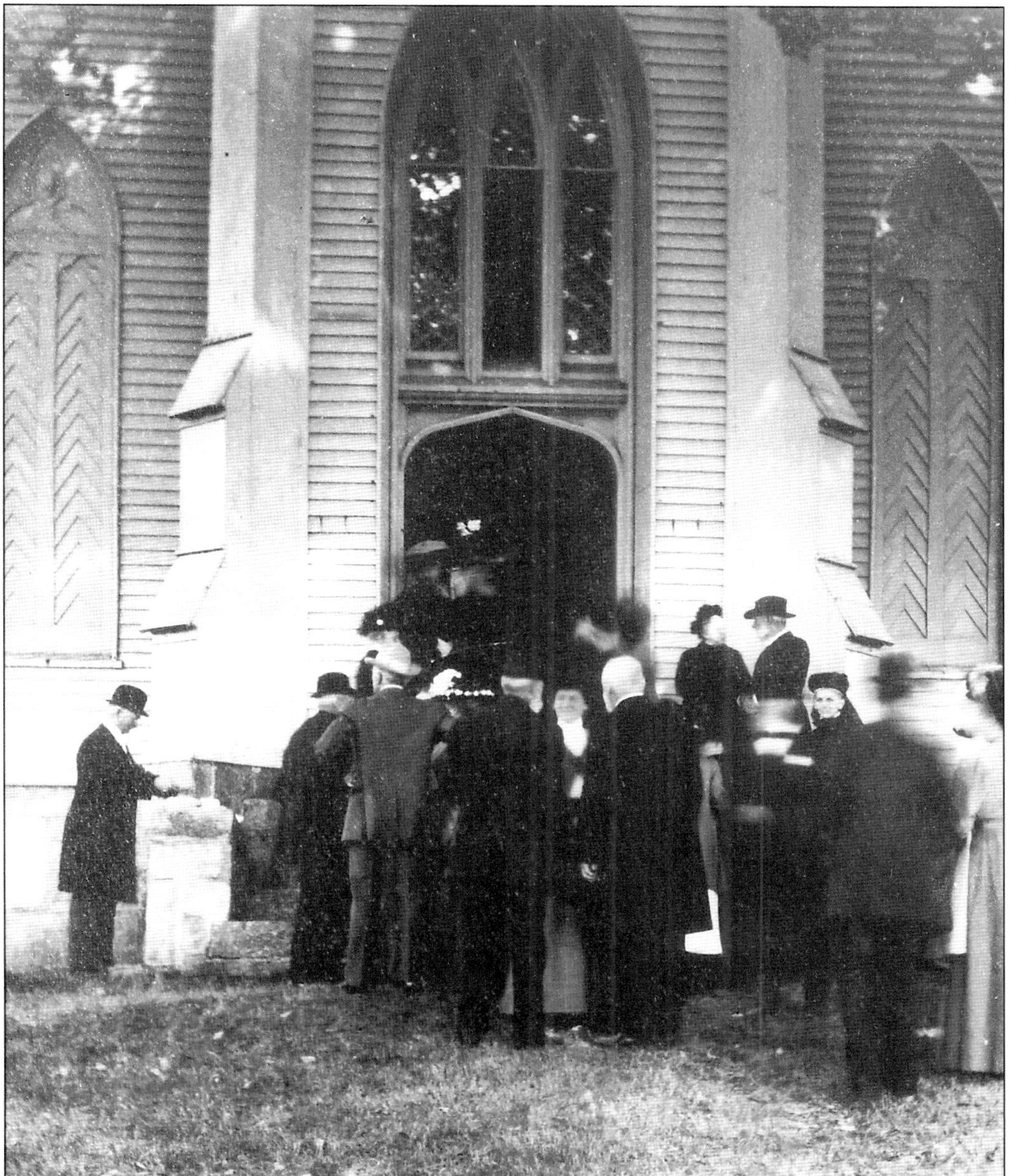

The congregation of Christ Episcopal Church visits outside the church after its 150th anniversary service in August 1910. Founded in 1760 during the closing days of the French and Indian Wars, Christ Church Tashua has now existed for 237 years. For a brief period during the American Revolution, local patriot groups insisted it remain closed "so that no prayers could be offered in support of the King." Another fact that might have given justification to the community's suspicions was the burial of Nathan Hubbell, a Tory, in the churchyard. Although there was, for a time, deep-seated prejudice against the Episcopal Church in America because of its historic ties to England, it soon won the hearts of all the colonists by its abiding faith and good works.

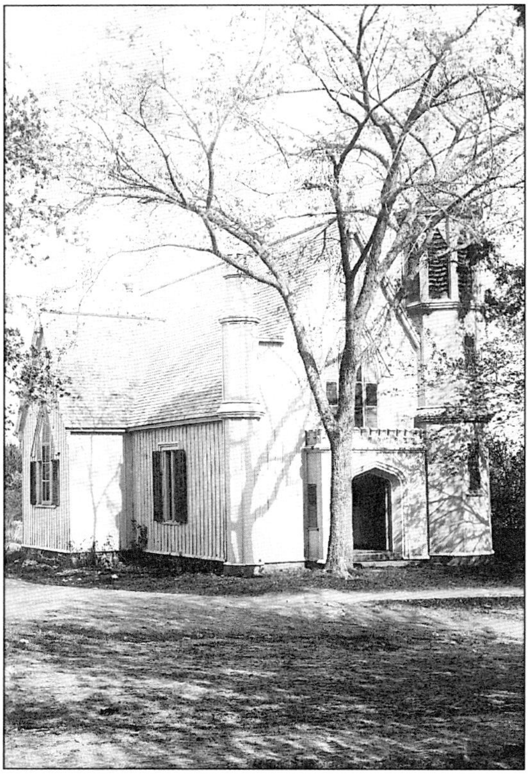

Although Episcopalians in Nichols had gathered to worship as a group in private homes with visiting clergy as early as 1815, it was not until 1847 that they could afford to build a church of their own, incorporating it as "The Ecclesiastical Society of the Protestant Episcopal Church in Nichols." The building, shown at left *c.* 1900, was located on a hill at the southeast corner of Jerusalem Hill and Huntington Turnpike. After ninety-four years at the Jerusalem Hill location, the parish was forced to move the building intact to Huntington Turnpike and Shelton Road because it was in the path of the newly planned Merritt Parkway. It served the parish well until it was destroyed by fire in 1969. A new church was dedicated in 1970. The pews and sanctuary of the original church are shown below.

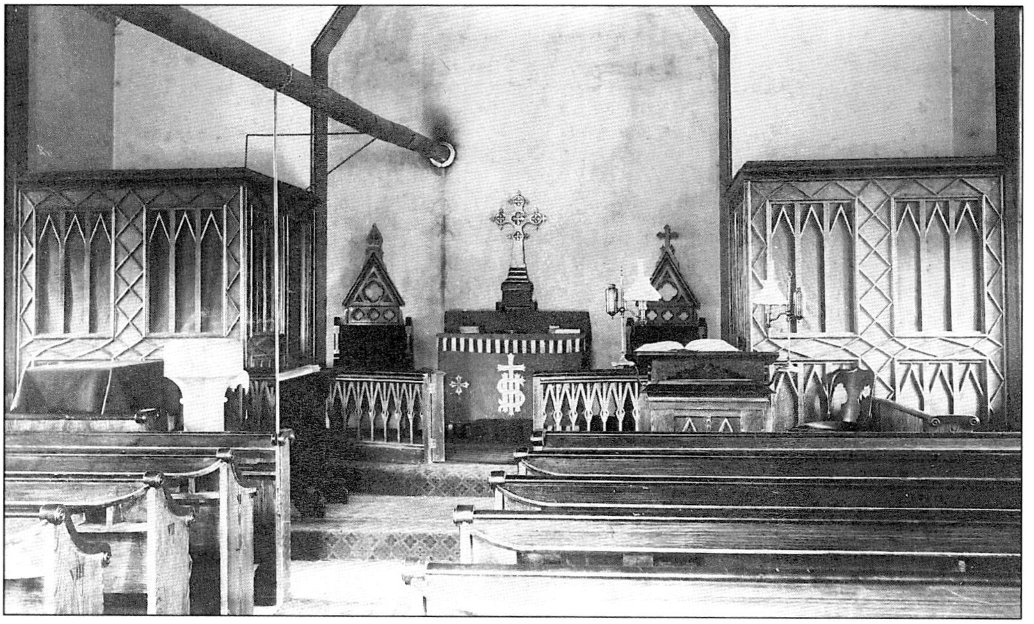

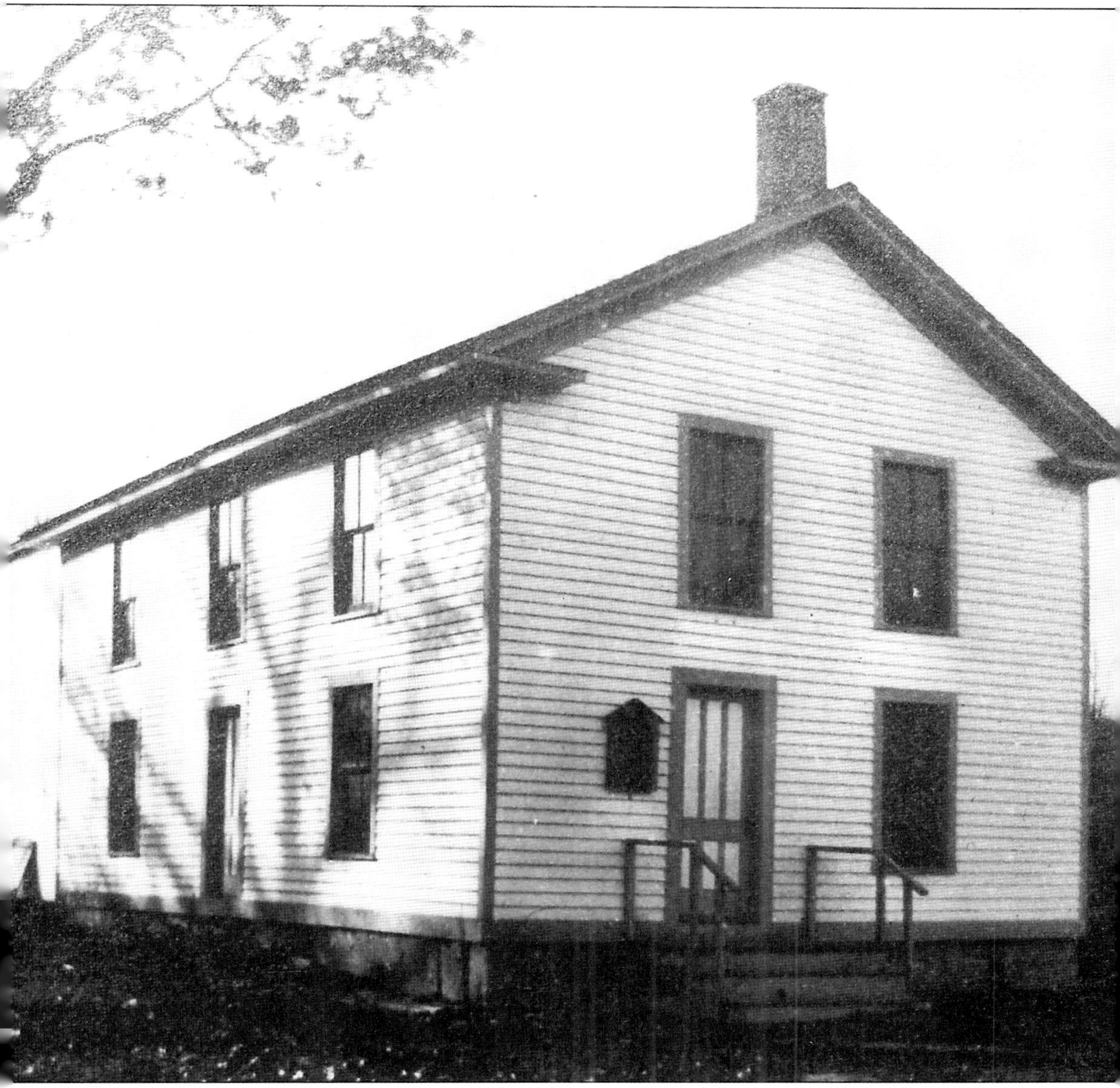

"The Hall," located on Main Street north of Long Hill Green, was purchased by the Long Hill Methodist Church for $150. The first service was held there on December 14, 1902. The ground on which it was built was very swampy and it was called "The Box in the Swamp." In 1917 the Hall was sold to the Bridgeport Hydraulic Company and the congregation moved into their new church on Elizabeth Street.

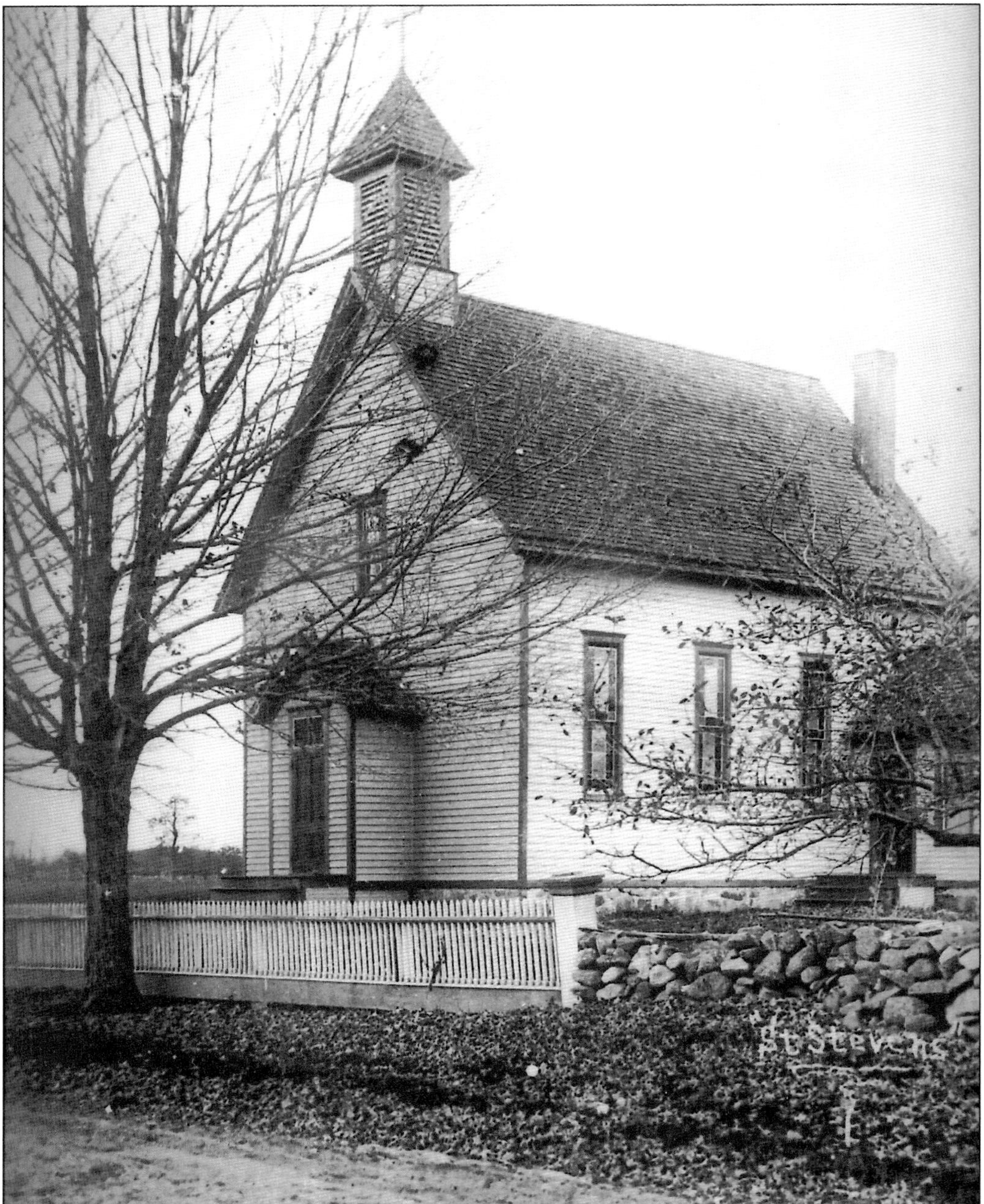


Saint Stephen's Roman Catholic Church, located on Main Street in Upper Long Hill, was a mission church of St. Rose's in Newtown. Erected in 1890 on land donated by Michael Honan, the church was heated by a pipeless wood furnace. The original white clapboard church, which had a seating capacity of 125, was almost demolished by a hurricane two weeks prior to the dedication of the present brick church on December 10, 1950.

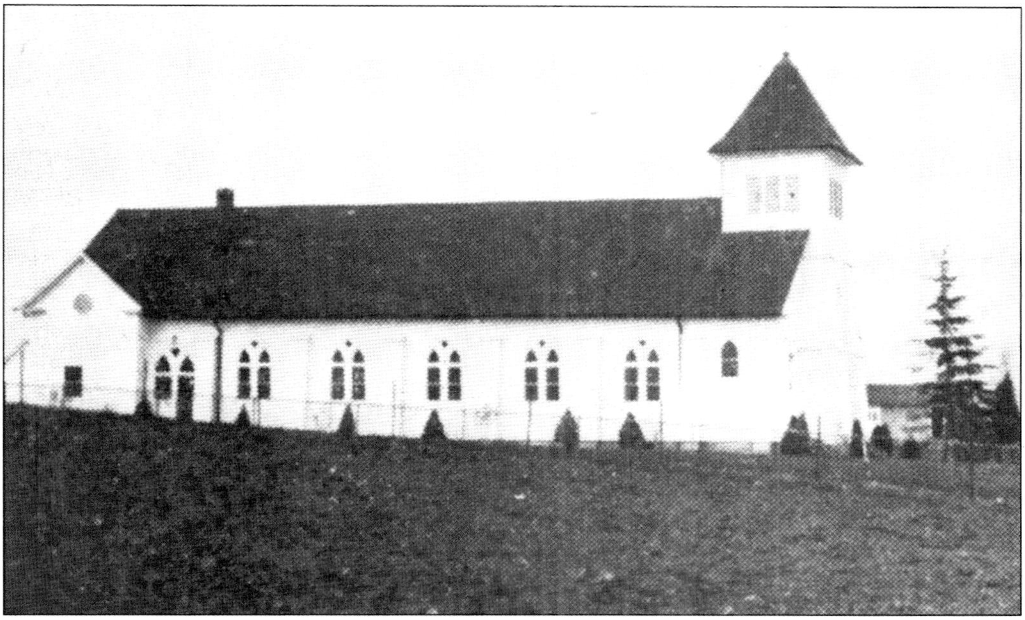

St. Theresa's Roman Catholic Church, a small white wooden frame building of colonial design on Main Street, was dedicated in 1935. As the parish grew, the original structure was razed in 1962 and replaced by a Norman-Gothic-style, stone church edifice.

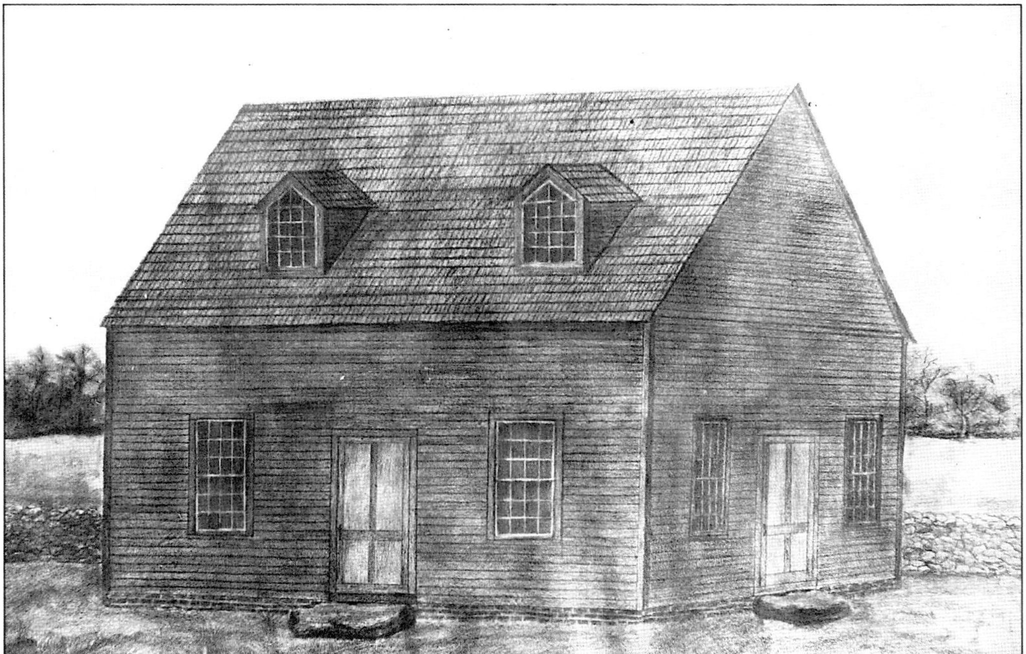

Lee's Chapel, named for its founder, was constructed in 1786. It was the first Methodist church built in New England. The 24-by-30-foot chapel was located on the western boundary of Trumbull on Park Avenue. It is shown as sketched by Louisa A. Hall of Plattsville Road in 1908, from information given to her by her first cousin once removed, Nelson T. Hall, in 1889.

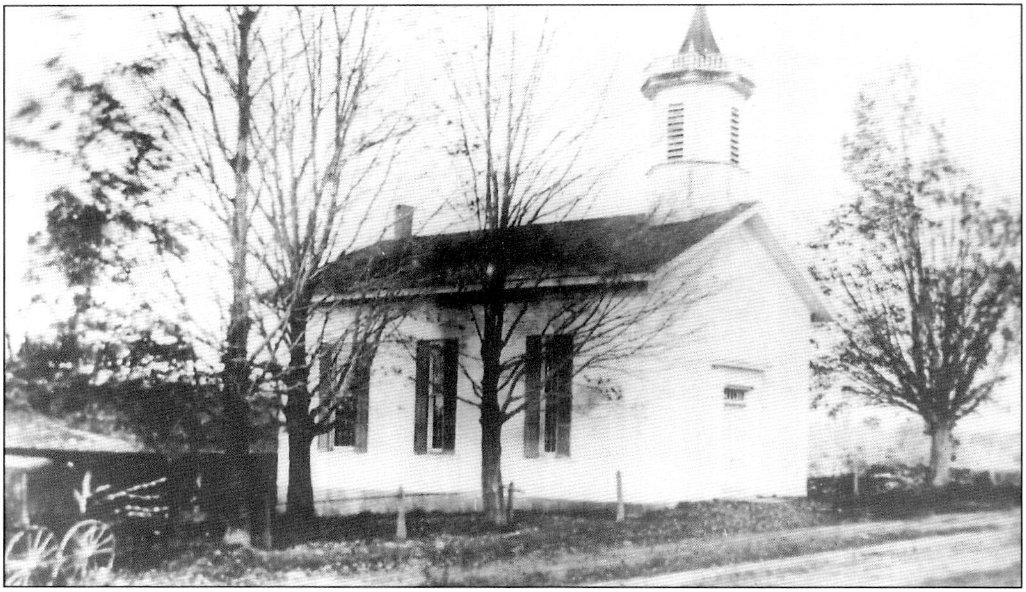

Reverend Henry Morgan preached for two years in Morgan's Chapel at the corner of Lake and Main Streets. The cornerstone was laid in 1857. Reverend Morgan left Trumbull to start Morgan Memorial, the forerunner of Goodwill Industries, in Boston, Massachusetts. The last service in the chapel was held in December 1902. The building was sold in 1911 to Campyon Cutter, who used it as the Long Hill Auto Station. The upper floor was a social room. In the 1930s the building became a grocery store until it was demolished in 1969. The interior of Morgan's Chapel is shown below.

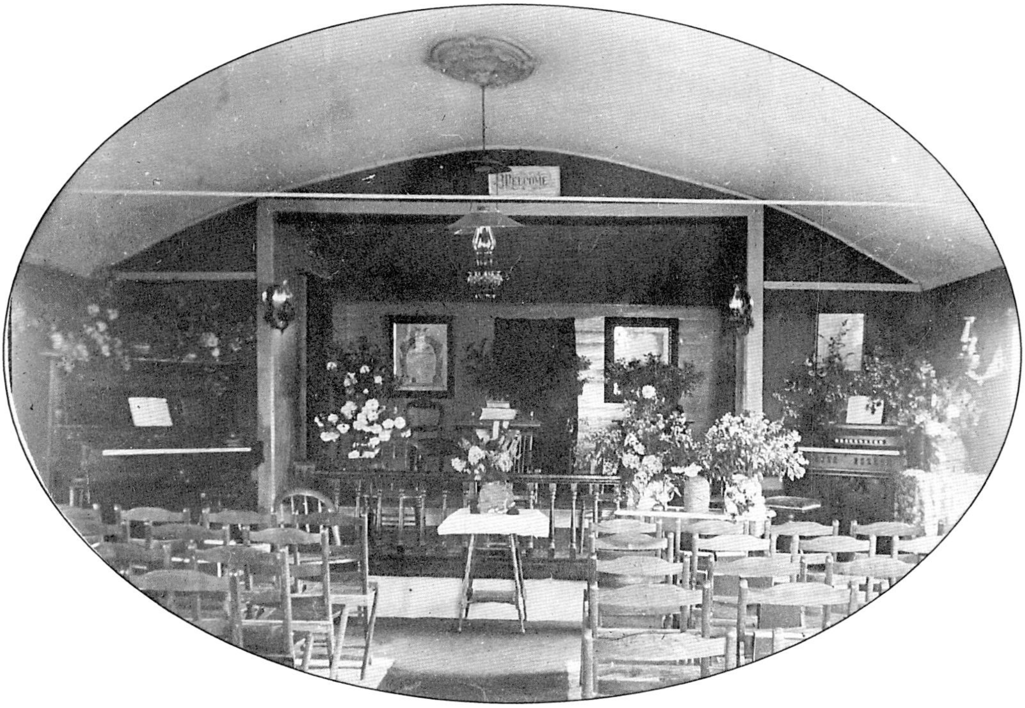

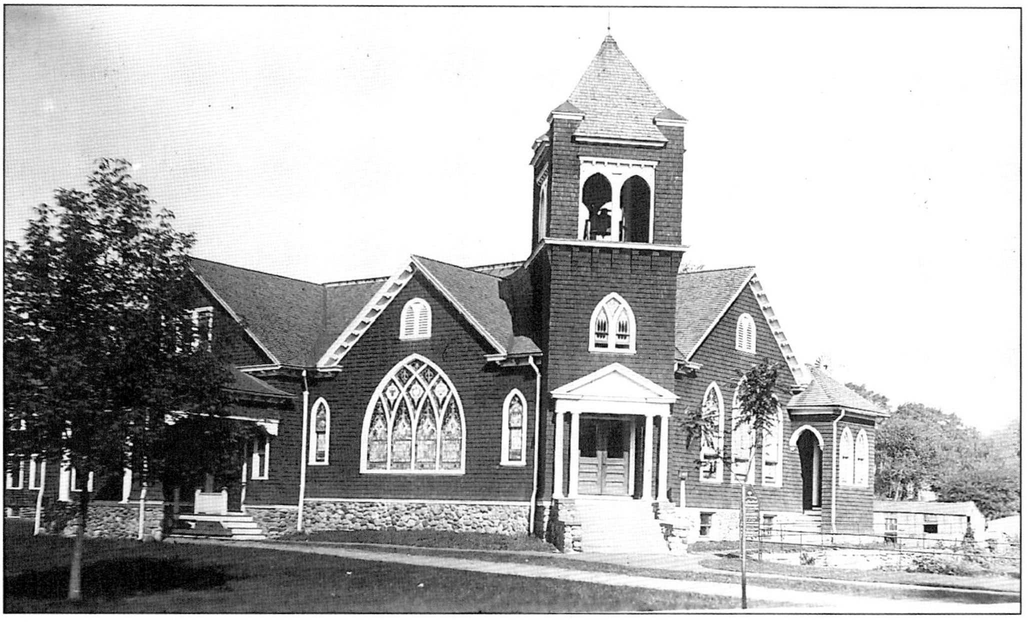

The Nichols United Methodist Church, north of the Nichols Green, is the result of reconstruction projects in 1905, 1960, and 1962. It was replaced in 1981 by an all-new structure, a red brick building topped by a white steeple.

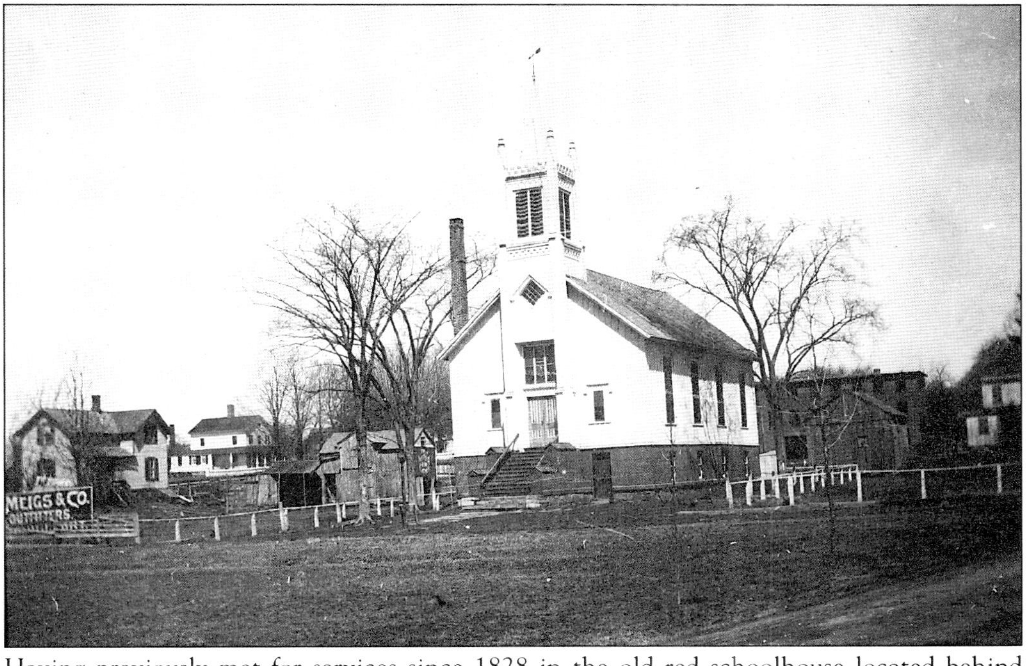


Having previously met for services since 1828 in the old red schoolhouse located behind the Nichols Fire Headquarters, the Nichols United Methodist Church, under diocese of Methodist Episcopal, North Conference, was built and dedicated in 1848. Located north of and facing the Nichols Green, it remained unchanged until 1905, when a fellowship and education center was added.

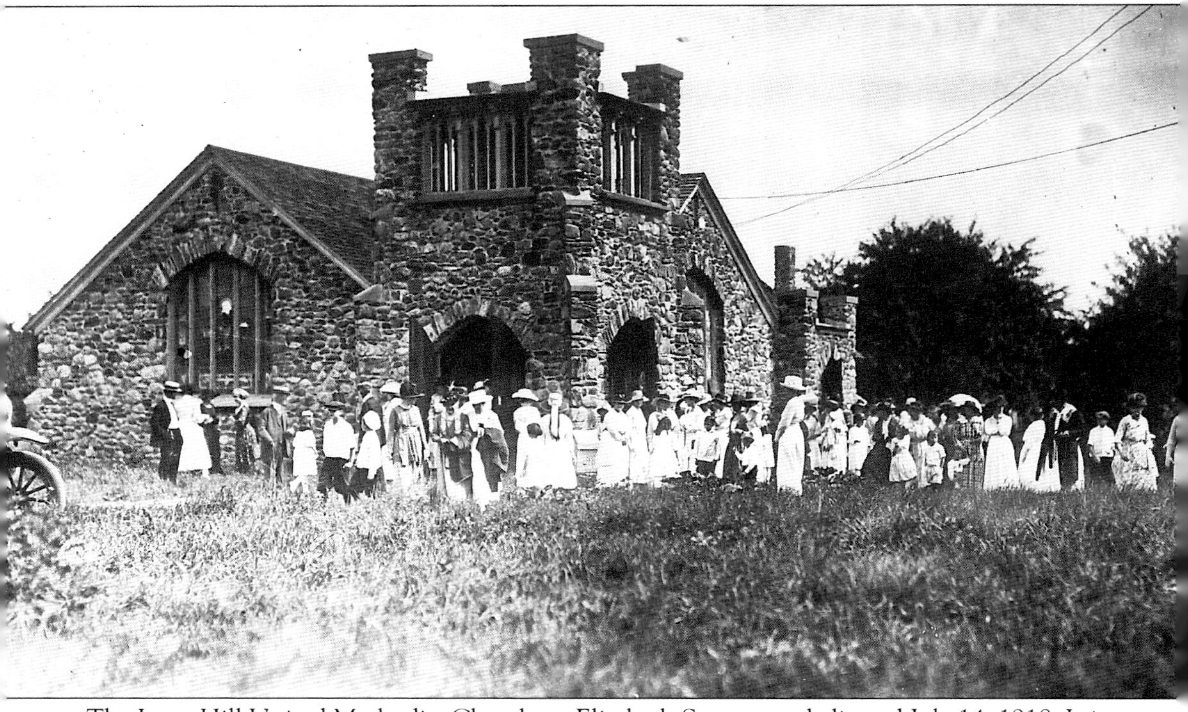

The Long Hill United Methodist Church on Elizabeth Street was dedicated July 14, 1918. It is noted for its three beautiful stained-glass windows. Stones for the church were supplied by the parishioners from surrounding farms. This scene shows the wedding of Clarice Bray and Walter Radcliffe on August 4, 1920.

*Three*

# Book Learnin'

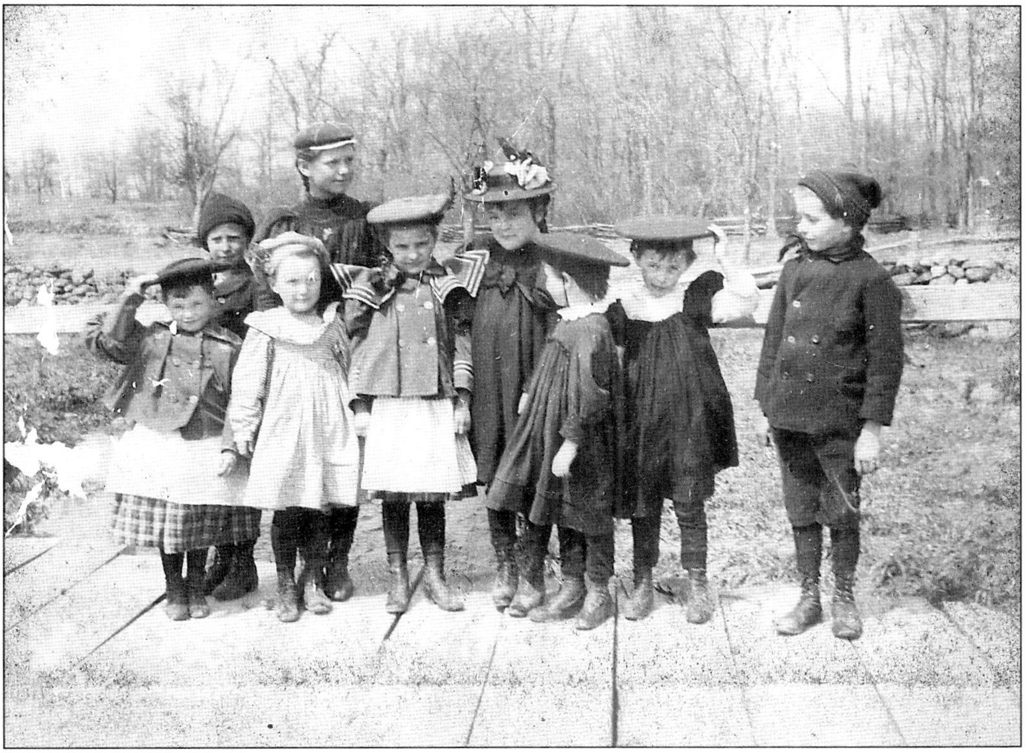

Students dressed in their very best clothes wait in line in front of Church Hill School for the school bell to ring the start of the school day.

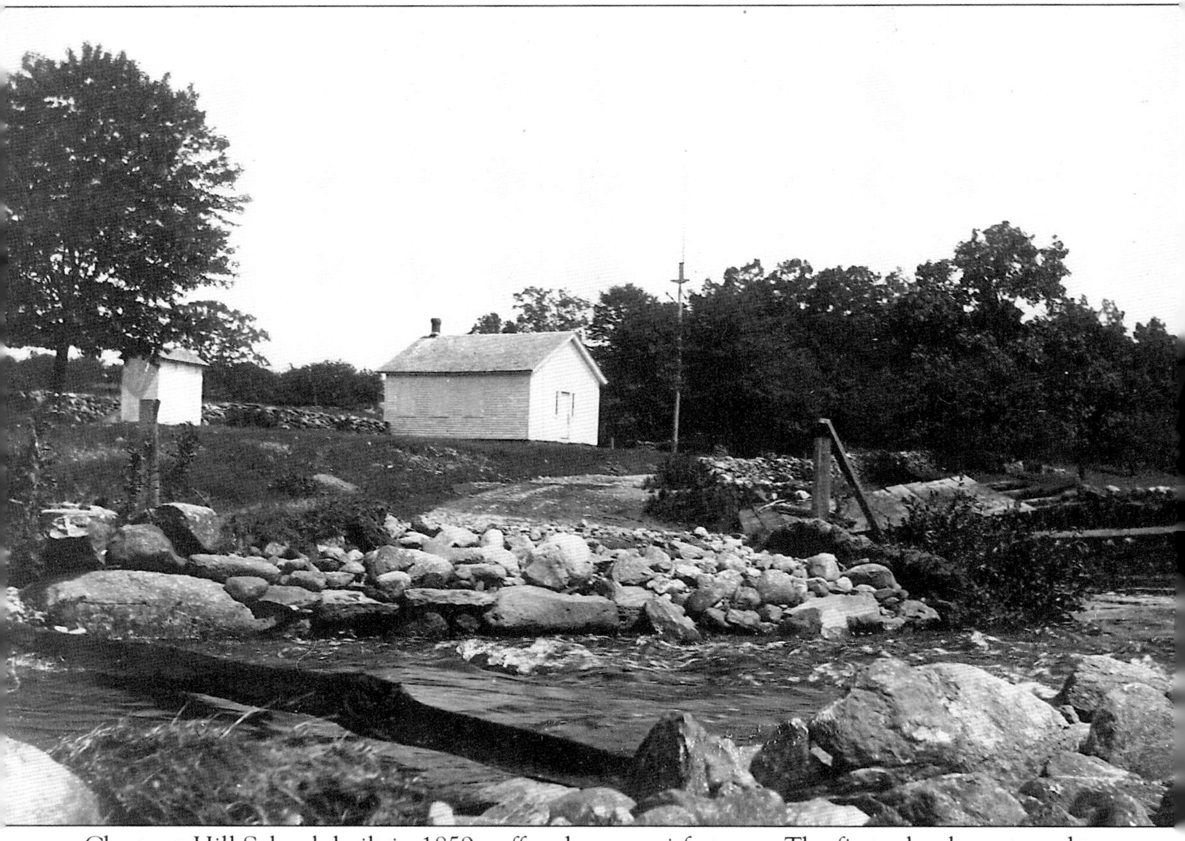

Chestnut Hill School, built in 1859, suffered many misfortunes. The first school was towed to the top of the hill by oxen. The next night it burned to the ground. A second and larger school was built on the same spot, but it burned down when a teacher put live coals into a barrel. The third school was built at the foot of the hill and Killian Avenue. This school was also damaged, this time in the flood of 1906 that caused Chestnut Hill Brook to overflow its banks, leaving large rocks strewn across the landscape as seen in this photograph. It was sold in 1930 for $200 and is now a private residence.

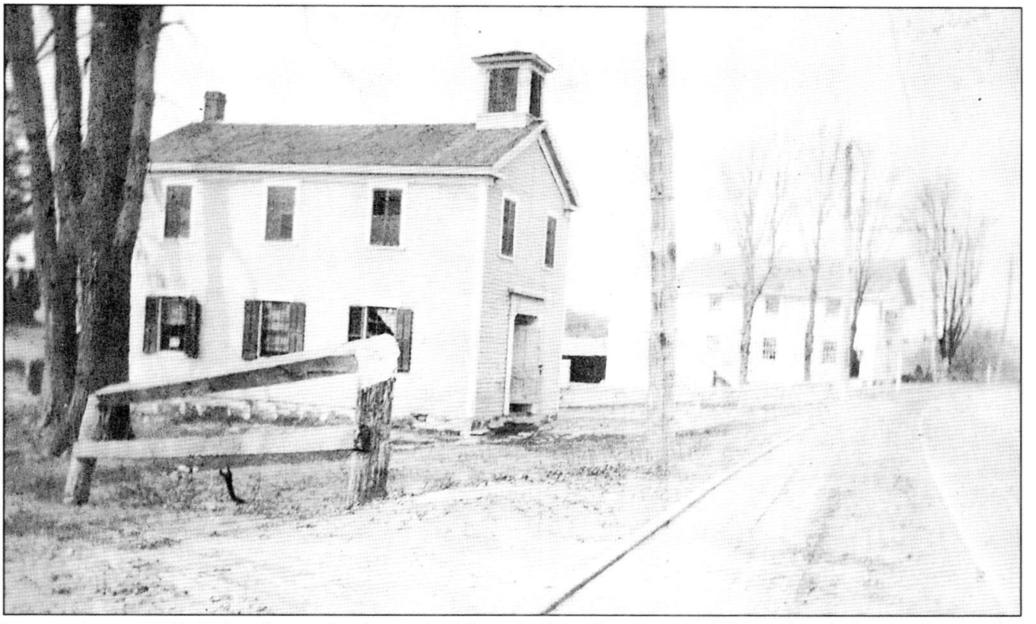

Lower Long Hill School was built in 1856 and closed in 1919. The school, located at Lake Avenue and Main Street next to Morgan's Chapel, taught children between the ages of four and seventeen. The teacher was paid between $18 to $25 per month and had to board with the students' families. In the 1890s the school was expanded to a two-room schoolhouse with classes upstairs and down. After the school closed, the building was moved to the south side of Lake Avenue, where it stands today as a private residence. Long Hill Trolley tracks can also be viewed in this photograph. Shown below are the students in Mr. Frank Seeley's class in 1895.

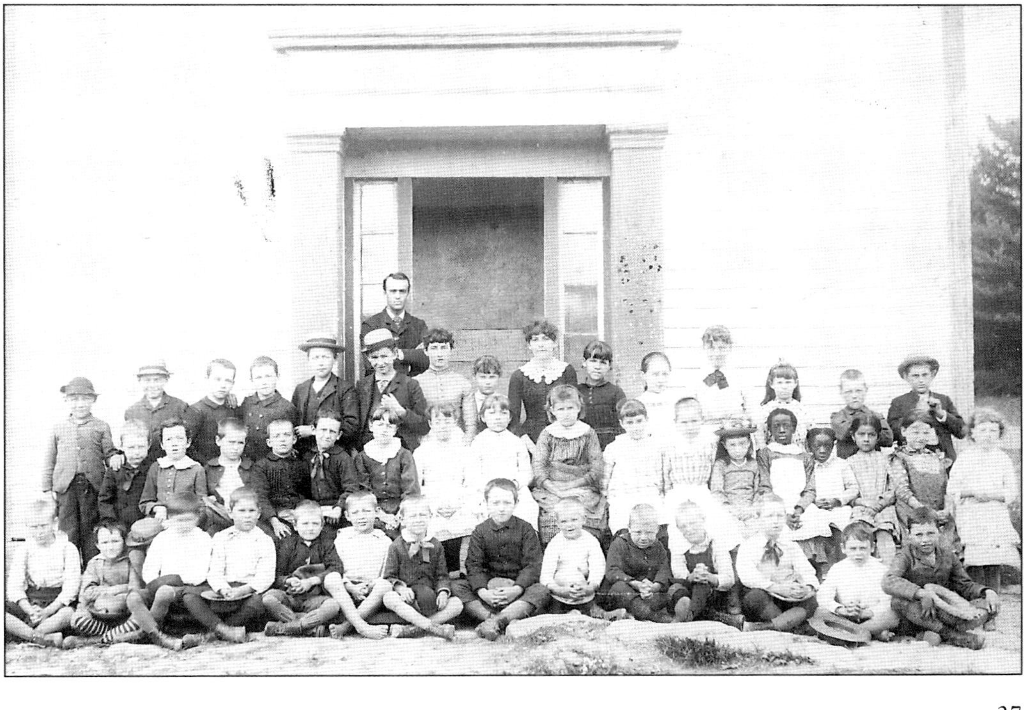

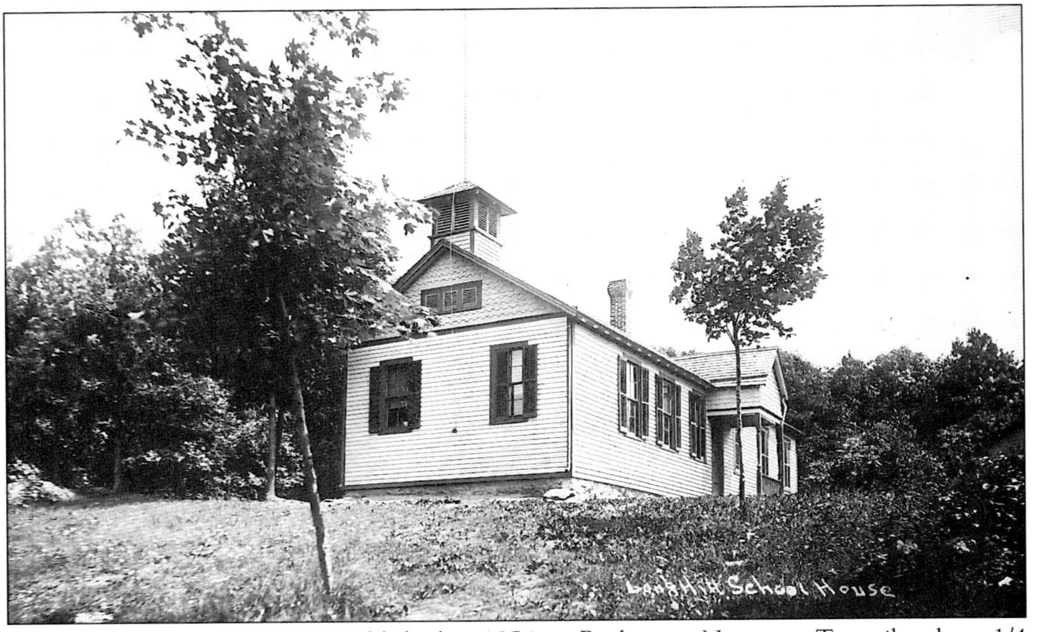


North Long Hill School was established in 1854 on Bridgeport-Newtown Turnpike about 1/4 mile north of the Long Hill Green on land donated by Peter Gabler. It was a small rural school. Desks and benches were used for all grades. In chilly weather, the stove was fired up daily by the teacher, a requirement of the position. The boys cut up the donated wood and carted it into the school for the teacher. While this schoolroom seems small and bleak by today's standards, it was a happy place to learn. The fine old stove in this picture is now the property of the Trumbull Historical Society.

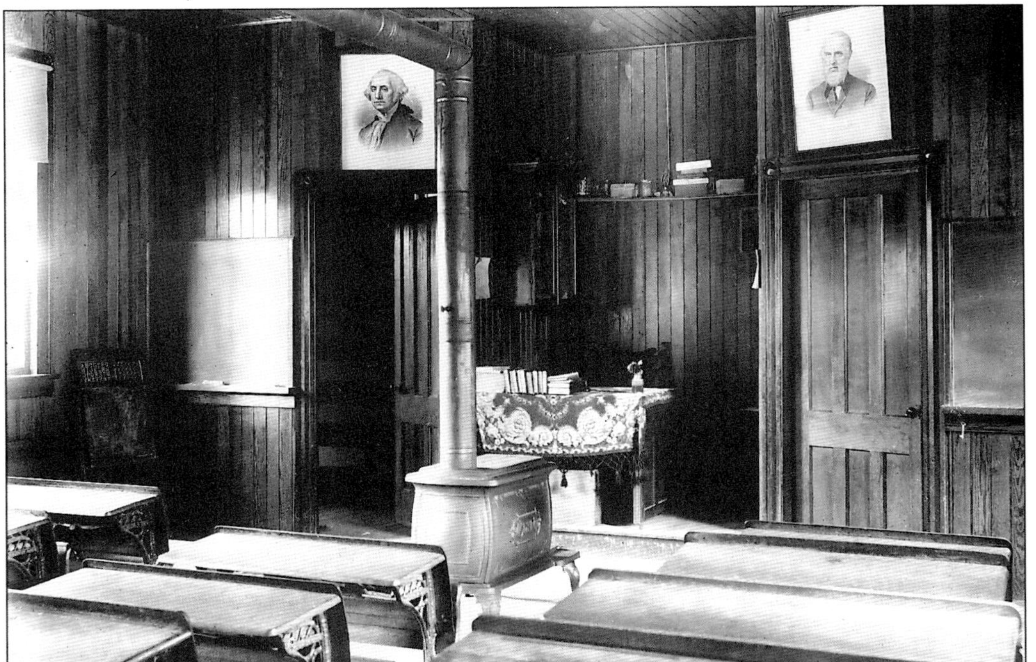

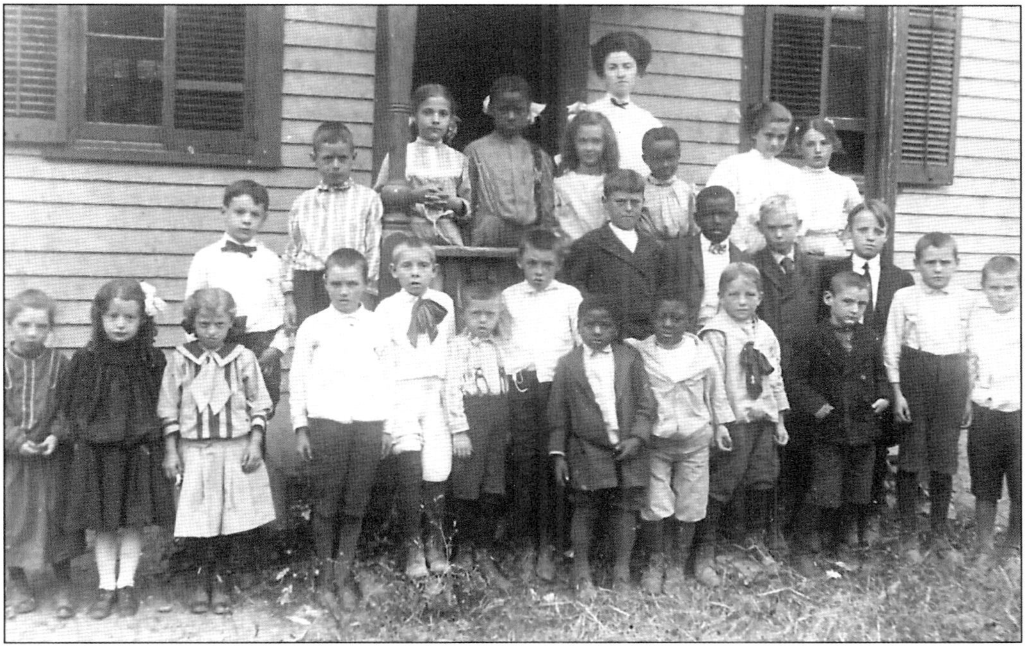

Teacher and students pose in front of North Long Hill School in 1910. In 1911 the school's name was changed to Upper Long Hill School. Students were taught at this site until 1920, when a new brick school was constructed on Main Street. This building is now a private residence on the hillside on the east side of Main Street, just north of Gisella Road.

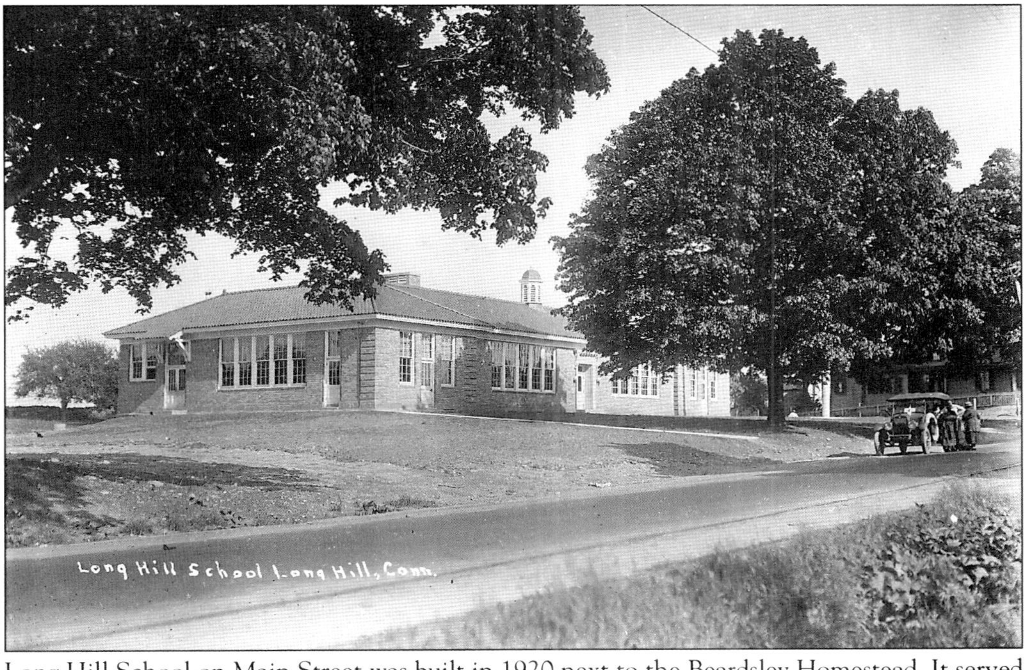


Long Hill School on Main Street was built in 1920 next to the Beardsley Homestead. It served as an elementary school until June 1980. Today it serves as the administrative offices for the Trumbull Board of Education.

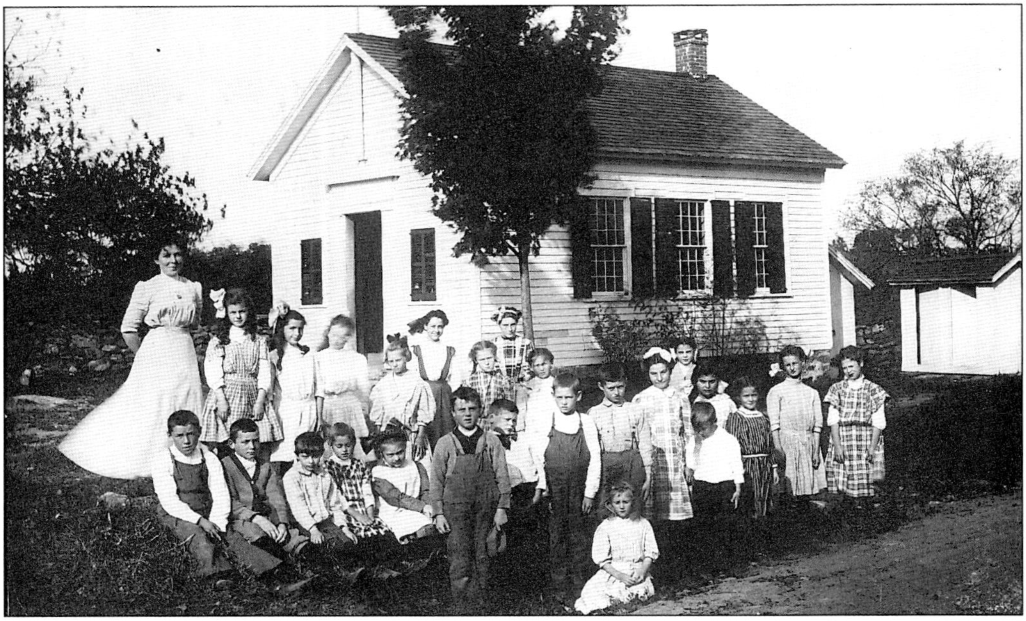

Tashua School, located at the northwest corner of the intersection of Madison Avenue and Fuller Road, is now a dwelling house. This school was used until 1920, when the students were transported to the new Long Hill School on Main Street by Henry Adams Sr., who was paid $5.18 per day to transport all students. Tashua School District, first formed in 1760, was named for the local Tamtashua Indians.

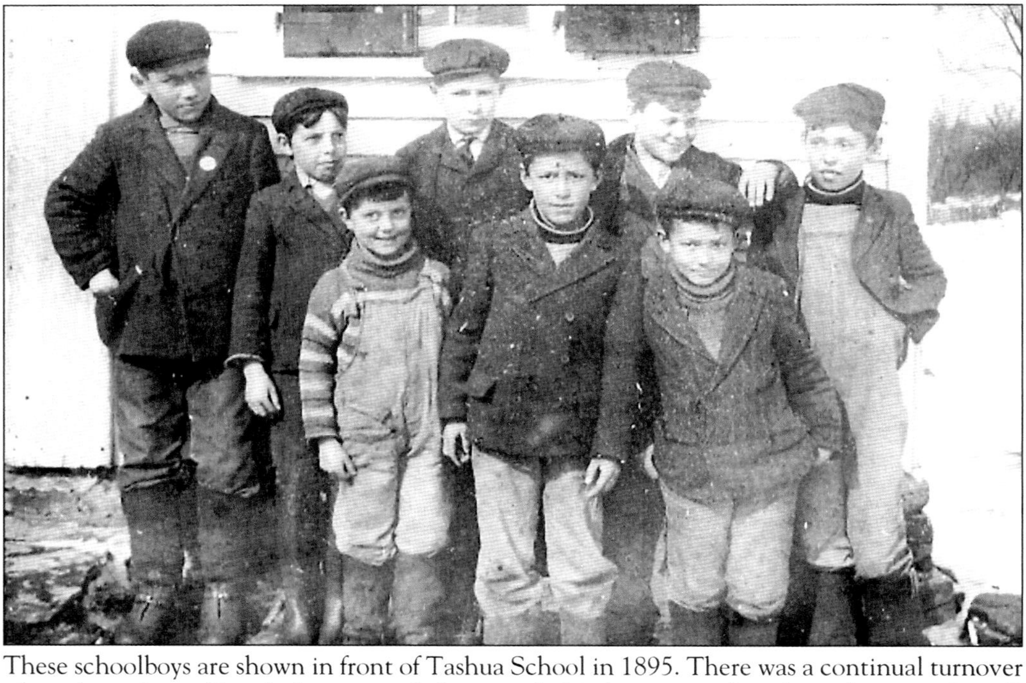

These schoolboys are shown in front of Tashua School in 1895. There was a continual turnover of teachers. It could only be assumed that unruly big boys, poor boarding places, and small salaries had something to do with it. The highest annual salary for a teacher in 1895 was $399.

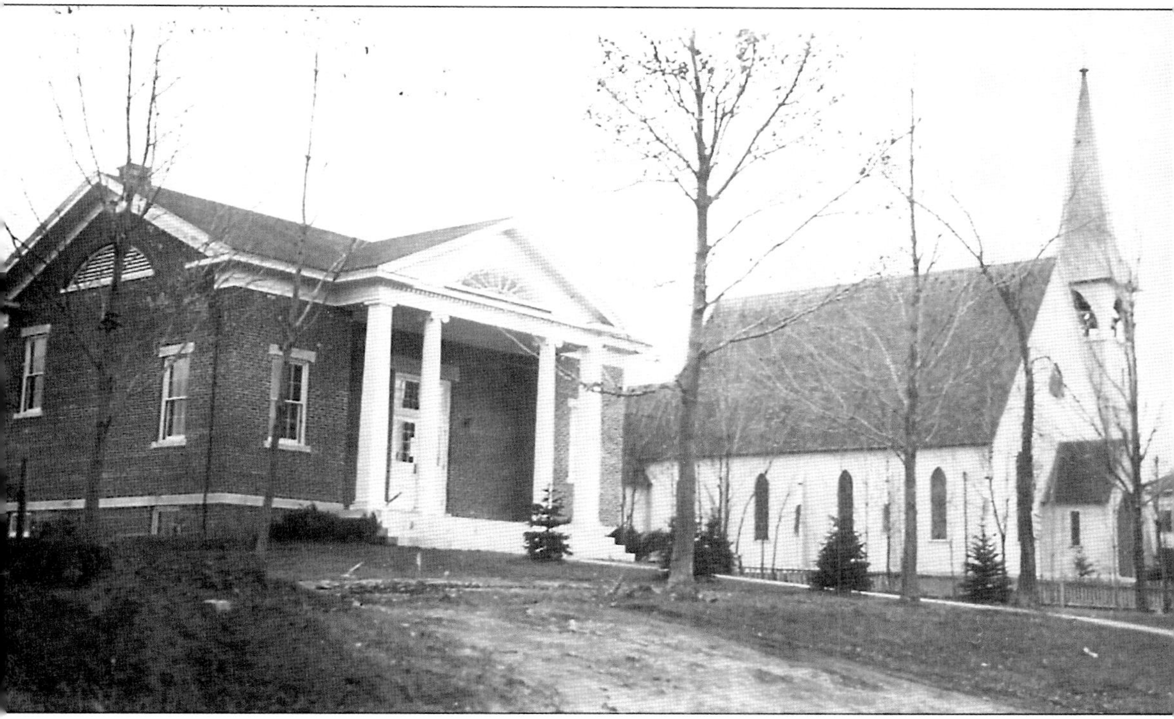

The Hawley Memorial Library on Main Street, a gift of Elizabeth Rand Hawley and Walter S. Hawley, was erected in 1936 in memory of David Banks Hawley and his mother, Isadora Abbott Hawley. The land was donated to the Long Hill Library Association in 1931 by Mrs. Anne Drew Miller, wife of Frank Miller. The library is pictured next to the old Grace Episcopal Church, which was built in 1881. This library was one of three libraries independently serving the town before the Trumbull Main Library was built on Quality Street. The Hawley building was sold. It is now a private residence which pleasantly echoes fond memories of literary pursuits.

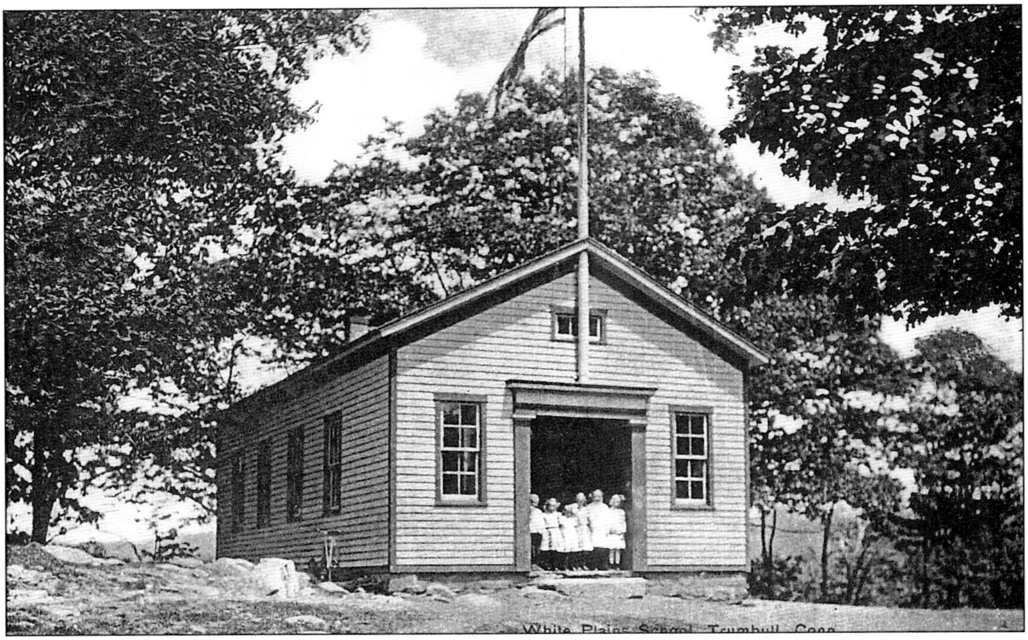

White Plains School, shown *c.* 1905, was originally one room, but was later enlarged to two rooms and, finally, a third room was erected south of the original. In 1926 the school annex was moved and used as part of the Trumbull Center Firehouse. In 1878, a teacher was paid monthly $32.00 if male and $31.78 if female. School expenses for the year 1878 totaled $2,316.73. The interior view shows the double desks at that time, with girls on one side of the room and boys on the other. A map of the United States is in the upper right. Single desks were purchased for the school in 1914.

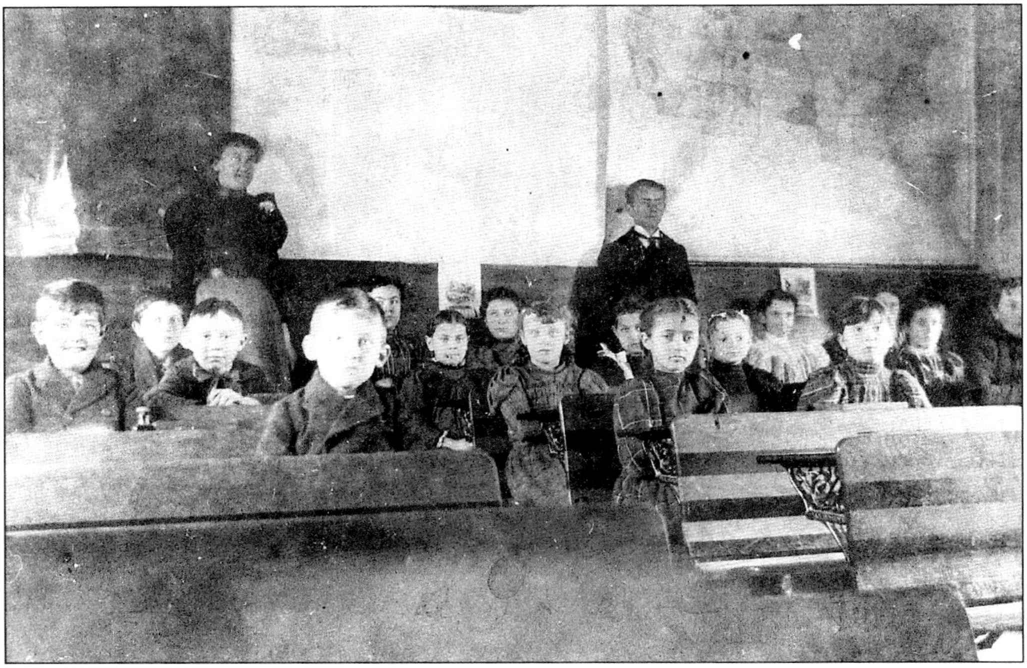

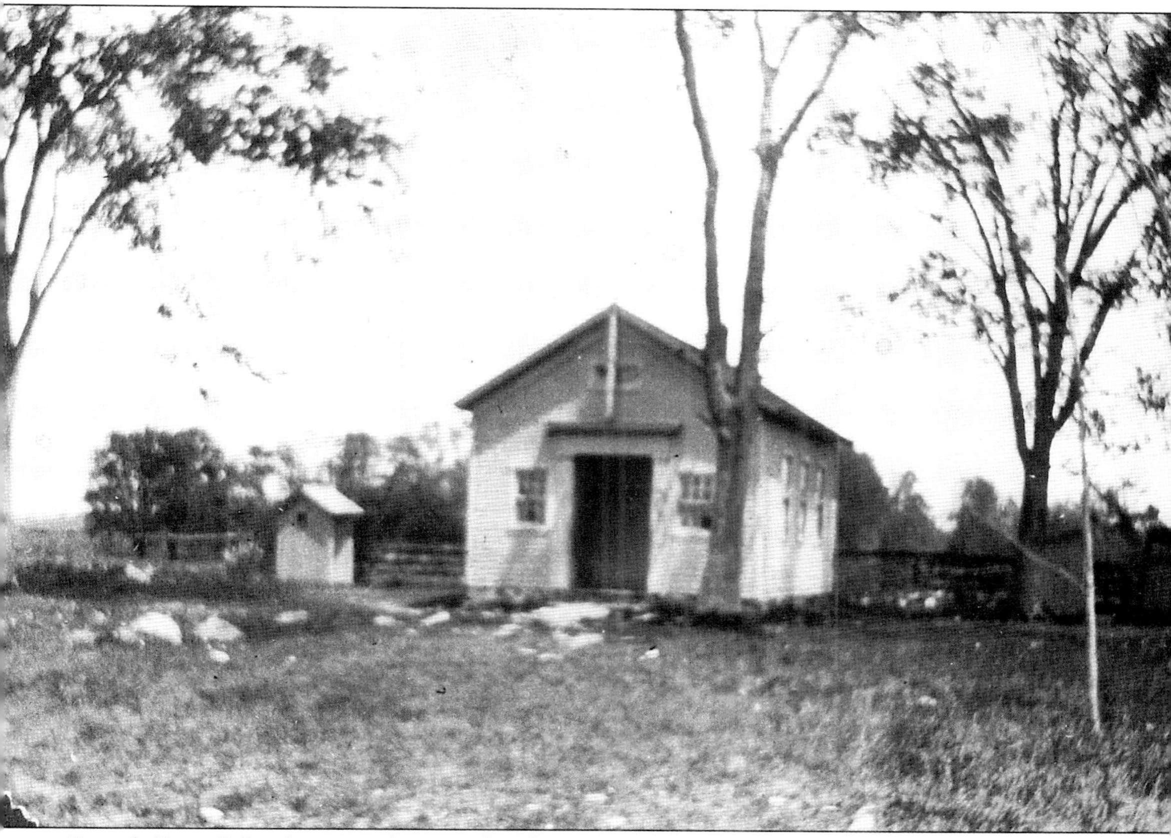

Daniels Farm School, a typical 1880 schoolhouse as it looked in 1907, is now a dwelling across the street to the south of Mohawk Drive. This small wooden building was a wonderful place to learn for many Trumbull youngsters. One among them was E. Merrill Beach, who later became a banker, and whose fine knowledge of Trumbull history has been a benefit to all. Notice, to the left of the building, an outhouse for the girls; to the right is a wood shed and an outhouse for the boys.

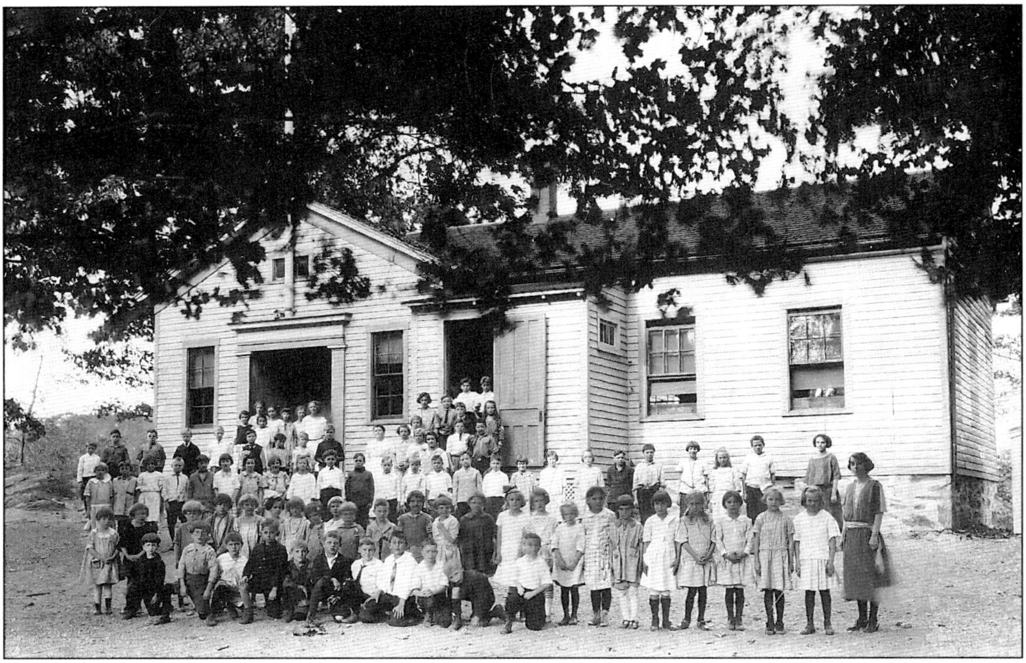

Students and teachers pose for a class picture in front of the White Plains School in 1924. The school districts were consolidated in the mid-1920s. In 1927 the town sold the school property and today it is a private residence. A visiting state nurse made an inspection of Trumbull schools in 1922 and reported no soap was found in any school.

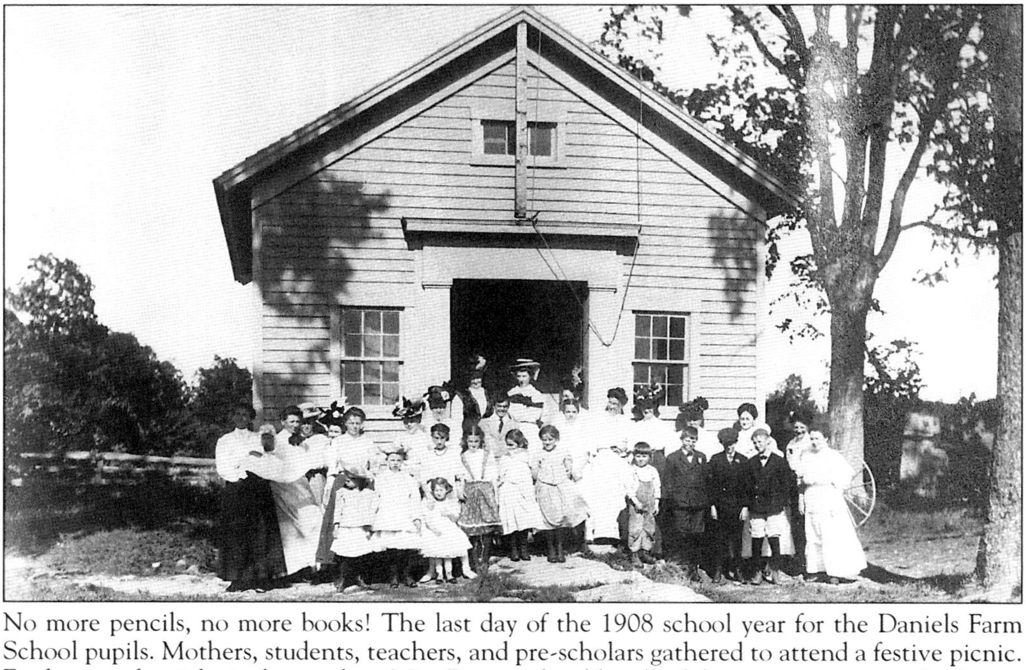

No more pencils, no more books! The last day of the 1908 school year for the Daniels Farm School pupils. Mothers, students, teachers, and pre-scholars gathered to attend a festive picnic. Farthest to the right is the teacher, Miss Bruce, who, like all of the youngsters, was also happy that the summer vacation was ahead.

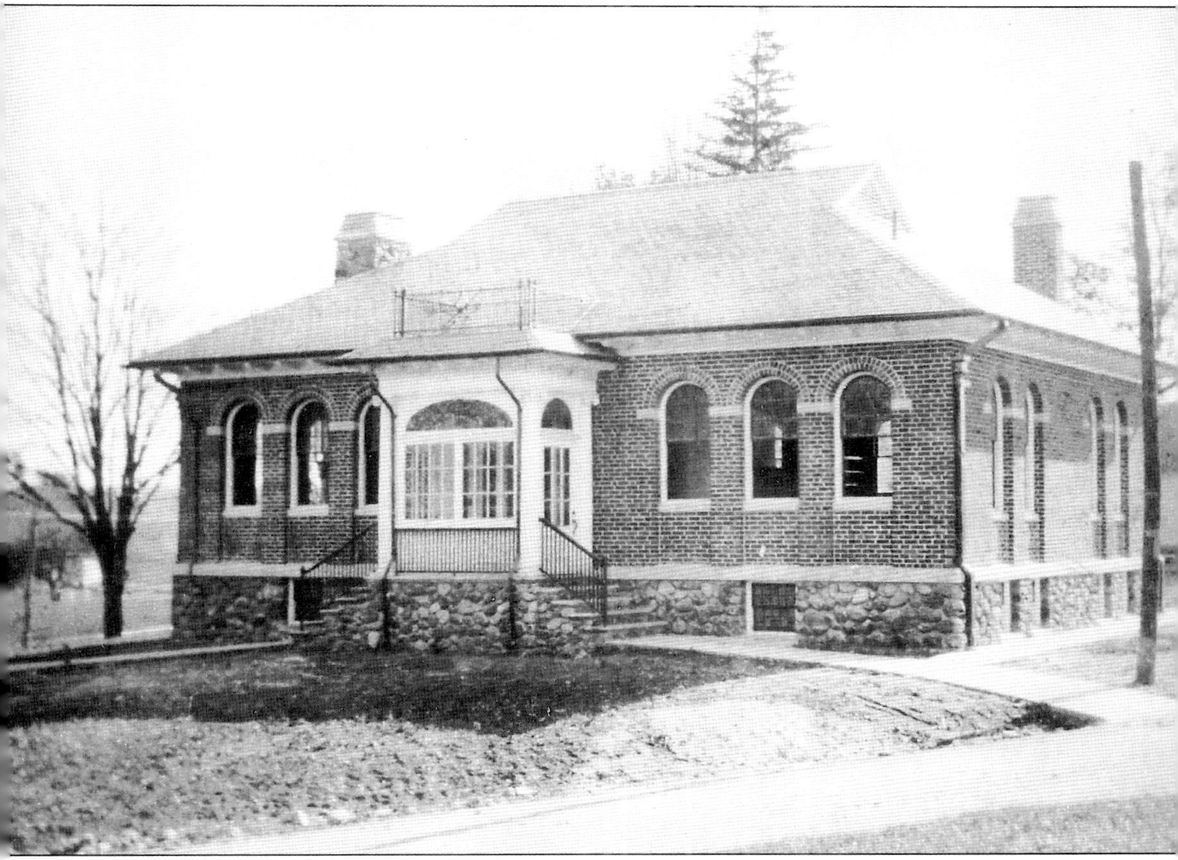

The Nichols Memorial Library was donated in 1922 by George Marcus Nichols and his sister, Mrs. Mary Nichols Merwin. The building is situated snug on a hillside on White Plains Road, Trumbull Center, uniquely placed between the Trumbull Congregational Church and parsonage. The donors were members of the church, and records show that when the building was no longer serving as a library, it would revert back to the church. It was one of the libraries phased out with the erection of the main Trumbull Library and it is now known as the Nichols Building, serving the church for special activities.

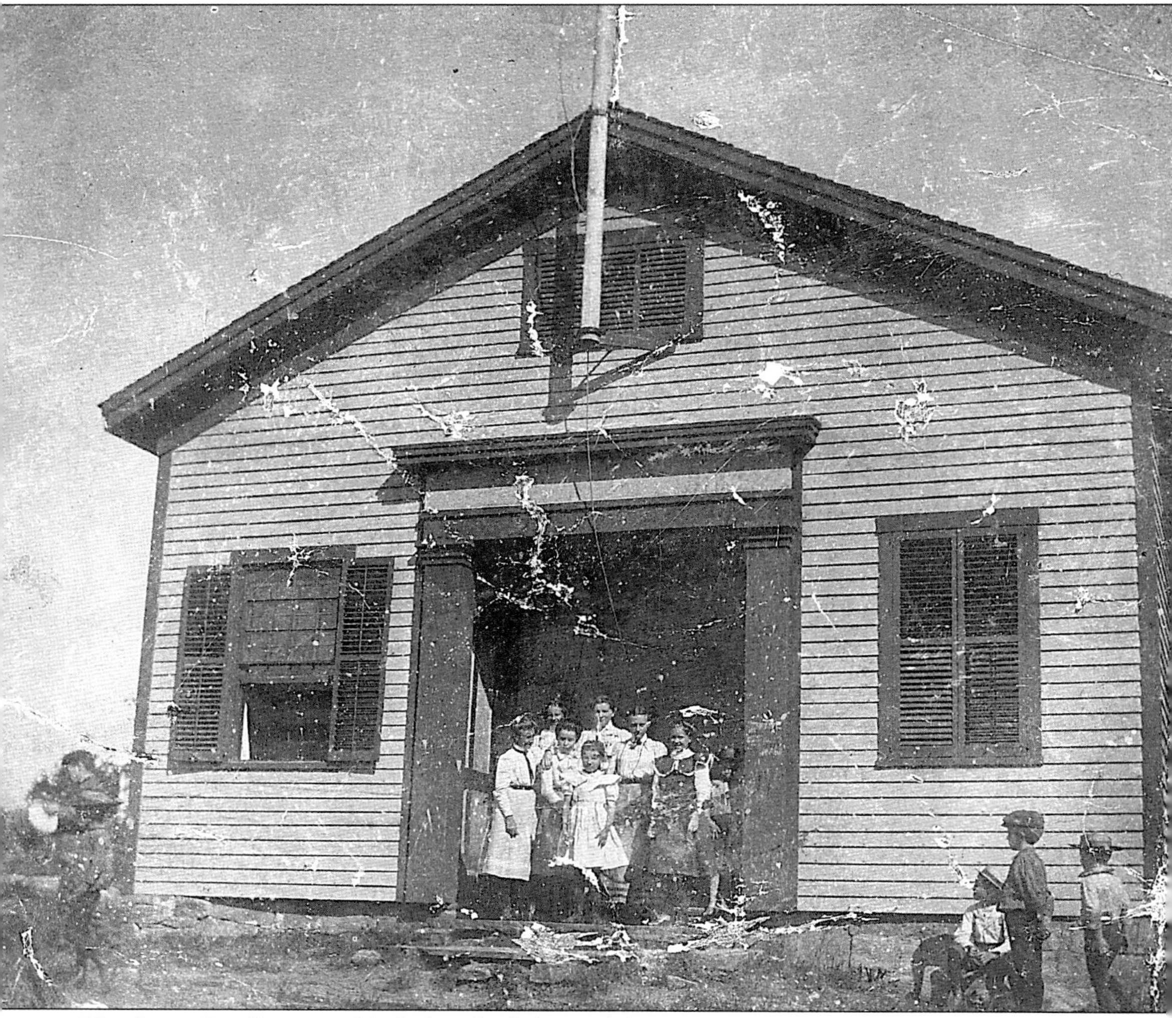

The first schoolhouse in Nichols, which burned down in the mid-1800s, was located on the east side of Huntington Turnpike on what is now Abraham Nichols Park. The children were temporarily taught in a room of Oliver Plumb's store until this one-room schoolhouse was built on Shelton Road in 1860. This building was remodeled into a two- and then a four-room building and was used as a school until 1920, when a new brick school was built on Priscilla Place.

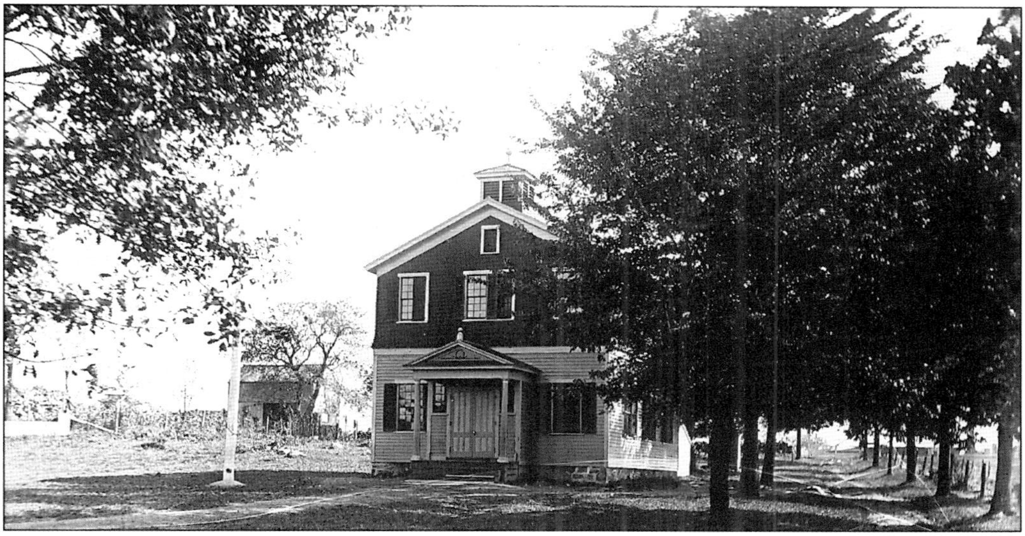

By 1893, an enlarged enrollment made it necessary to add another story to the Shelton Road schoolhouse. When the school was no longer needed in the early 1920s, the building was used by the Nichols Fire Department until its present firehouse was built on the site.

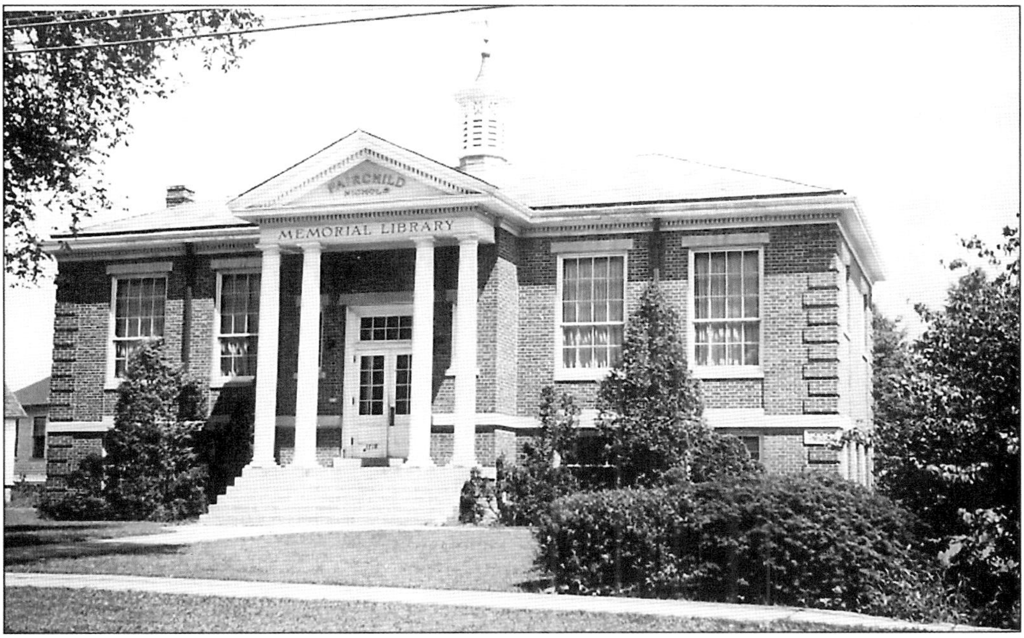


Fairchild Memorial Library moved into its modern building on Huntington Turnpike in September 1929. The library started with a total of a thousand volumes in one room of the old wooden firehouse behind the present Nichols Fire Headquarters in 1922. A gift of land and building materials by Erwin and Edith Fairchild made construction of a modern building possible. This library is the only branch library still in existence as part of the town library system.

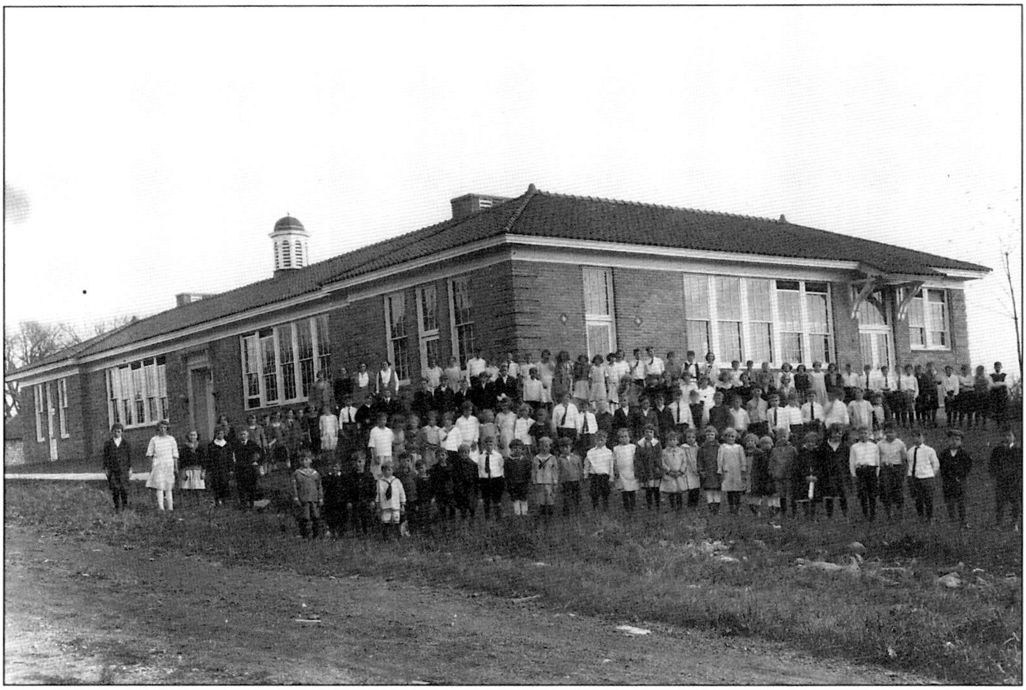

Nichols School on Priscilla Place (pictured) and its twin, Long Hill School on Main Street, were built in 1920 under the same contract for a total of $75,699 plus architect's fees of $4,000. The school contained four classrooms and a central auditorium. Teachers taught two grade levels per classroom. Miss Anne Merritt was principal and teacher of seventh and eighth grades in 1924.

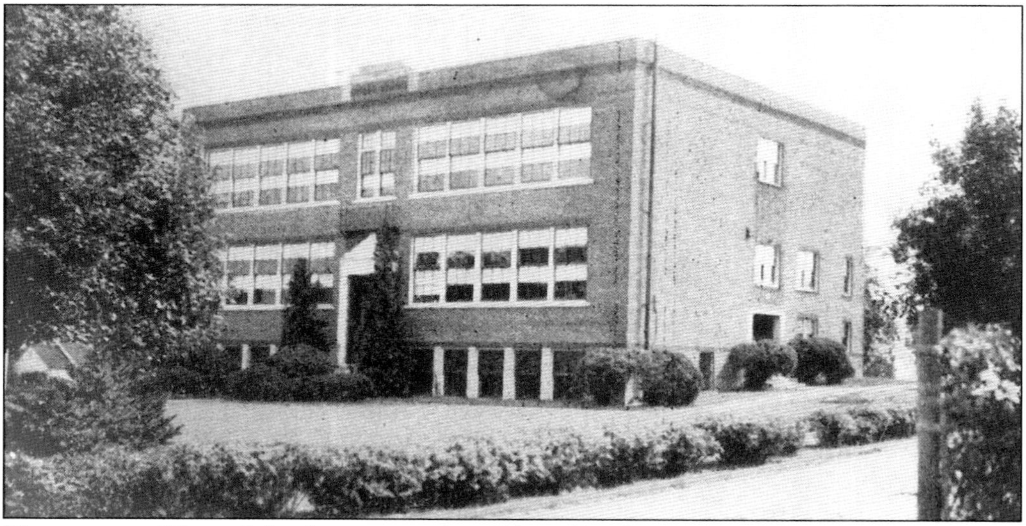

The six-room Edison School was erected on Edison Road in 1929. Four rooms were added in 1948 to serve the growing educational needs of lower Long Hill. The school was demolished in 1980. Today it is the site of Trumbull Police Headquarters.

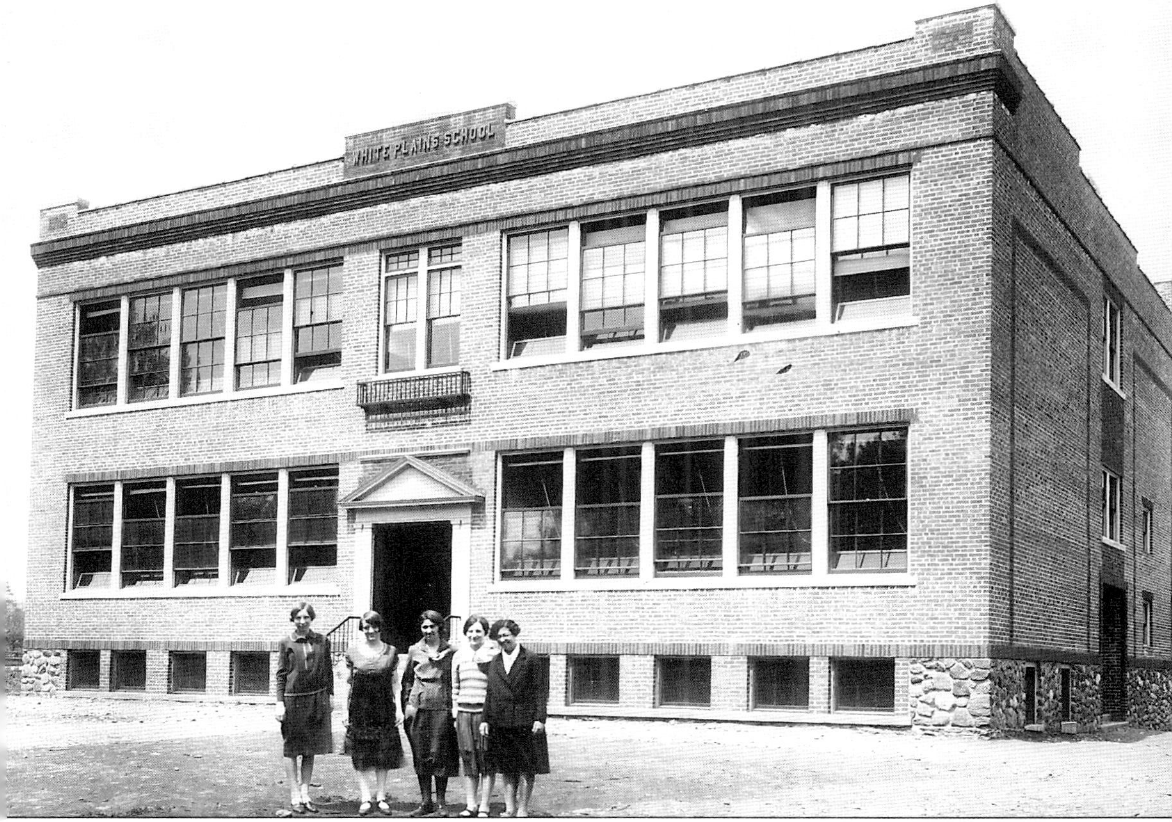


White Plains School, later known as Trumbull Center School, was located on White Plains Road next to the Trumbull Burying Ground. This photograph, taken in 1926, one year after the school was built, shows the five teachers. From left to right, those pictured are as follows: Frances Linley, Leverne Shipman, Beth Davis, Vera Hitt, and Marie Martin. Four rooms were added to the school in 1936. In 1985 the school was demolished and today a bank and professional offices are located on the site.

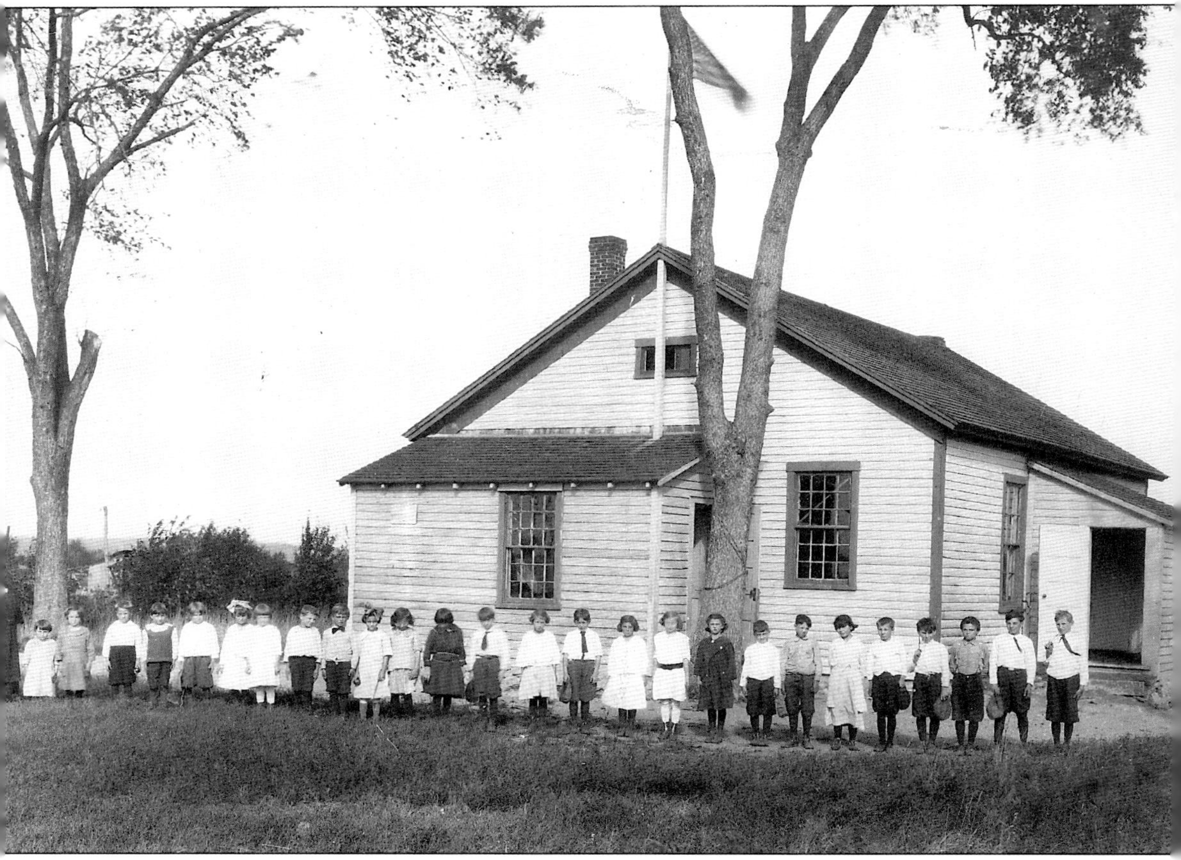

Daniels Farm School stood on the east side of the road about half a mile north of Strobel Road. This photograph was taken about 1915 and shows the school after it went from one to two rooms. The shed affair on the front included the added luxury of a "cloak room." In 1921, the school was closed and the children in the Daniels Farm District were bussed to Nichols to the new brick schoolhouse on Priscilla Place.

# Four

# Making a Living

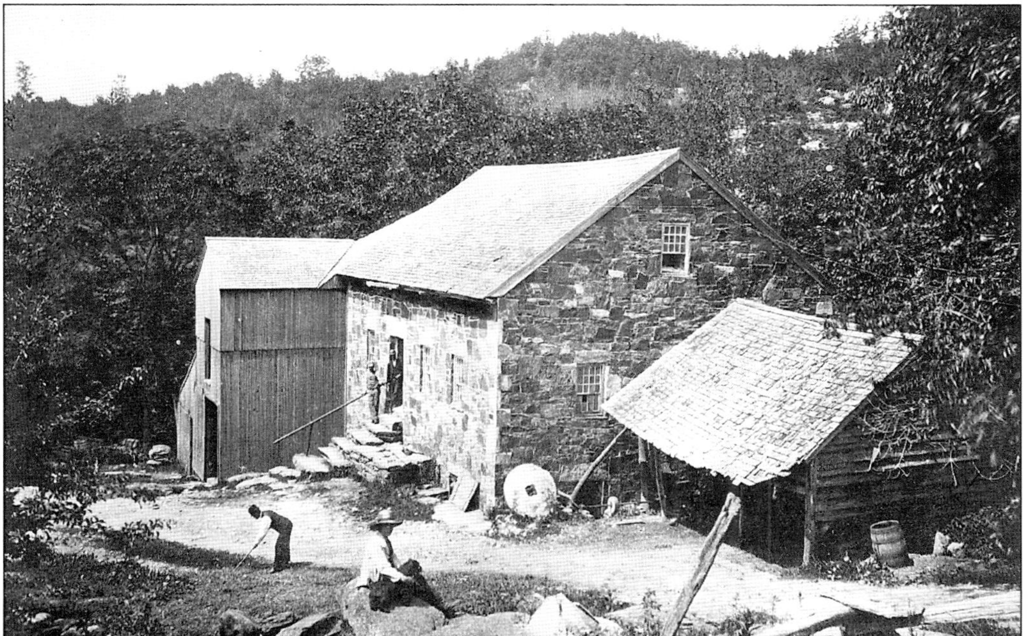

Beer's Gristmill (1885) on the Pequonnock River used water power from Parlor Rock Falls to operate. Seated in this picture is Charles Hubbard, who lived across the street from the mill. The wooden building in the rear housed a generator that supplied electricity to Parlor Rock Park.

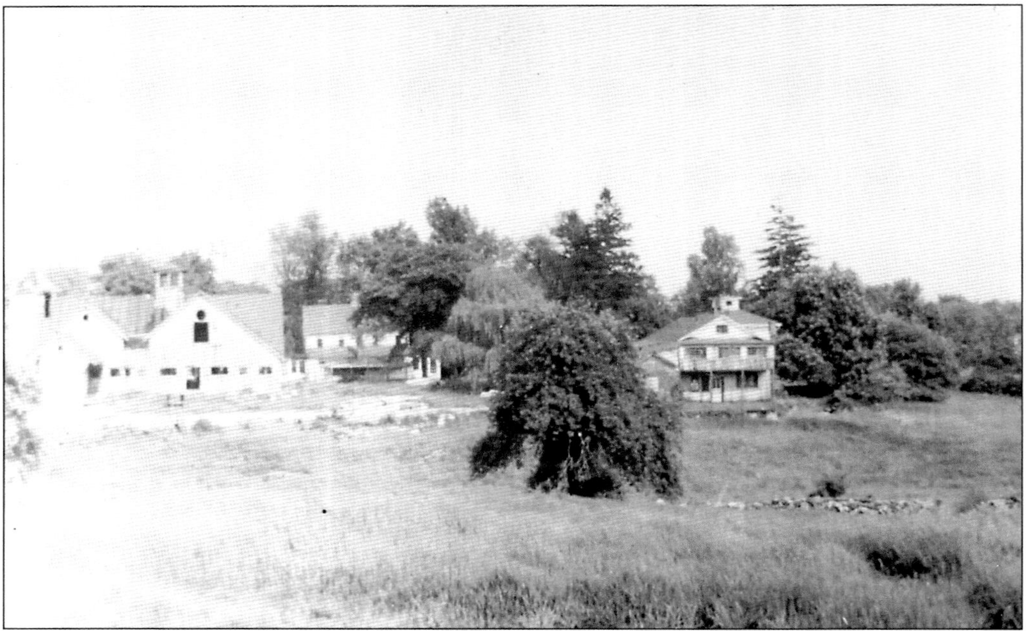

This large farm owned by John Nichols was on Huntington Turnpike north of Unity Road. In the photograph above, taken from the rear pasture looking toward the turnpike, the cupola of the Starkweather House is on the right. The house in the center was built as a rental property for extra income. The beautiful farm buildings seen in the close-up below were the pride of the family. It is said the lumber used to construct them was perfect—"no knots." By 1955 the last vestige of the farm was gone. The pasture is now heavily wooded and the grounds and remaining house are now home to the Nichols Improvement Association.

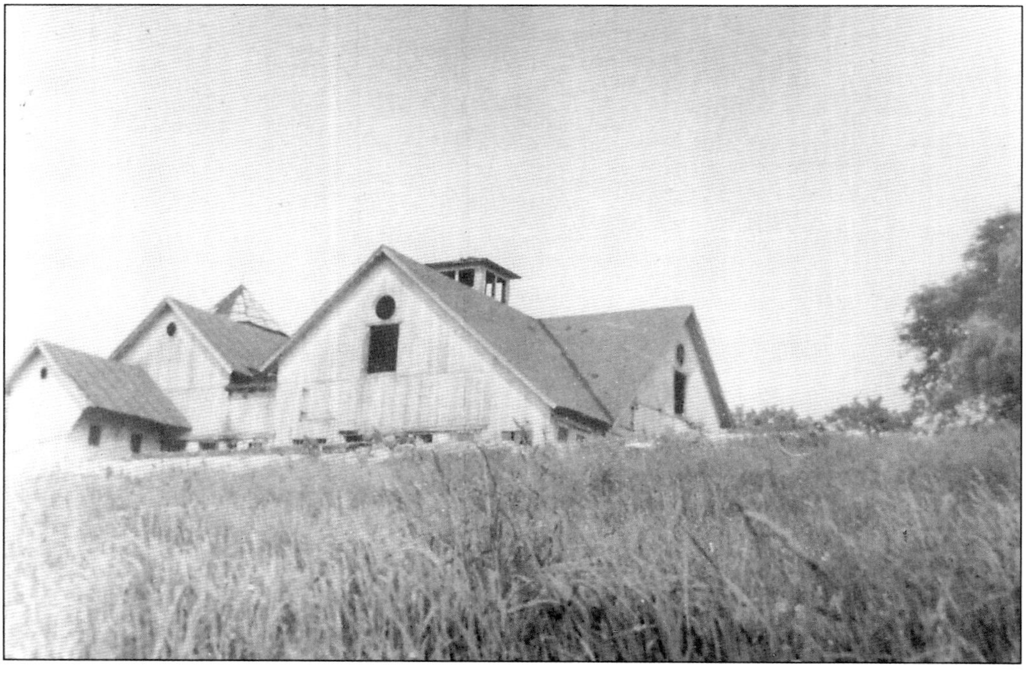

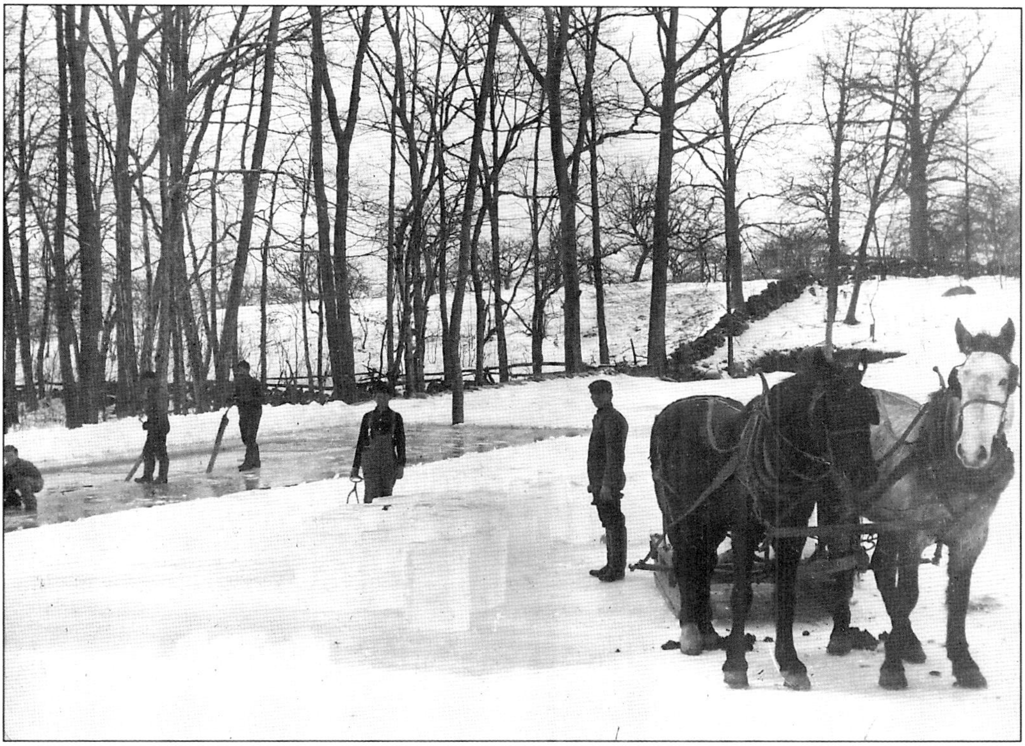

Men are cutting ice on Buck Hill Pond at Agur Beach's farm in 1906. The water was frozen to a depth of 10 to 12 inches, and saws were used to cut the ice into blocks. The ice was then pulled by horses for storage in Mr. Beach's ice house.

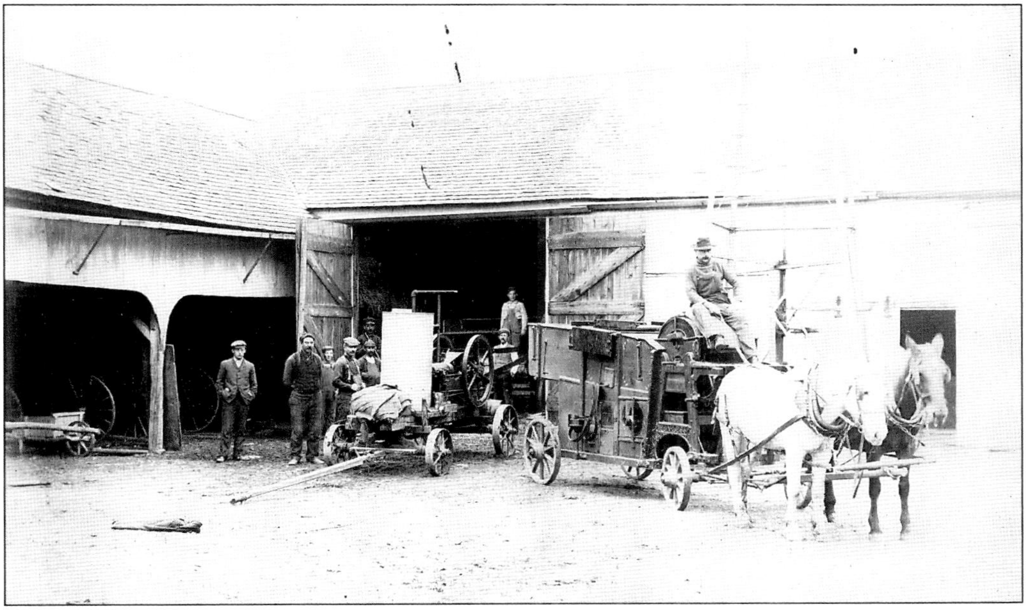

Workmen anticipating a busy day gather their harvesting equipment at Agur Beach's barn on Plattsville Road.

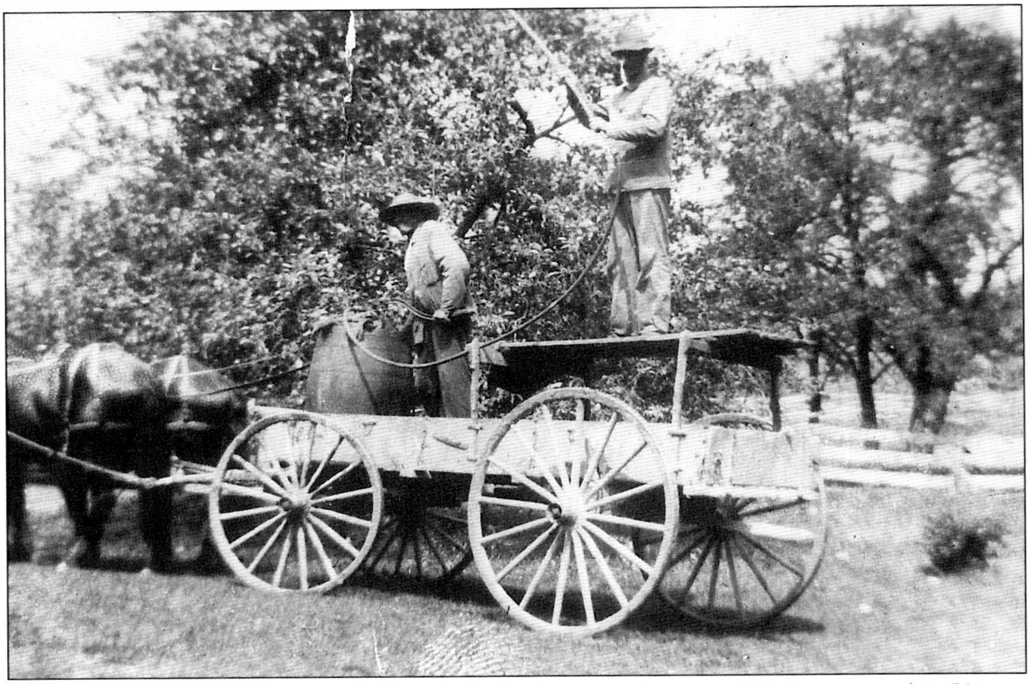

In 1915, a photographer snapped Sam Seeley's picture as he sprayed fruit trees on his 50-acre farm. A Seeley family deed shows that part of their property on Seeley Road was purchased in 1795, two years before Trumbull officially became a town.

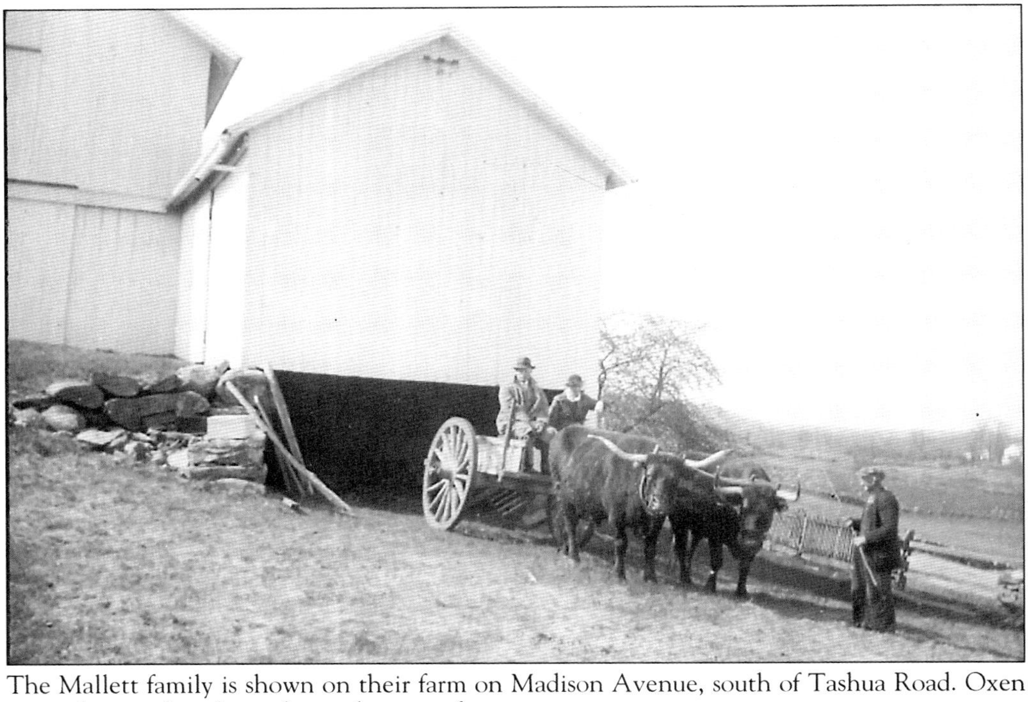

The Mallett family is shown on their farm on Madison Avenue, south of Tashua Road. Oxen were often preferred over horses by many farmers.

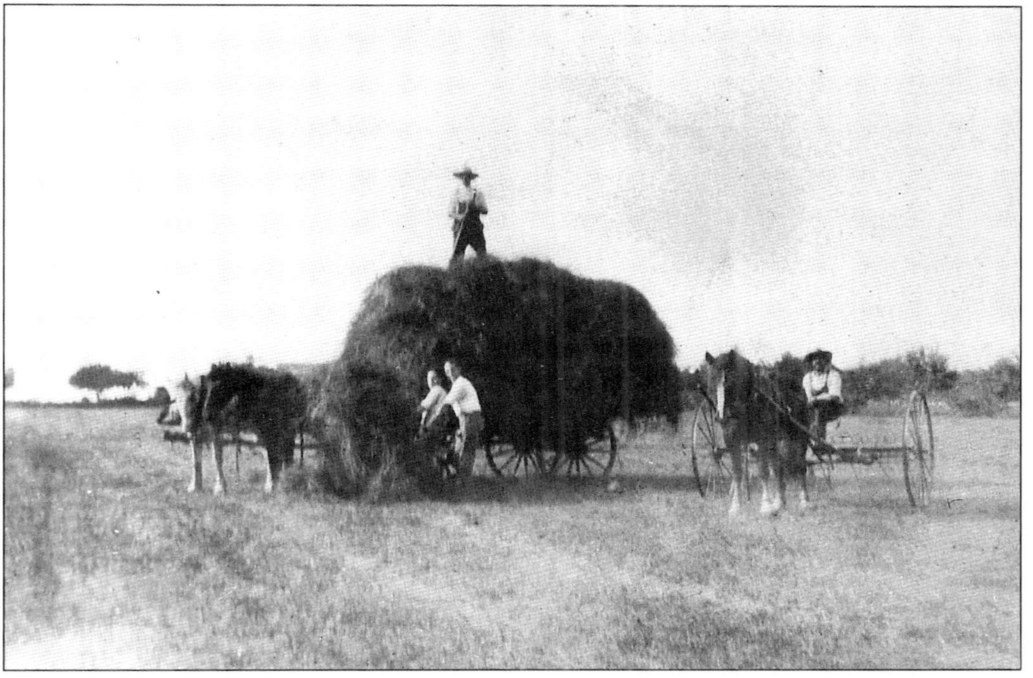

Banford Beach stands atop his hay wagon in 1910. The farm, located where Daniels Farm School stands today, consisted of 85 acres and cost Mr. Beach $2,040 when it was purchased.

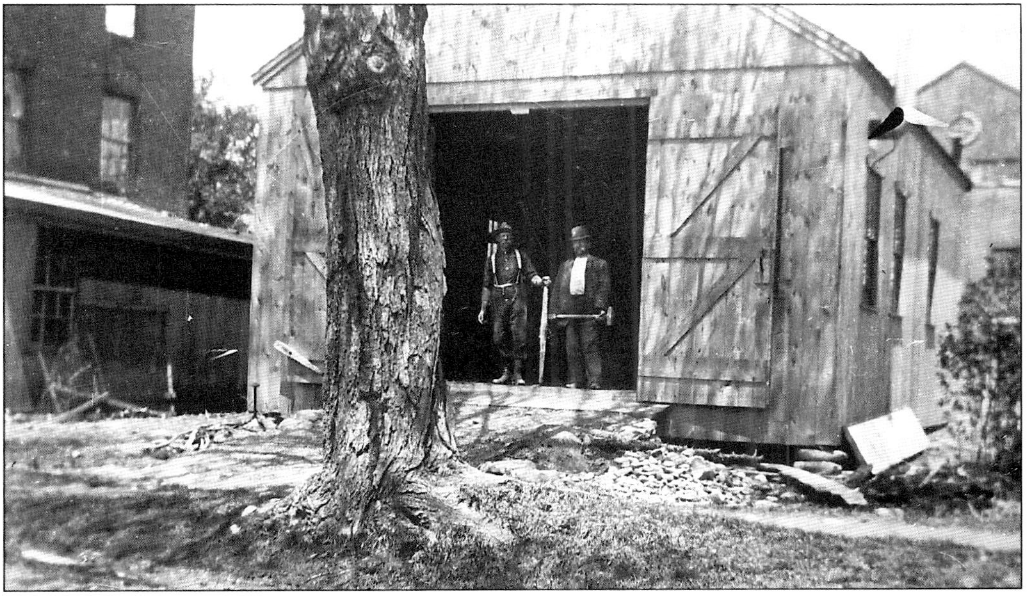

Ernest L. Hitt, the village blacksmith, moved to Trumbull from Monticello, New York, in 1905. His blacksmith shop was located next to his home on Center Road in Nichols. Mr. Hitt repaired carriages, wagons, and saddles. He also forged the ironwork that holds the bells for the old Nichols Methodist Church and the iron for the eagle atop the flagpole on Nichols Green. The E.L. Hitt Blacksmith shop was forced out of business in 1916 due to declining business caused by the increased use of the automobile.

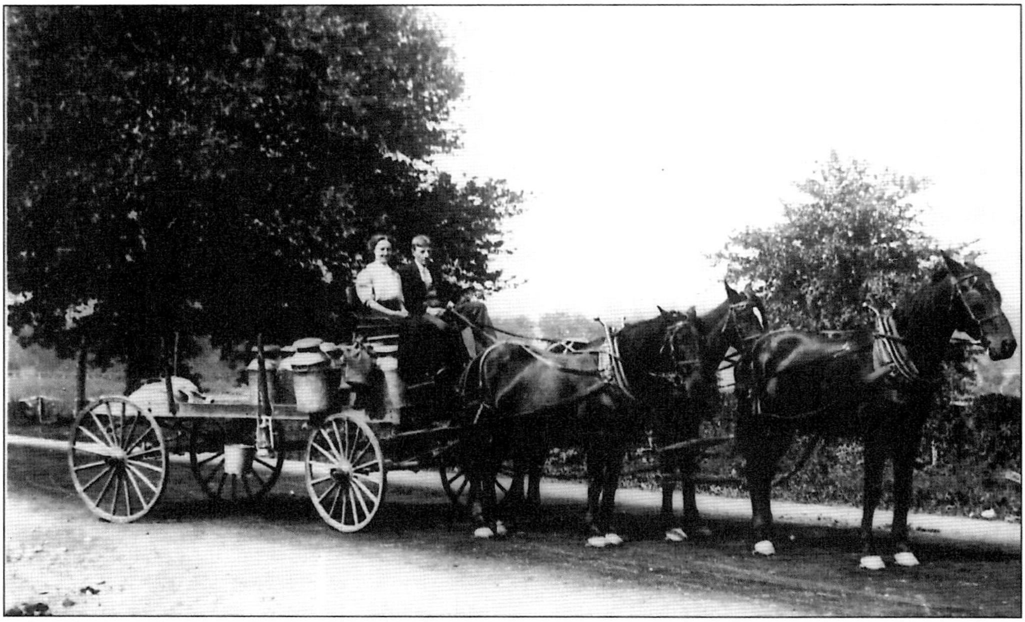

After the Civil War, as Bridgeport grew, dairy farming became the main occupation in Trumbull. Jobe's Dairy of Long Hill peddled milk by horse and wagon. The milk was stored in the large cans from which they would fill a measure and place the milk into a customer's waiting pail or bottle. Those who called at the farm received a lower price for the milk. The Jobe Homestead is still standing on the northeast corner of Whitney Avenue and Broadway.

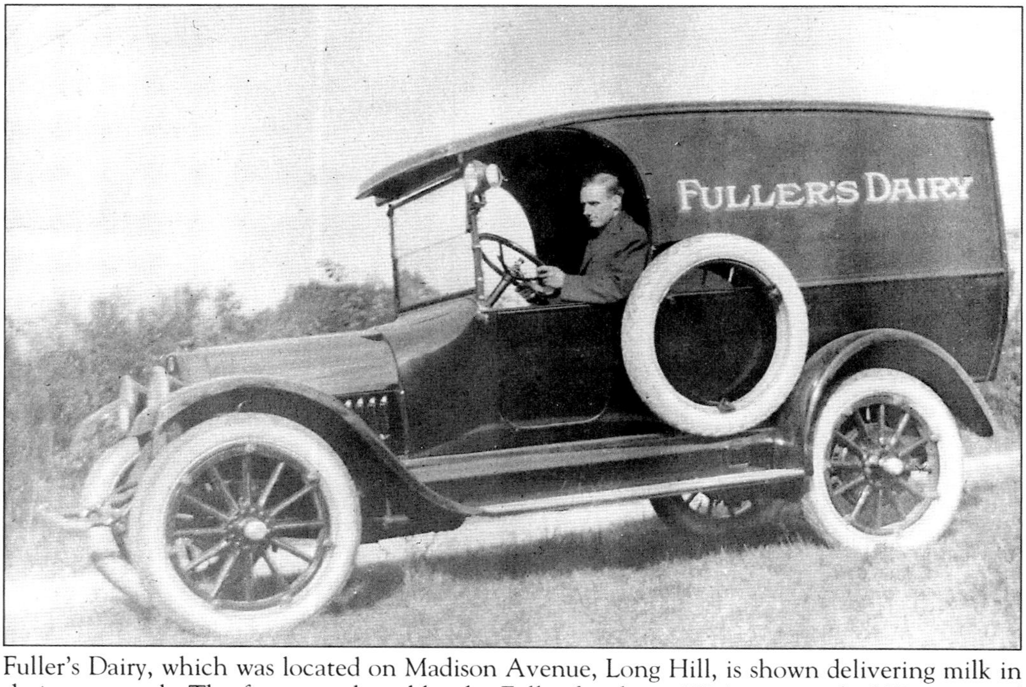


Fuller's Dairy, which was located on Madison Avenue, Long Hill, is shown delivering milk in their new truck. The farm, purchased by the Fuller family in 1904, consisted of 58 acres and remained in the family until 1951.

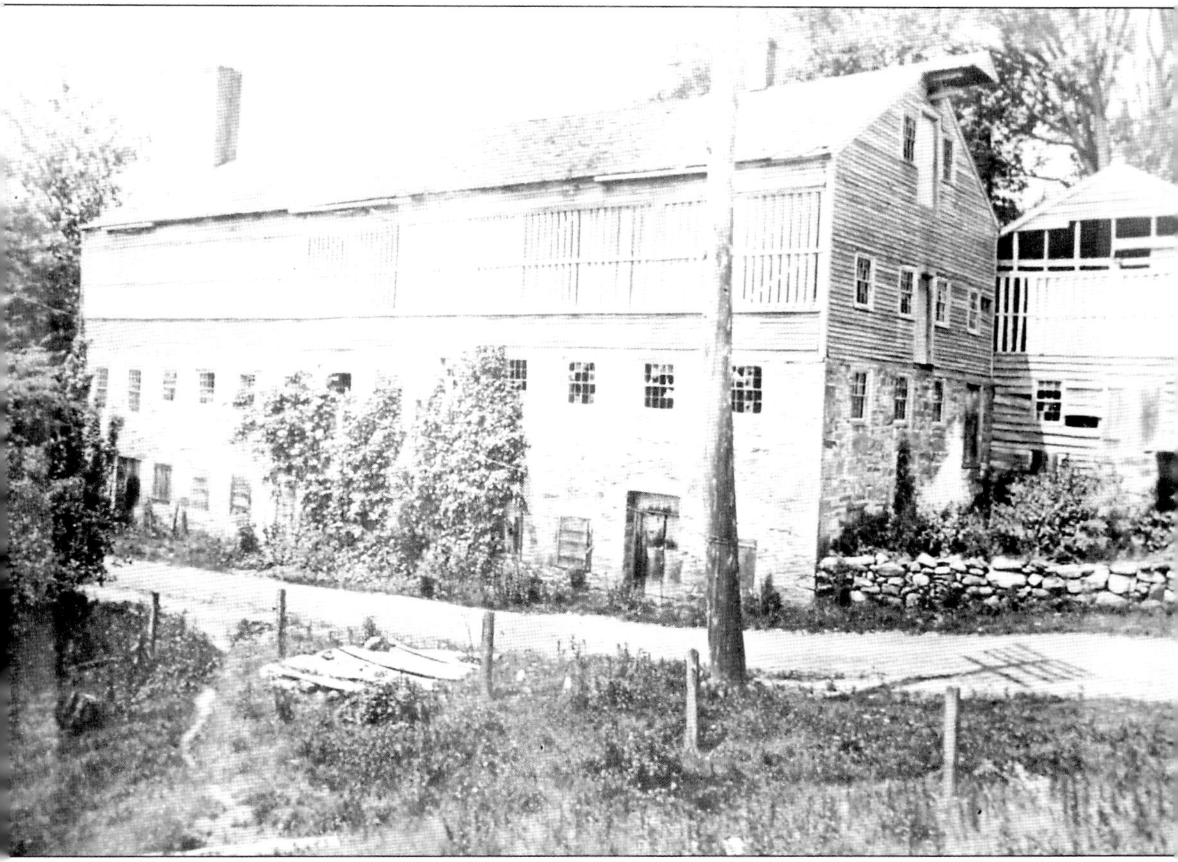

Reuben Fairchild and his brothers, Daniel and Eben, built the Fairchild Paper Mill in 1826. They were guided in their endeavors by Andrew Tait, who had learned the art of papermaking in Scotland. Fairchild Paper Mill was the first mill to make white note paper. The company ran a boarding house for its female employees. The mill stood to the west of White Plains Road at the "Falls" on the Pequonnock River, near what is today the entrance to Fairchild Memorial Park.

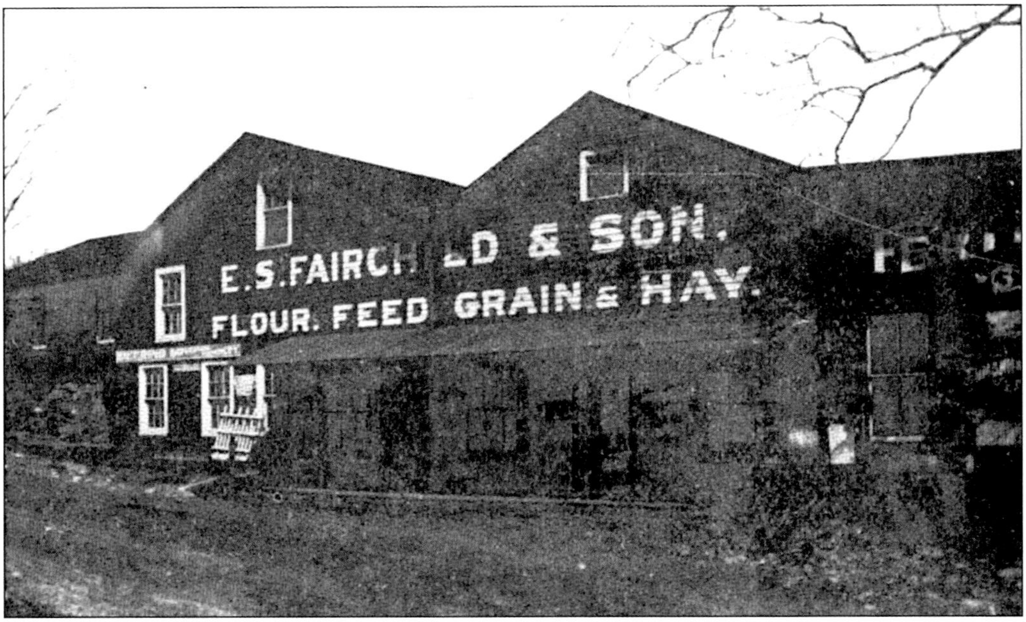


Erwin S. Fairchild's store and mill was located on Huntington Turnpike where it now intersects with Erwin Street. Mr. Fairchild was also known for clearing the roads of Nichols with his homemade snowplow, which was a regular sled with two planks in front nailed together to form a V.

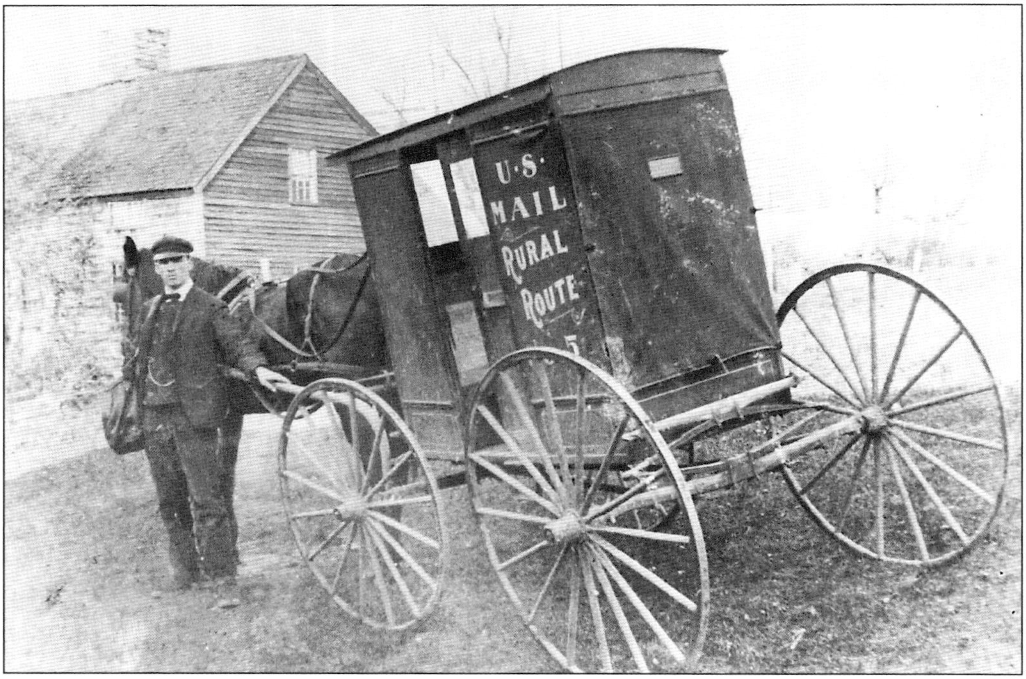


The United States Post Office Rural Free Delivery service was important to support Trumbull's many businesses flourishing in the 1800s and 1900s. Robert Staines is pictured with his mail wagon.

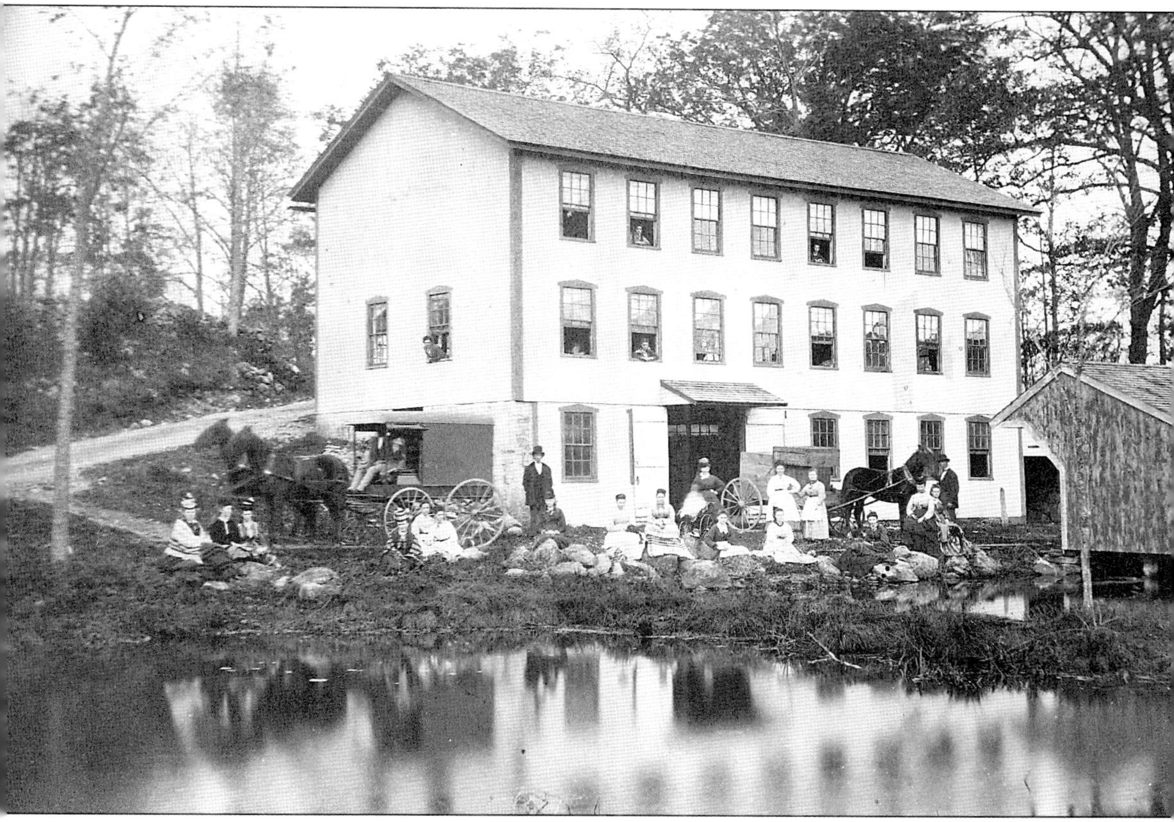

The Tousey Shirt Factory began operation in the 1860s when Wheeler P. Tousey acquired the property on Broadway in Upper Long Hill. The factory, which manufactured men's shirts and undergarments, employed many local people.

After Mr. Tousey's death in 1889, his son, Rinaldo C. Tousey, operated the factory, which not only provided a livelihood for many, but also served the social needs of its workers, who often attended dances held in the upper work room. The workers posed for an official portrait in this 1895 scene.

Rinaldo Tousey died in 1906, and his wife, Ellen A. Tousey, and his sister, Lamora A. Hawley, continued to operate the business until September 1918, when it was sold to William A. Gabler of Oxford. He sold the property in 1923 to the Stepney Witch Hazel Company.

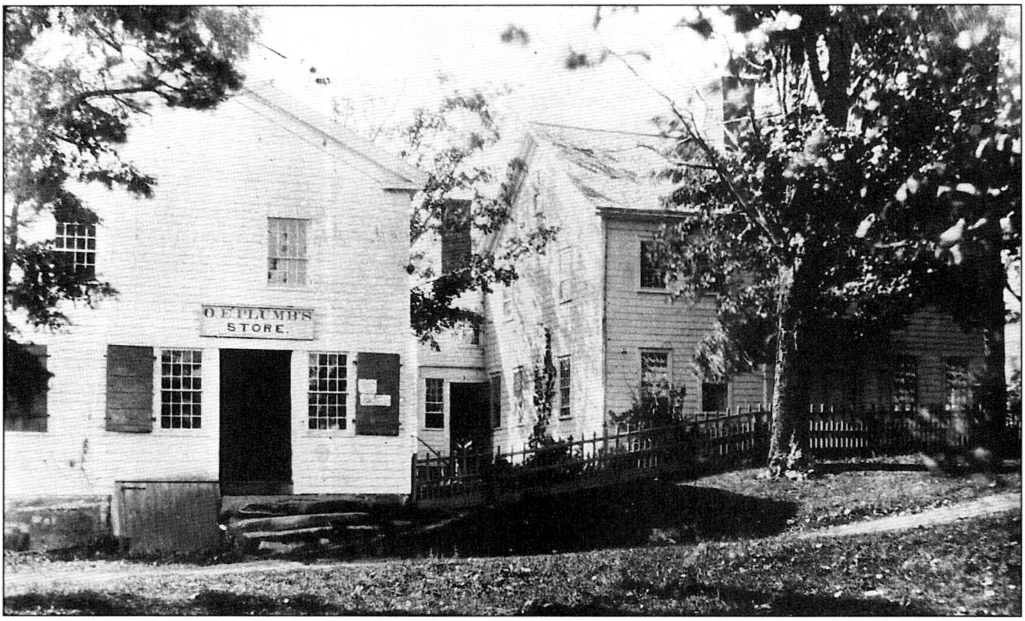


On Huntington Turnpike, Oliver E. Plumb operated a store that was attached to the original homestead of Joseph Plumb, his grandfather. He sold general merchandise, including the products of a slaughterhouse located behind the buildings pictured. The store was operating in the 1860s; the original house was constructed *c.* 1750.

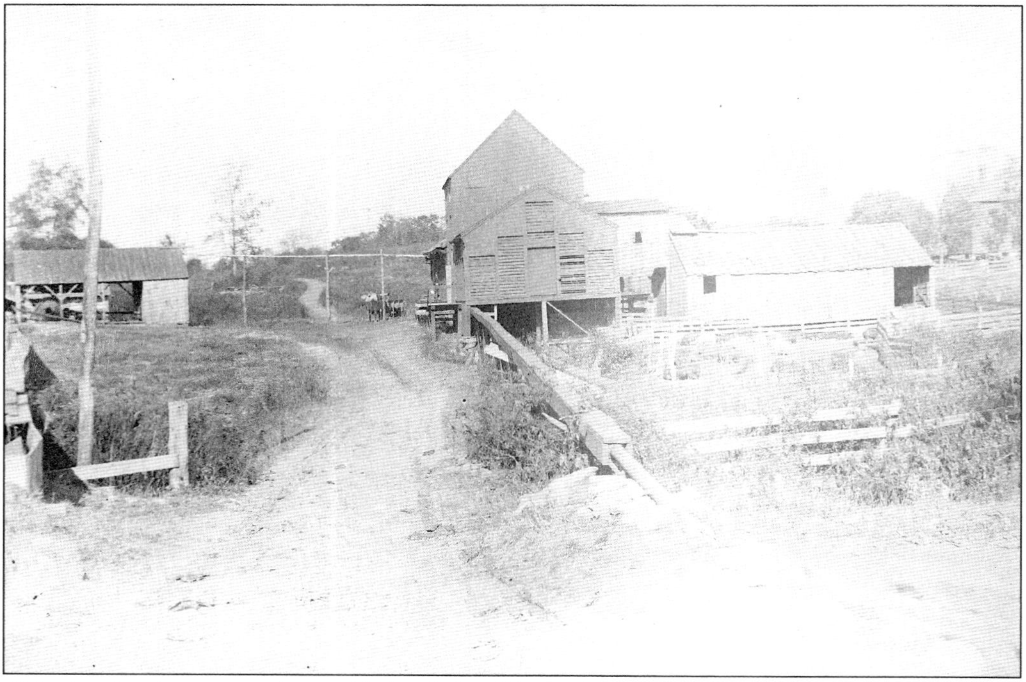

This slaughterhouse was located behind the Oliver E. Plumb store on Huntington Turnpike. Local farmers could have their livestock butchered here for their own use. Freshly cut meat was also sold at the Plumb store.

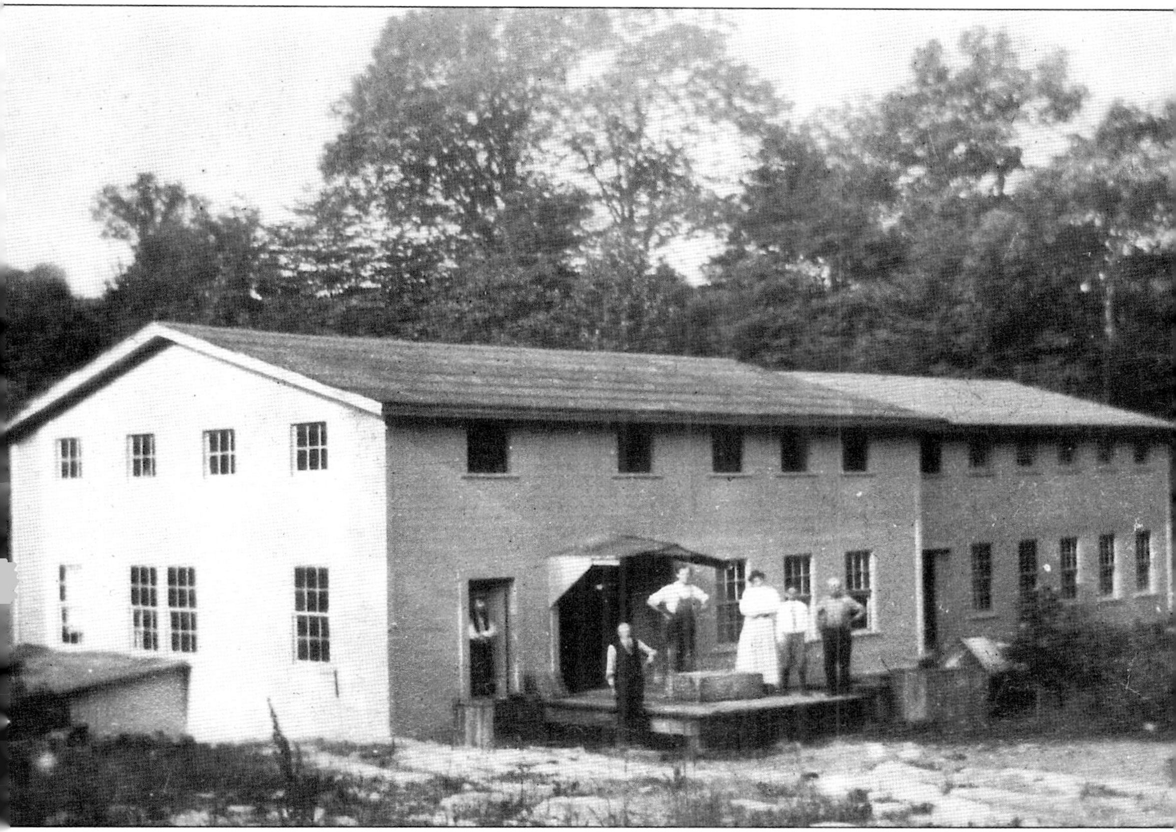

The Charles E. Radcliffe & Bros. Woolen Mill was a busy factory making such things as knit wristlets for canvas gloves. It was located just south of the Whitney Avenue bridge on the east bank of the Pequonnock River. The water turned a huge waterwheel for power, but the mill was also equipped to use steam when the river was low. The factory was forced to close in 1937 after 124 years of production when water from the river was diverted to the Easton Reservoir.

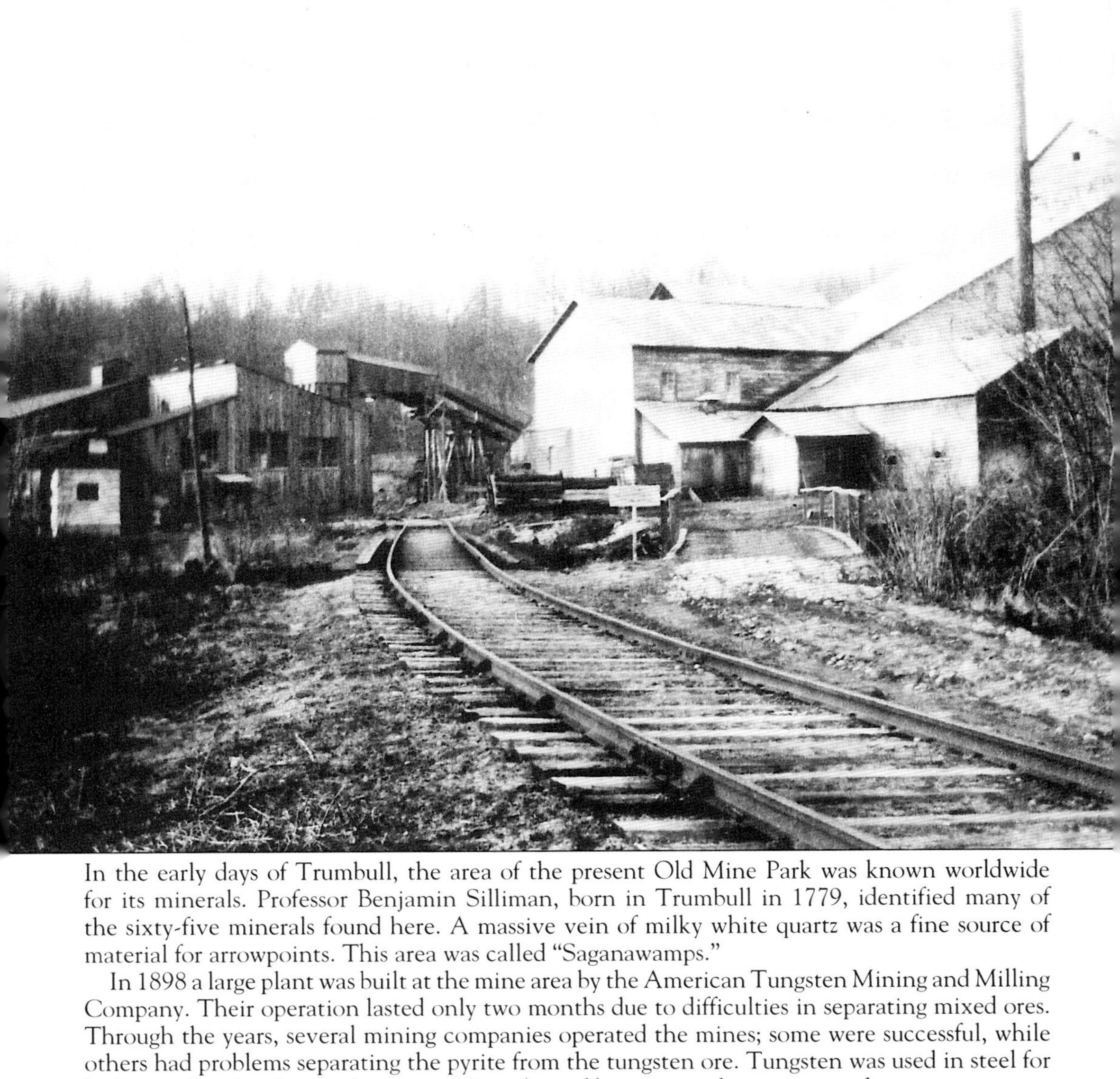

In the early days of Trumbull, the area of the present Old Mine Park was known worldwide for its minerals. Professor Benjamin Silliman, born in Trumbull in 1779, identified many of the sixty-five minerals found here. A massive vein of milky white quartz was a fine source of material for arrowpoints. This area was called "Saganawamps."

In 1898 a large plant was built at the mine area by the American Tungsten Mining and Milling Company. Their operation lasted only two months due to difficulties in separating mixed ores. Through the years, several mining companies operated the mines; some were successful, while others had problems separating the pyrite from the tungsten ore. Tungsten was used in steel for high-speed tools, electrical contact points, lamp filaments, and tungsten steel.

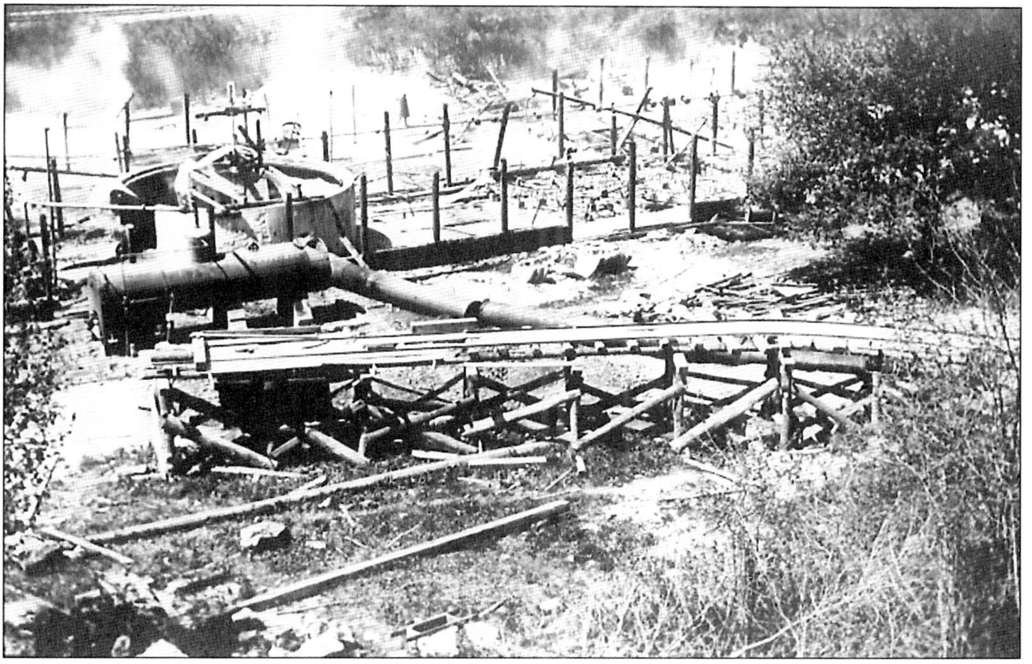

On May 21, 1916, a fire completely destroyed all the buildings of the mining plant, with a loss of $200,000 to $300,000. At that time, the New Reform Tungsten Co. of America was operating the mine. The fire was of suspicious origin. The property was never owned by the company and, at a much later date, was taken over by the Town of Trumbull for nonpayment of taxes. After the fire, the mines were not reopened for business. Due to changes in manufacturing techniques, the mines would not have been a lucrative investment. Today the site provides Trumbull residents with open space for hiking, picnicking, and swimming.

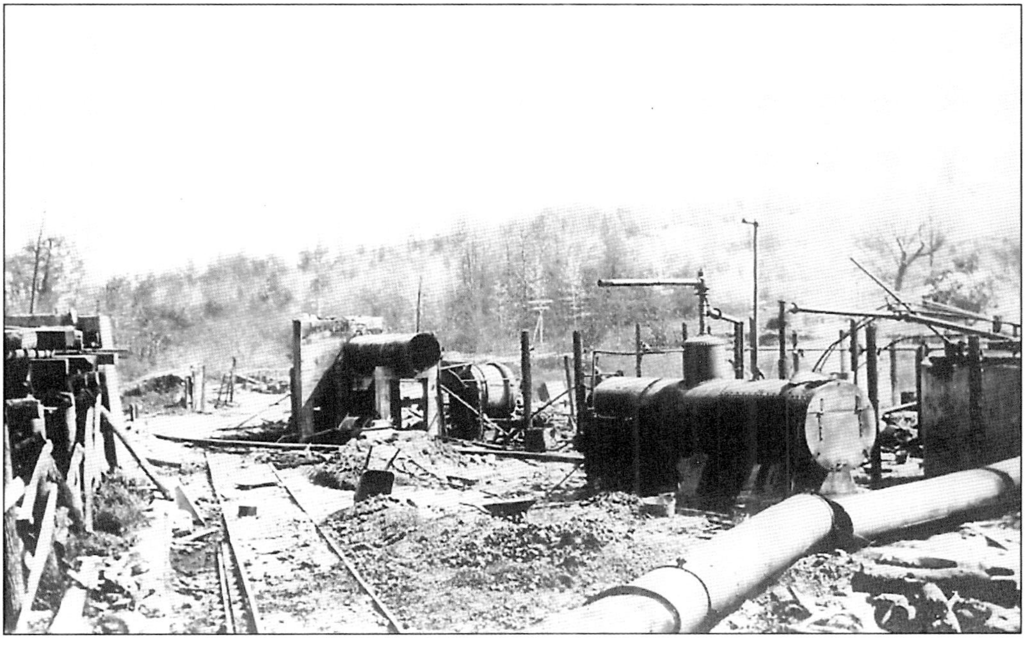

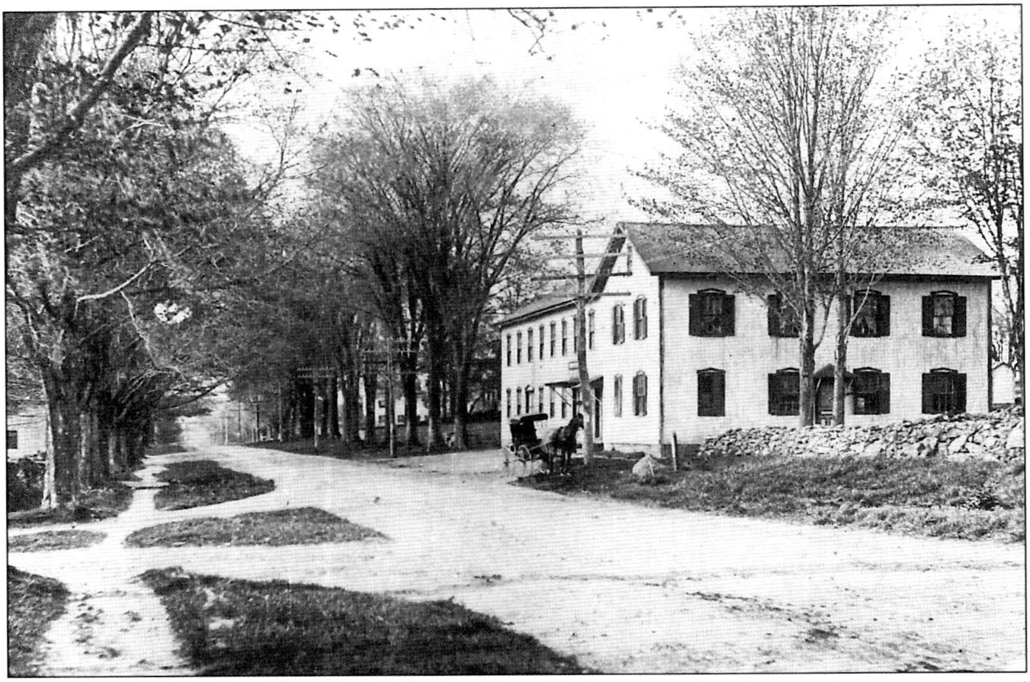

In the 1860s Harvey Hubbell moved from New York and built a factory that manufactured men's flannel shirts and drawers (underwear) on Main Street, Long Hill. In the early 1900s Mr. Hubbell patented a pull chain for electric lights and the company made other electrical accessories. The company later moved to Bridgeport. The original ironing room of the shirt factory is presently a florist shop. An unpaved Stonehouse Road is visible on the left side of the photograph above. Pictured below are workers of the Hubbell-Hadley Shirt Factory.

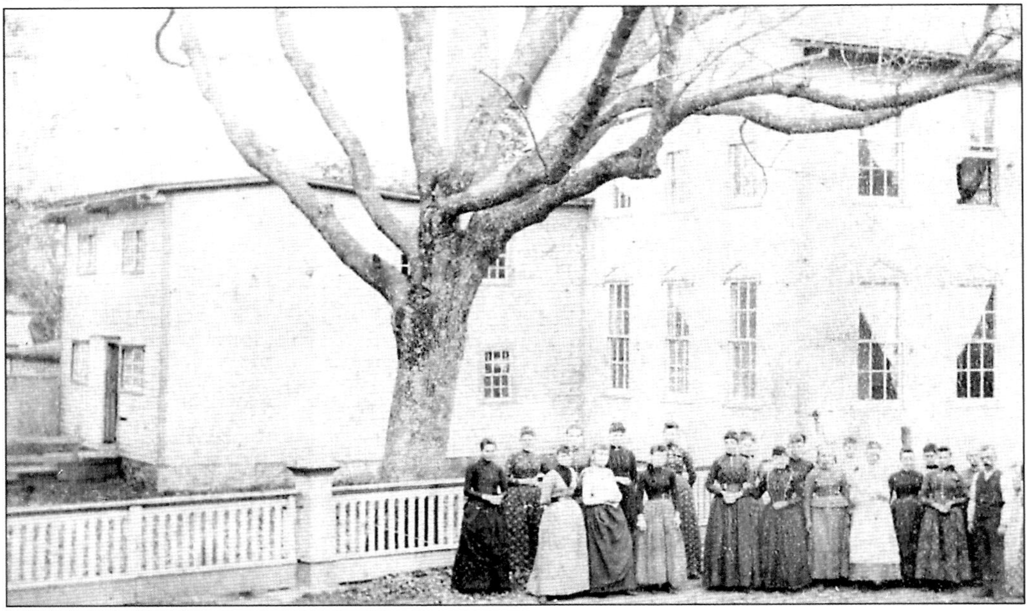

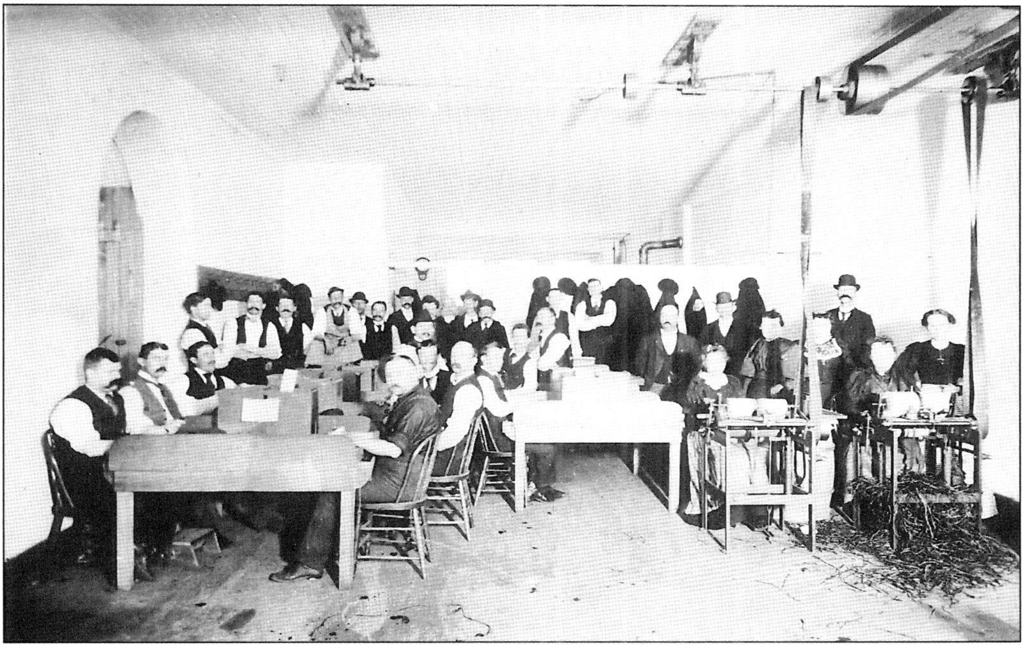

The cigar business was active in Trumbull from 1870 to 1950. This is an interior view of David S. Leavitt's cigar factory that was located in the rear of his home on Main Street. Young people were employed as readers at the cigar factories. They read aloud from periodicals and newspapers, as the cigar makers plied their trade. Mr. Leavitt was the last to operate a cigar factory in Trumbull.

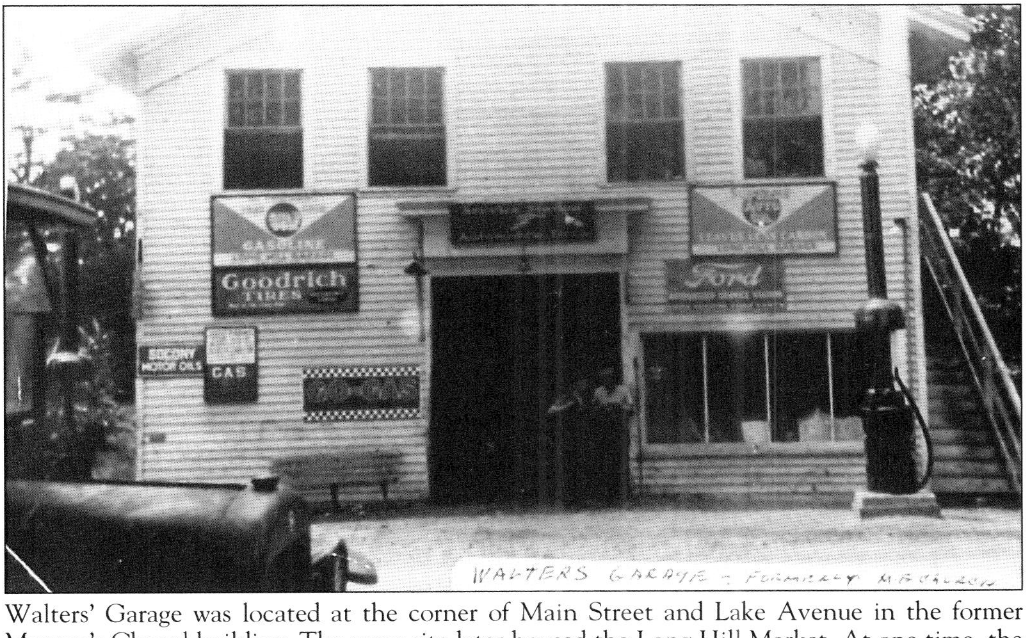


Walters' Garage was located at the corner of Main Street and Lake Avenue in the former Morgan's Chapel building. The same site later housed the Long Hill Market. At one time, the upstairs was a dance hall, and it was later converted to apartments. In 1969 the building was demolished and today it is the site of a modern brick service station.

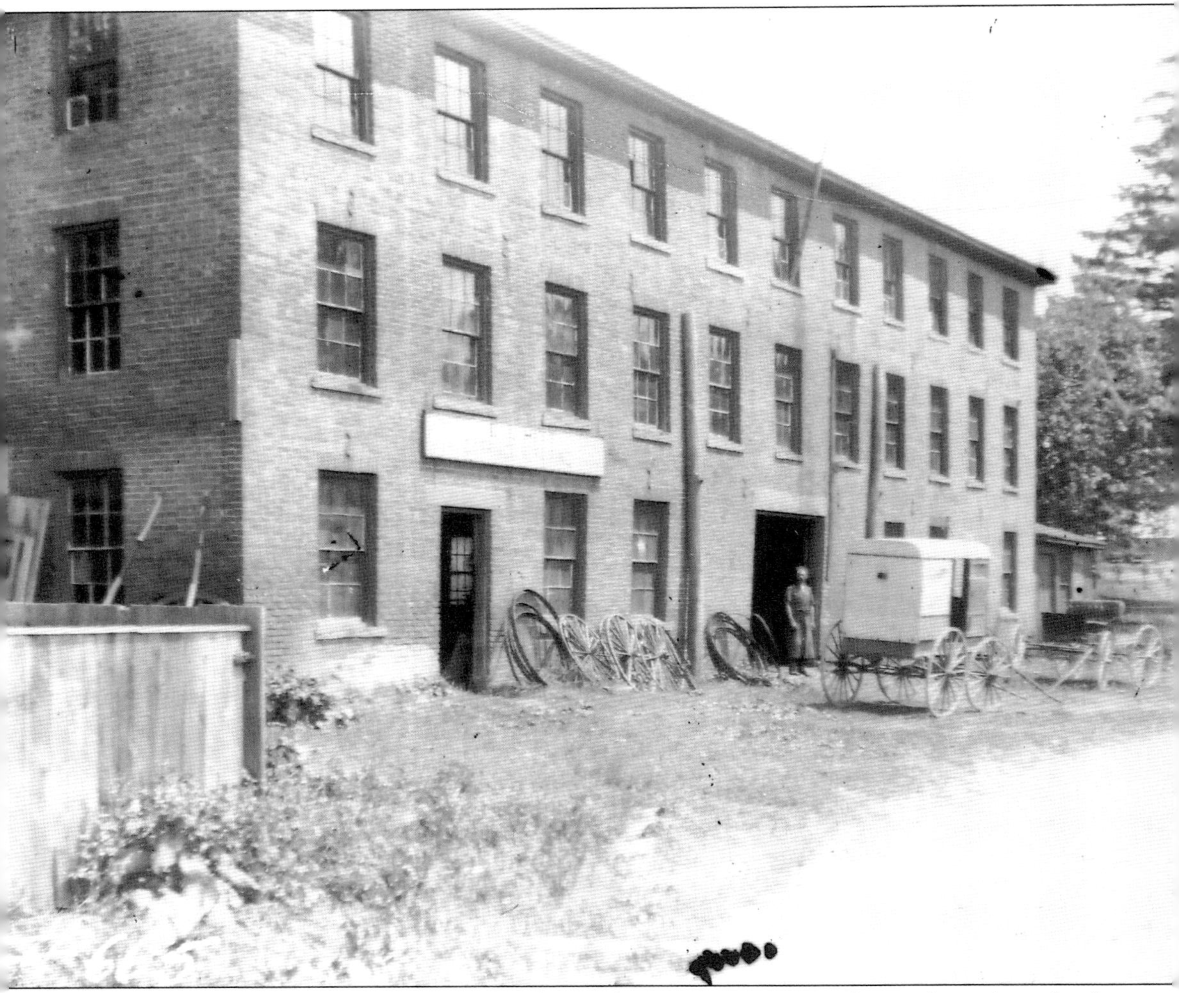

Prior to the Civil War, horse-drawn coaches and carriages were manufactured in a large brick factory on Center Road in Nichols by Nichols, Peck and Co. A substantial portion of their production was consigned to the Australian market. Later blacksmith E.L. Hitt operated a carriage repair business in the building. Cook's Hall was upstairs over the carriage factory. Social events, dances, basketball games, and even a professional appearance by P.T. Barnum were produced for local entertainment here. The building now houses a machine shop.

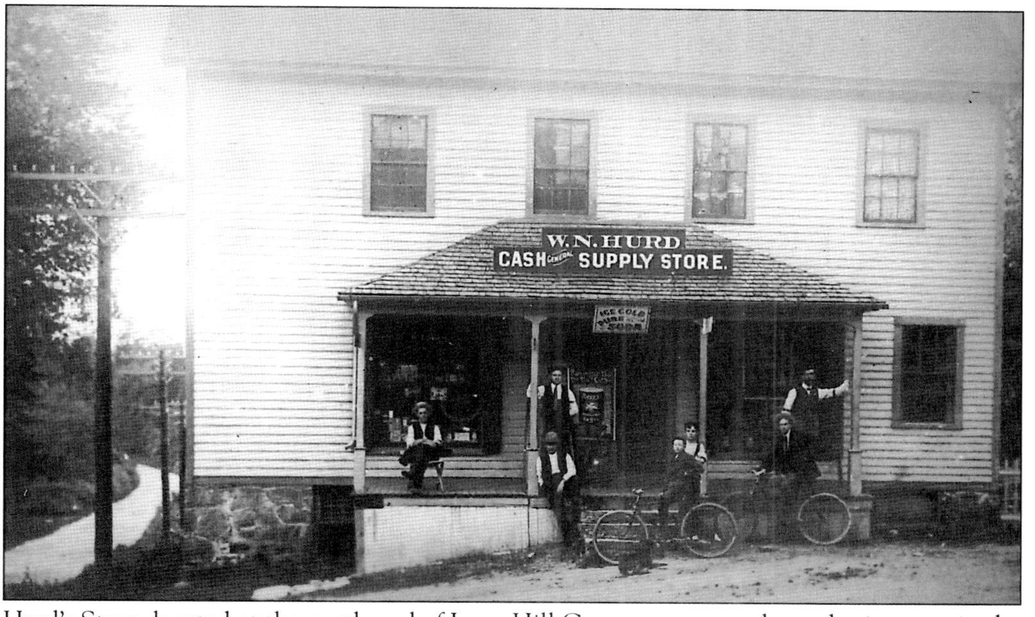


Hurd's Store, located at the north end of Long Hill Green, was a popular gathering spot in the late 1800s. Here, Frank Hurd (second from left) and store employees pose in front of the pipe rail where customers could tie up their horses while they shopped. The store was sold to George Smith in 1921.

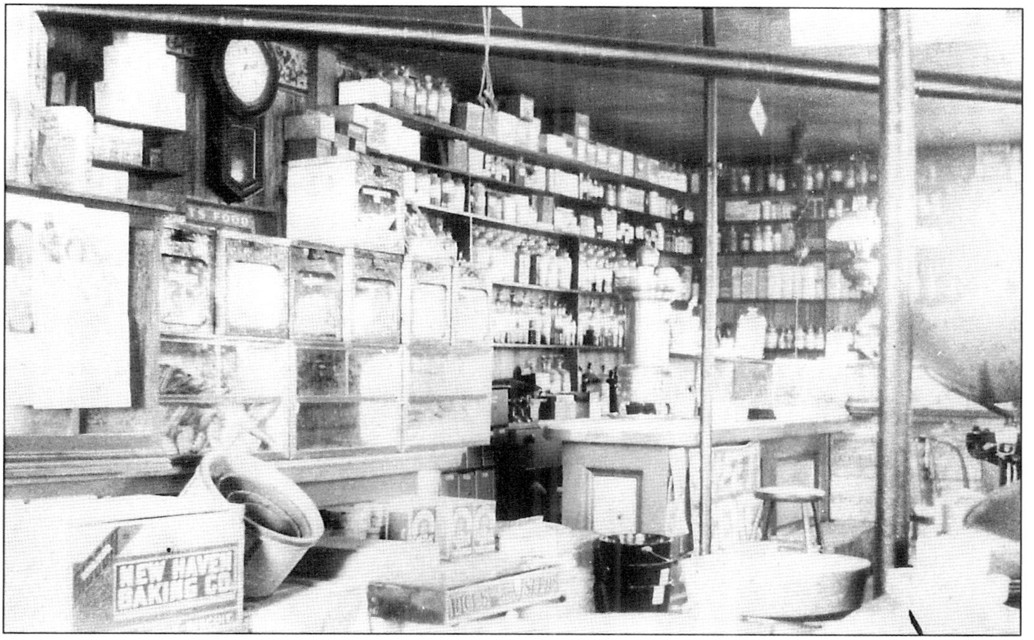


The interior of Wilson N. Hurd's store shows an abundance of merchandise. Most products were delivered in bulk in wooden containers, which were recycled into firewood. A single clerk would fill your order and most folks kept an "account," which was recorded in a ledger and paid monthly. The building was demolished in 1974 for a planned exit ramp from Route 25 that was never constructed.

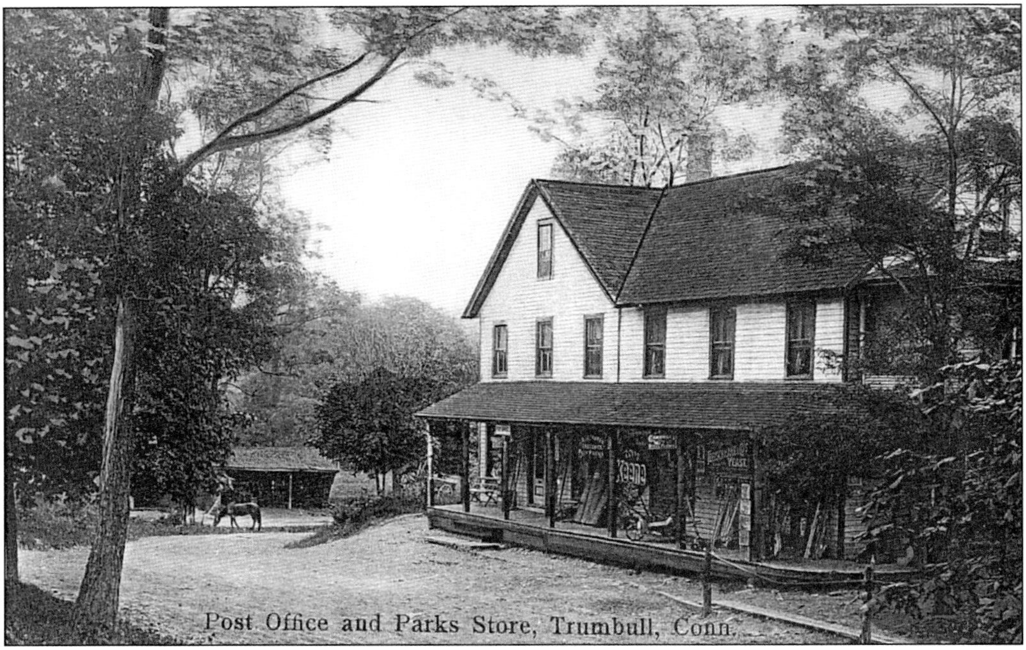


Parks' Store and Post Office was situated at the intersection of White Plains Road and Daniels Farm Road. The business was sold to Emanuel Kurtz in 1918 and operated by the Kurtz family for many years until it was replaced by a gas station.

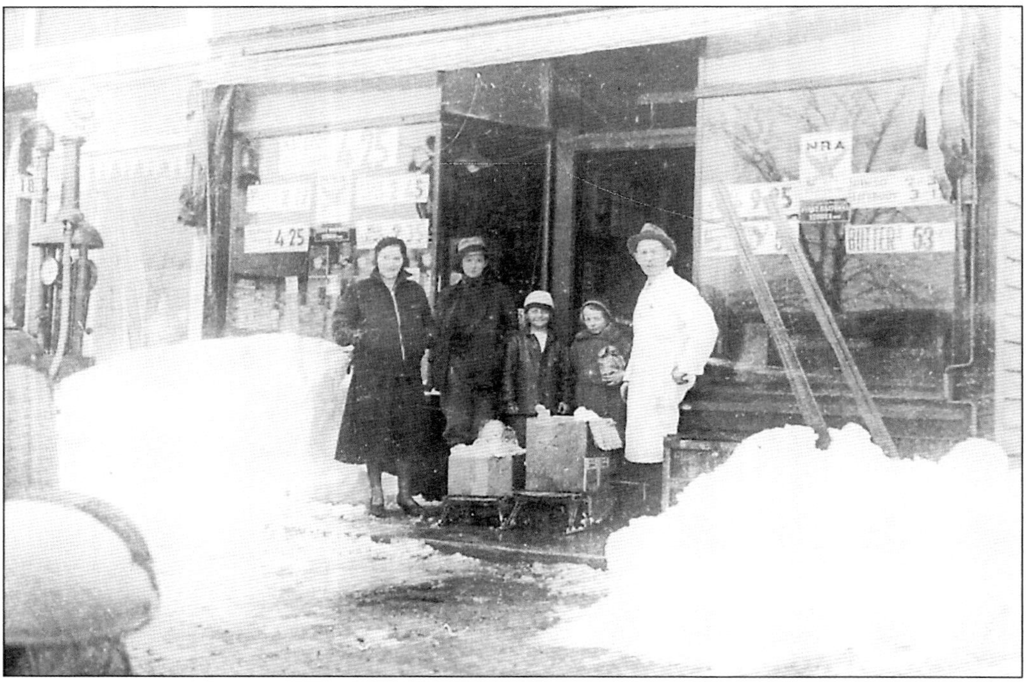


The First National Store was located on Main Street where the Merritt Parkway bridge is now. It was managed by Patsy Kohler, who is shown here with members of his family. Note the bargain prices posted in the windows.

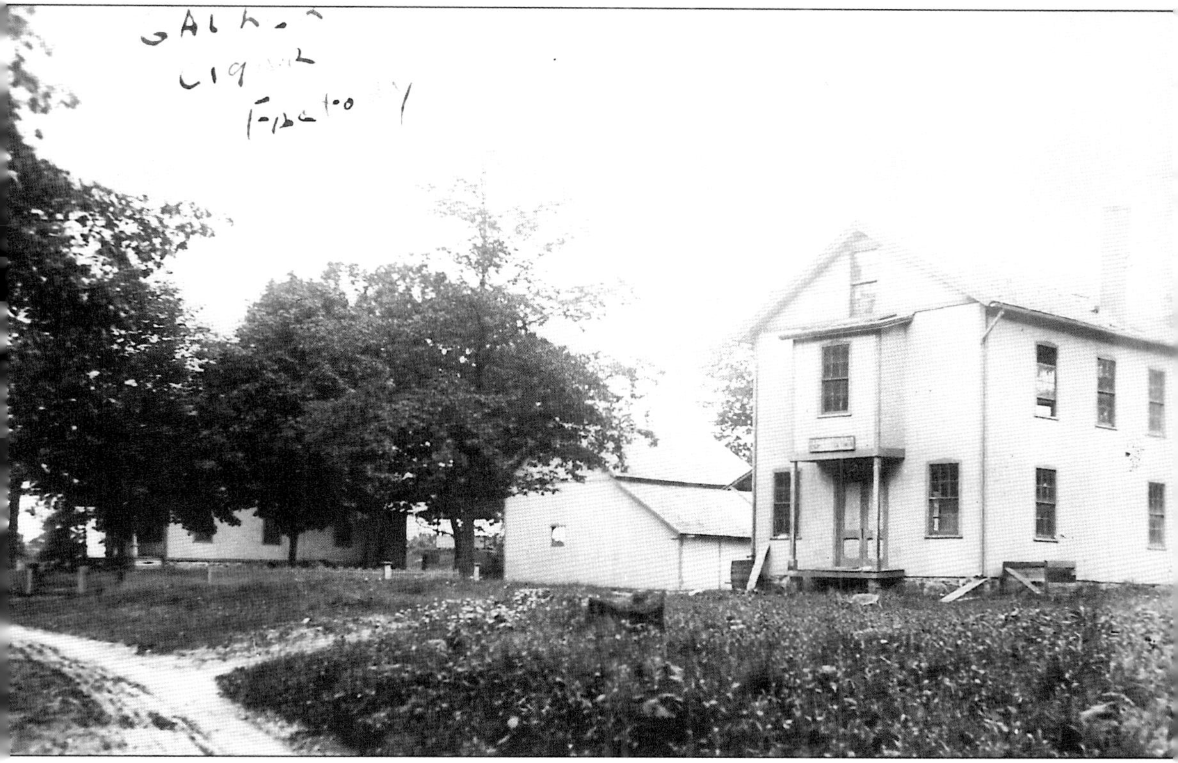

The Peter Gabler Cigar Shop on Broadway, Long Hill, was built in 1882. Upon his discharge from service in the Civil War, Mr. Gabler settled in Trumbull and opened a shop on Long Hill Green. As business increased, he opened this larger shop. When he died in 1921, his sons, Fred and Leo, continued the business. In 1935, "Gabler's Judge Cigar—Every Puff A Pleasure," was still making advertising headlines. In 1976, this shop was made into a pretty home by Arthur Gabler (another son) who celebrated his ninety-ninth birthday here in 1981.

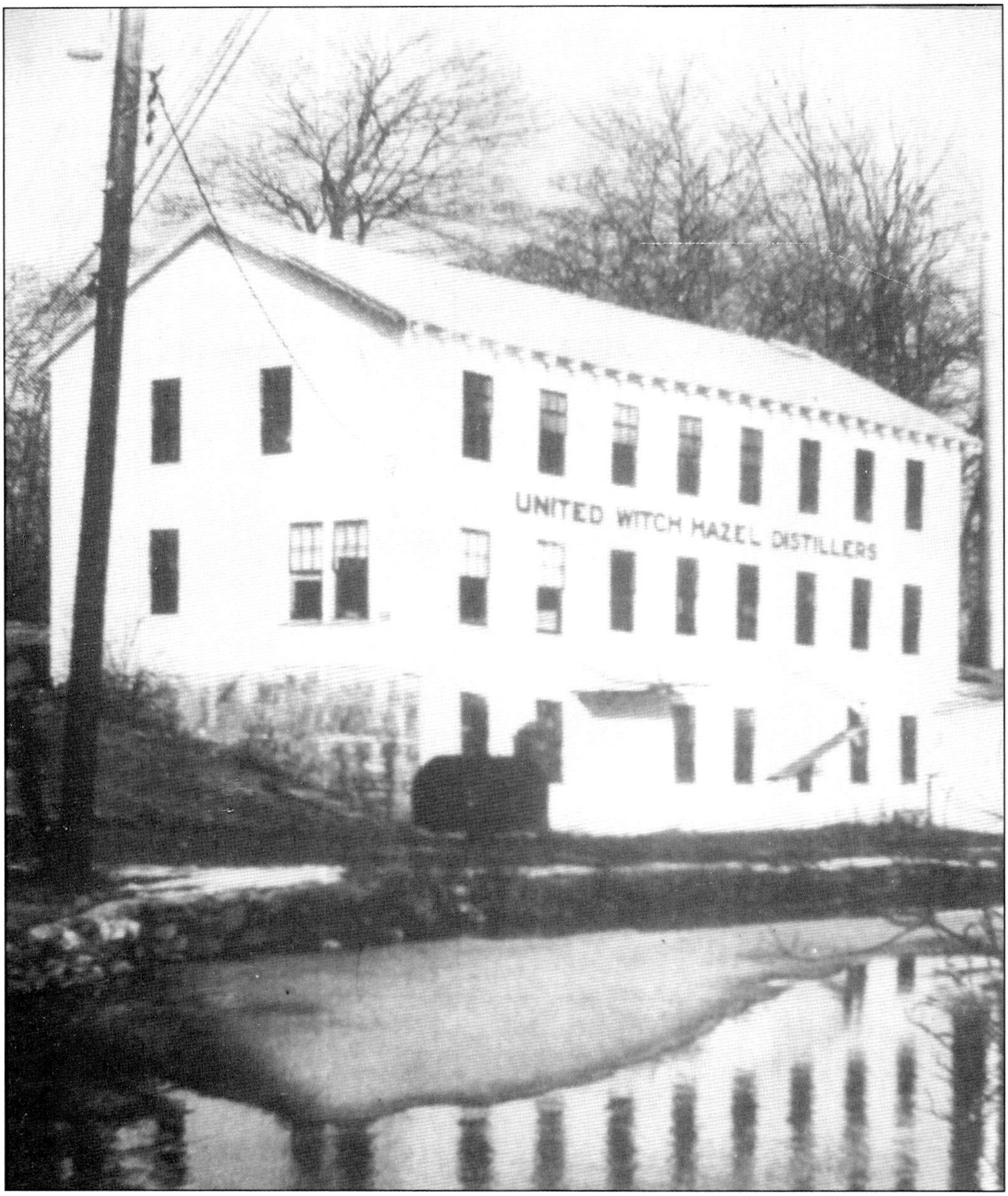


Witch hazel, an alcohol-based lotion used to treat bruises, sprains, and minor skin problems, was produced in Trumbull for over half a century. Located on the site of the former Tousey Shirt Factory on Broadway in Upper Long Hill, the witch hazel operation began in 1923 when the Stepney Witch Hazel Company, owned by Chester G. Emack, purchased the property. The Hoyt Brothers, Inc. continued to operate at the site from 1935 until 1951, when Humphreys Pharmaceutical Company of Rutherford, New Jersey, took over. Witch hazel is a shrub with yellow flowers native to Connecticut. The harvesting of the plant's bark and leaves began in the fall in the Kent and Canaan areas of the state, and the plant material was brought by truck for processing in Trumbull. Operating from November to May, the company manufactured 1,000 gallons of witch hazel per day and as many as 185,000 gallons per season.

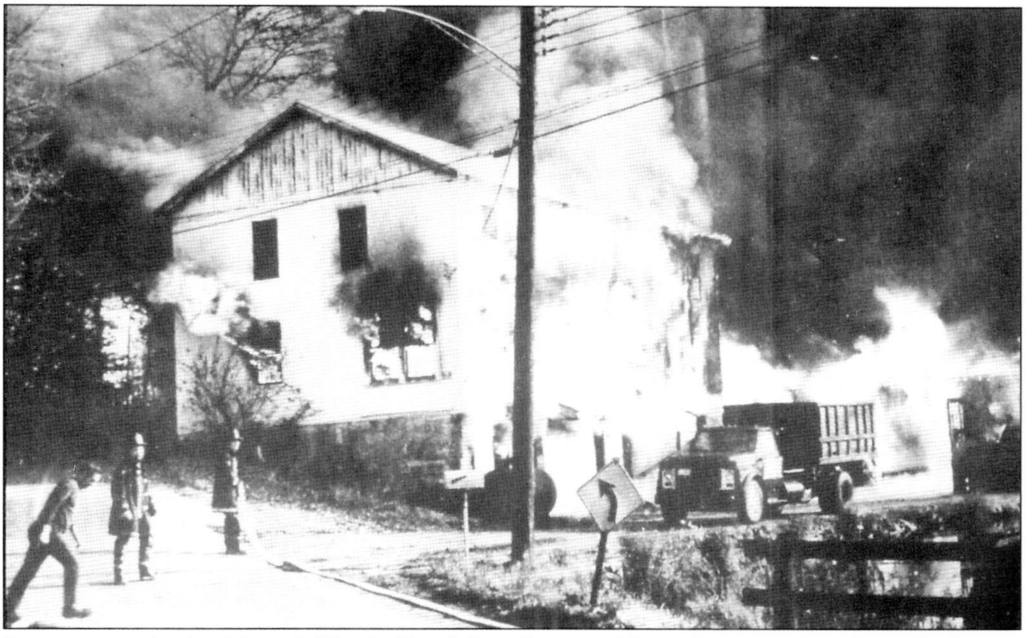

Disaster struck the United Witch Hazel Distillers on November 1, 1974. A spark from a defective switch to an electrical pump connecting two alcohol tanks caused a flash fire. The fire, which broke out three days into the processing season, resulted in a total estimated loss of $325,000.

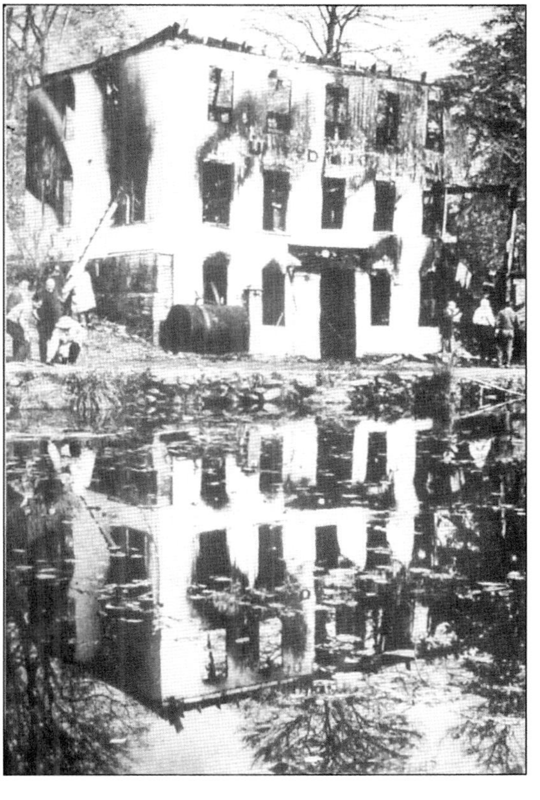

The Long Hill Volunteer Fire Department battled the blaze with the help of the Trumbull Center, Nichols, and Stepney Fire Departments. At the time of the fire, United Witch Hazel Distillers was one of only three factories in the nation manufacturing witch hazel. The factory was demolished and was never rebuilt.

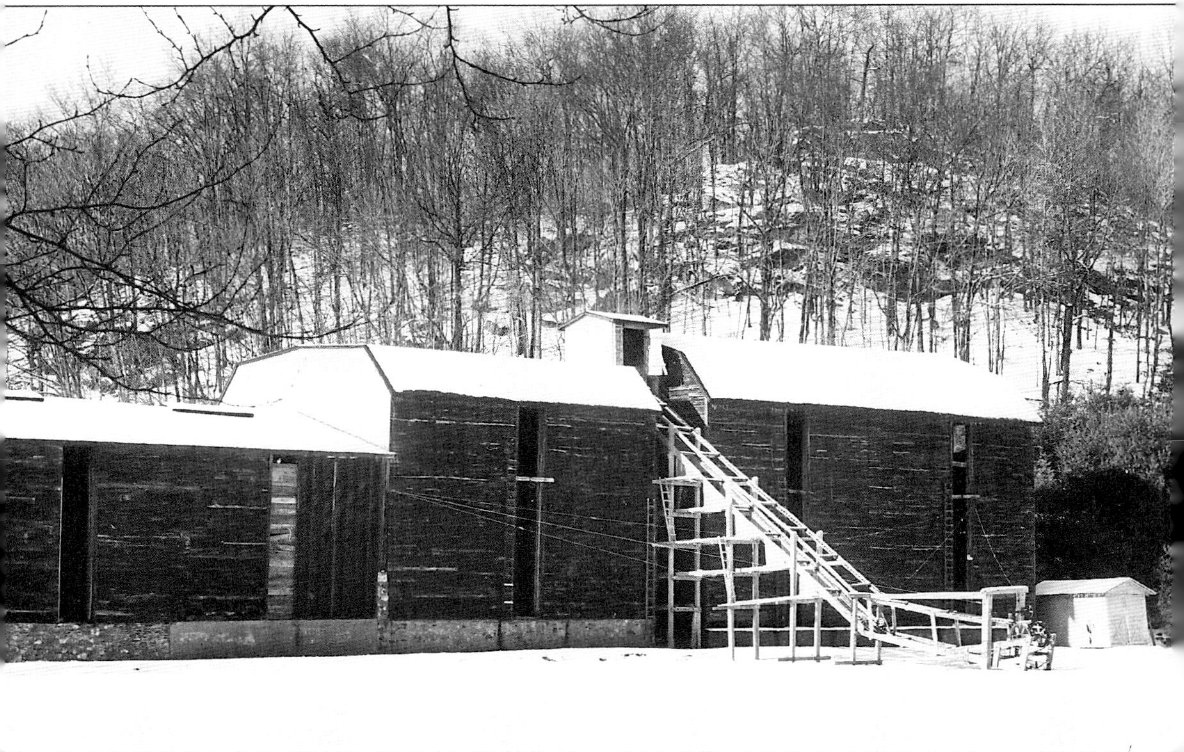

The historic Kaatz Ice House was located on Whitney Avenue on the shore of Kaatz Pond, where ice was harvested commercially from 1908 to 1955. New England was the main source of ice for Southern plantations and the West Indies sugar islands during the late eighteenth and early nineteenth centuries. Though dating from the early twentieth century, Kaatz Ice House was a rare structure representative of the New England ice industry. Kaatz Ice House survived until the 1950s because Bridgeport's more exclusive hotels and a selective clientele preferred natural ice rather than the artificial ice produced in refrigeration plants. Although accepted into the National Register of Historic Places and believed to be the only structure of its kind standing in Connecticut, if not New England, it had deteriorated to such an extent that it was razed in 1978.

*Five*

# Getting Around

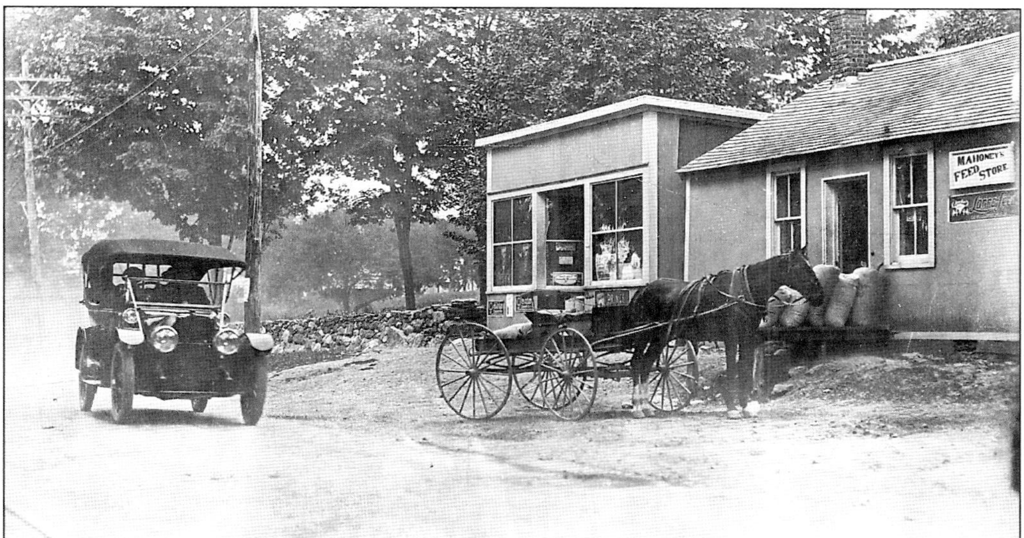

Trumbull's horse-drawn vehicles found rivals not only in 1840, when the Housatonic Railroad opened its line, but also at the turn of the twentieth century, with the advent of automobiles. This 1916 photograph shows John P. Mahoney's Feed and Grocery Store on Main Street. Many businesses operated on this site over the years including a cigar shop, post office, a paint store, a Diversity shop, and a florist. The store building was originally part of the Hubbell-Hadley Shirt Factory.

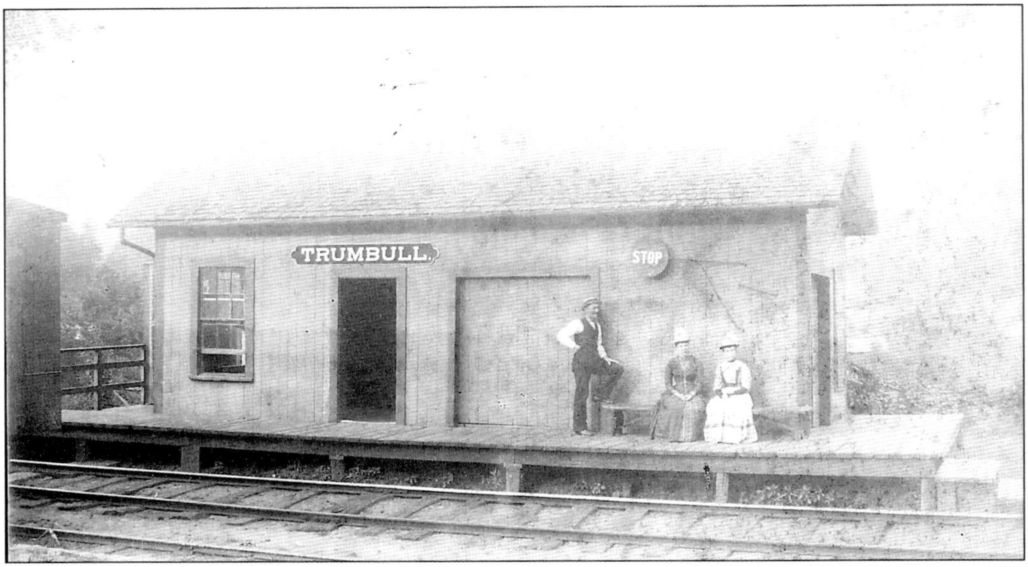


The first Trumbull Railroad Station was located west of the old town hall, now the Helen E. Plumb Building. The stop was known as Trumbull Church since it was near the site where the second and third Trumbull Congregational Church buildings stood. Arthur E. Plumb, father of Helen, was a station agent in the late 1880s. He is pictured with Ida Plumb, Helen's aunt, and her friend Emily Burton.

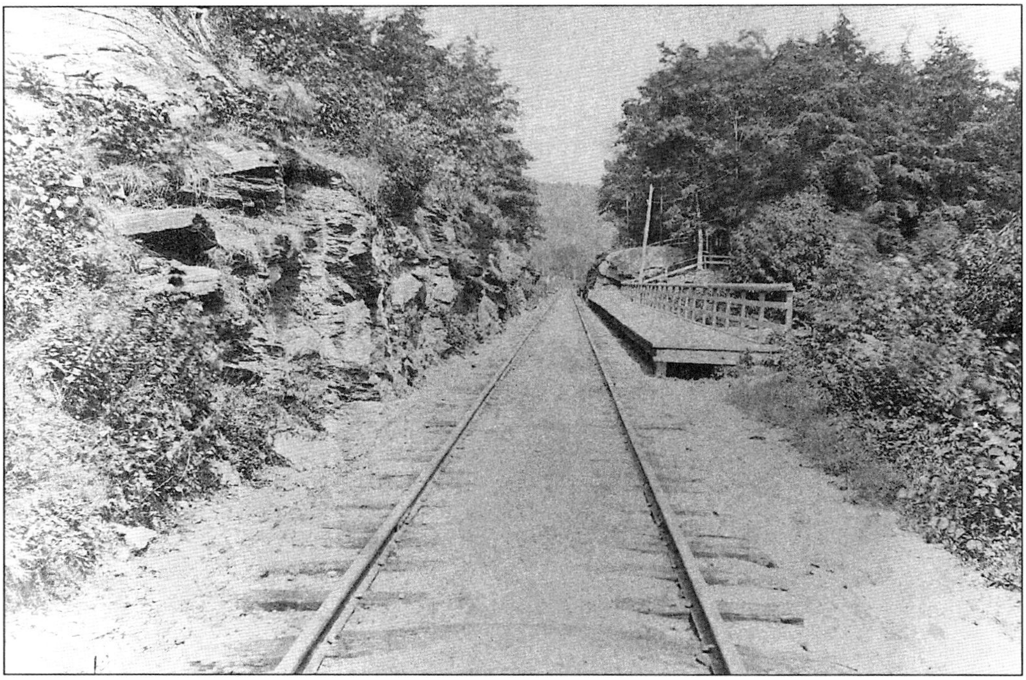

A quiet moment in the busy schedule of the Housatonic Railroad shows an empty Parlor Rock platform waiting for the train to arrive and disembark a happy crowd of visitors. They would have climbed up the wooden stairway to the Parlor Rock Grove for entertainment, sports, and picnics in the beautiful natural surroundings of the Trumbull valley.

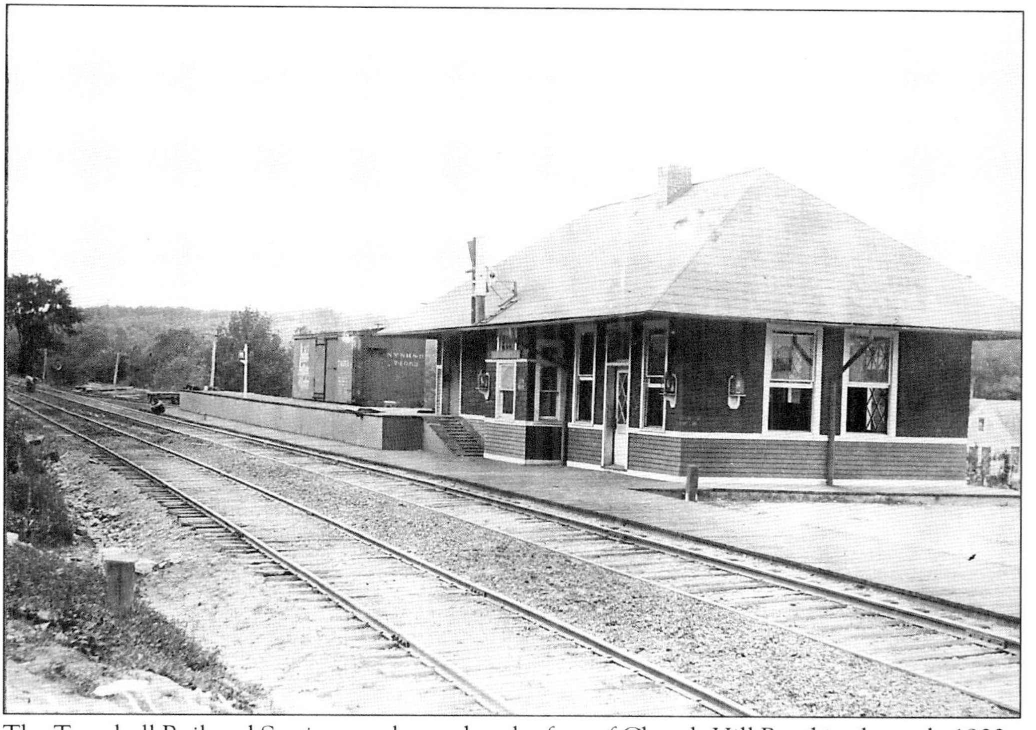

The Trumbull Railroad Station was located at the foot of Church Hill Road in the early 1900s. Trumbull was the first station stop after North Bridgeport on the Housatonic Railroad, which ran from Bridgeport to New Milford in 1840.

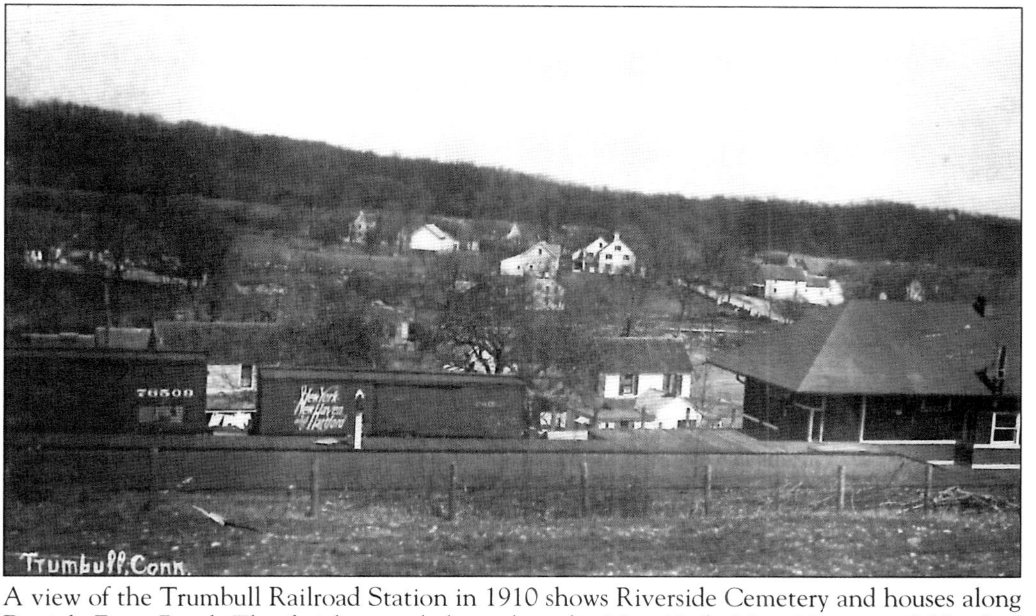


A view of the Trumbull Railroad Station in 1910 shows Riverside Cemetery and houses along Daniels Farm Road. The freight cars belonged to the New York, New Haven and Hartford Railroad, which took stock control of the Housatonic Railroad in 1892.

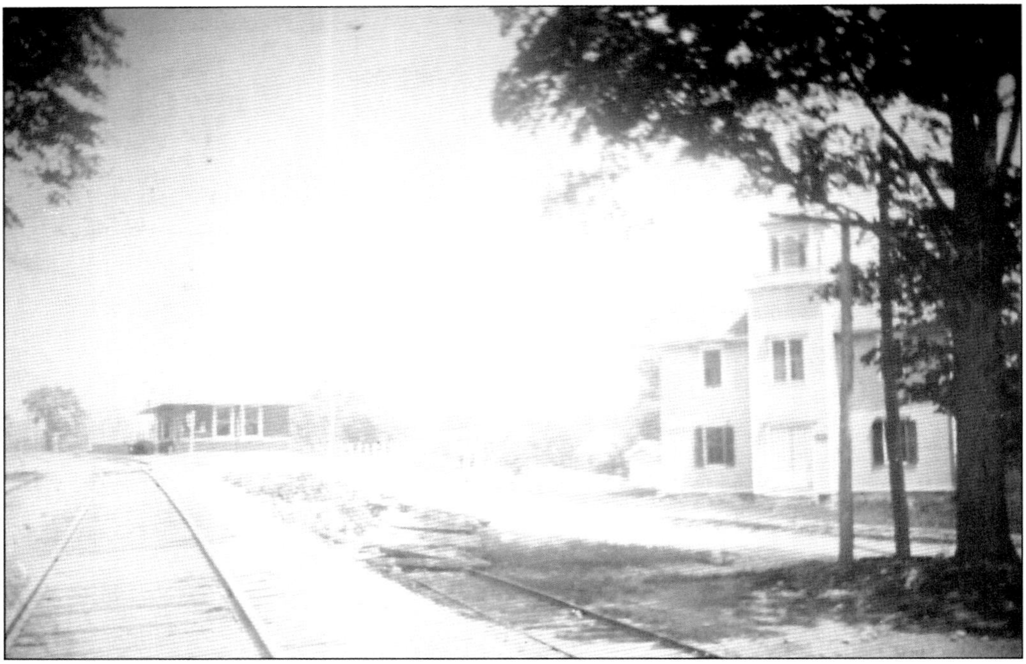

The Trumbull Railroad Station, Trumbull Town Hall, and the Housatonic Railroad tracks are shown here at Church Hill Road. The steep hill leading down to Trumbull Center was an ideal spot for sledding before automobiles became plentiful. In 1849, the railroad tracks were extended to Pittsfield, Massachusetts, paralleling the Housatonic River and known as the Berkshire Line. The railroad served manufacturers in small towns and carried produce and milk from farmers.

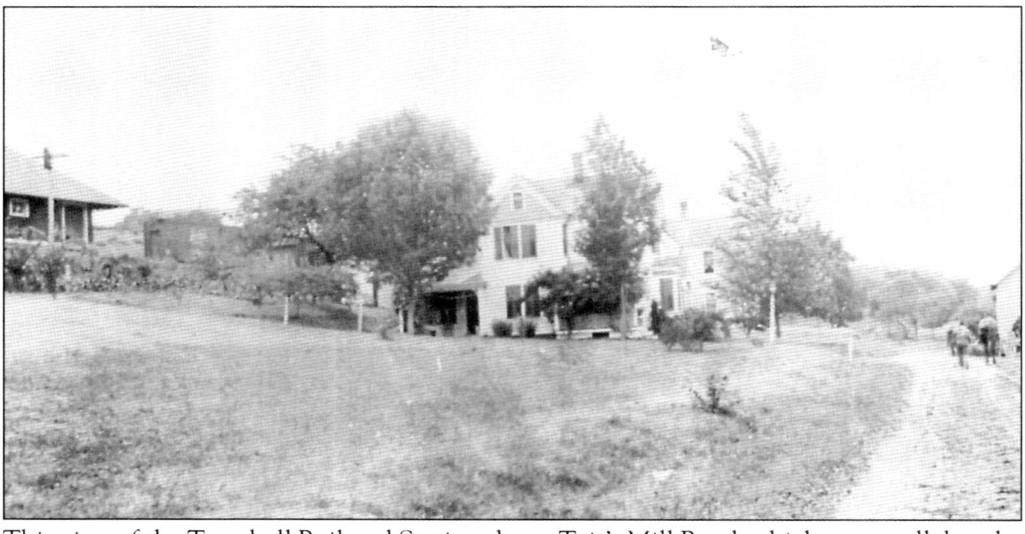

This view of the Trumbull Railroad Station shows Tait's Mill Road, which ran parallel to the railroad tracks. Andrew Tait built a mill on the Pequonnock River in 1836 to manufacture paper and strawboards. After his death, the mill was run by his son and grandsons. The property was purchased by Bridgeport Hydraulic Company in 1895 after the business moved to North Bridgeport.

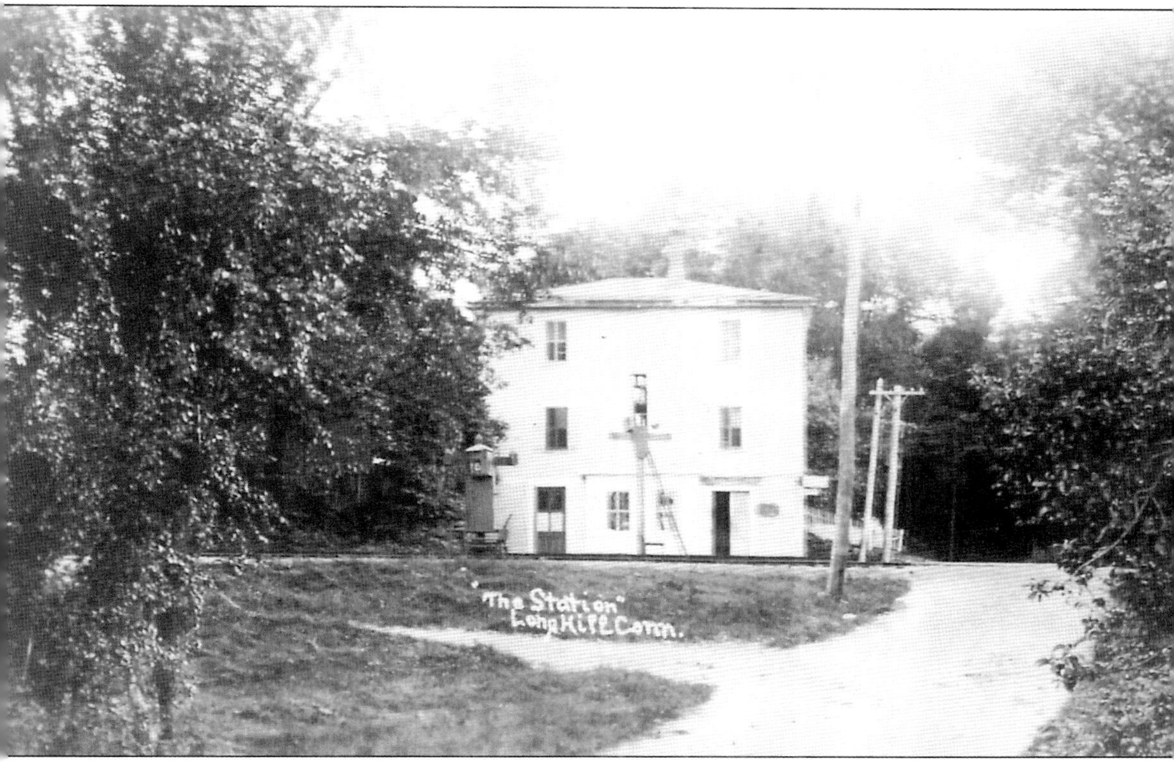


The Long Hill Railroad Station was in use from 1840 until the early 1930s. Long Hill Depot, as it was called, was located only 3 miles from the Church Hill Road Station. In its early days, Long Hill Depot was a "flag station." People would have to wave a white handkerchief in the daytime, or burn newspapers at night, to get the train to stop. In its heyday, Long Hill Depot was an active freight station and the delivery point for coal for the Radcliffe Woolen Mill and tobacco for the local cigar shops. Ironically, one of the last uses for the old Housatonic Railroad tracks was to haul materials for the construction of the Merritt Parkway. The railroad service was disbanded in 1932.

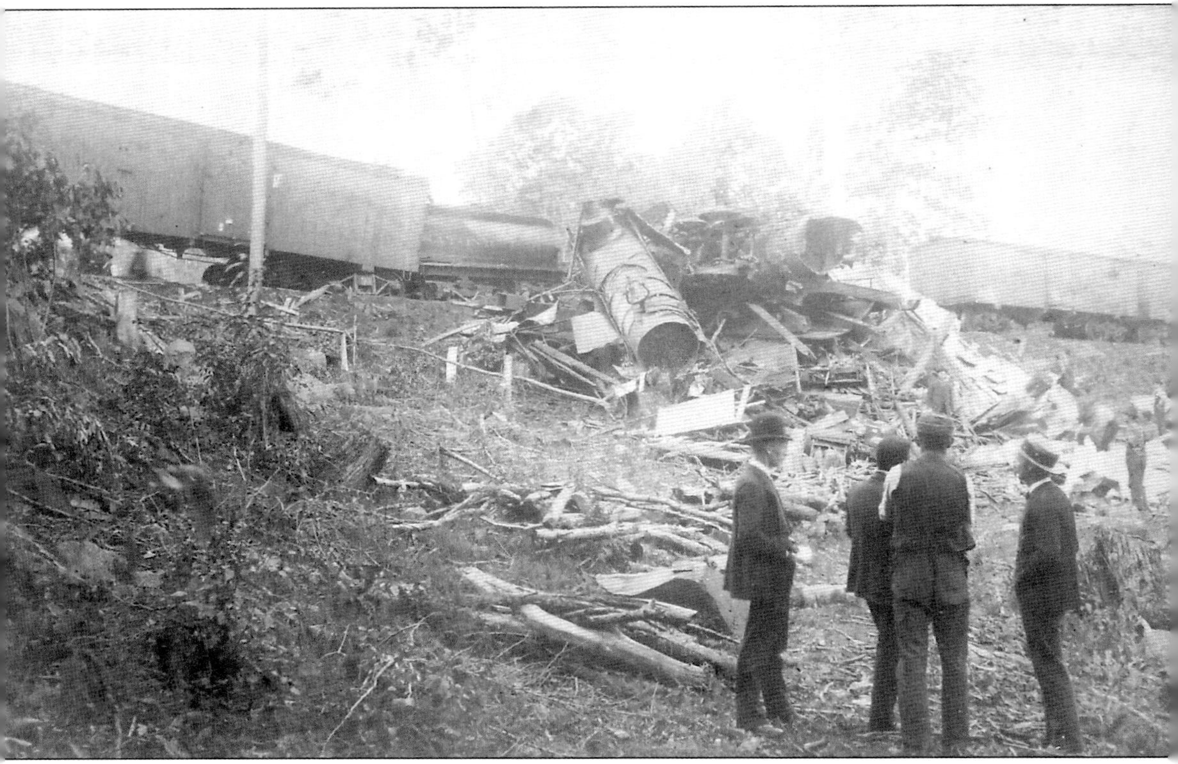

As the railroad trains steamed and chugged through the valley at about 10 miles per hour, the engineers were on constant alert for natural disasters on the tracks: wandering cattle, wild animals, rocks, fallen trees, and other obstructions. They were also ever-vigilant for fires caused by hot coals. This picture of a New York, New Haven and Hartford Railroad wreck occurred September 30, 1901, just south of the Long Hill Depot. Engineer Holt, running past a freight train from Hawleyville to Bridgeport, had received orders from the dispatcher to remain on switch at Stepney until the regular "up-freight" passed. Holt dozed off and met the other train head on.

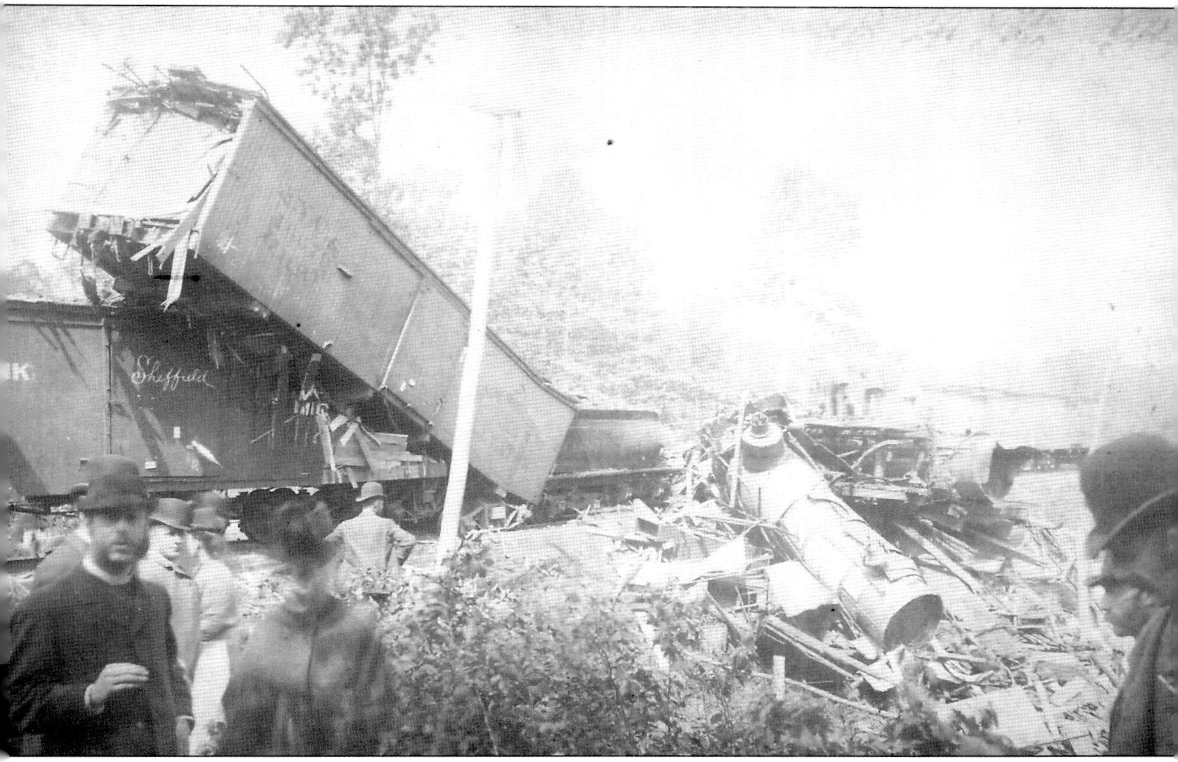


It was a massive wreck. Two locomotives and eighteen cars were destroyed. Holt's life was spared, but he did lose one arm. Five others were killed and many were injured. Among the passengers was J.G. Nichols, who was transporting his prize ox, weighing 4,300 pounds, to the Newtown Fair. Neither he nor the ox was injured and, although the ox was the winner at other fairs, it missed this one. The railroad line proved a valuable aid to the progress of the area despite its numerous accidents.

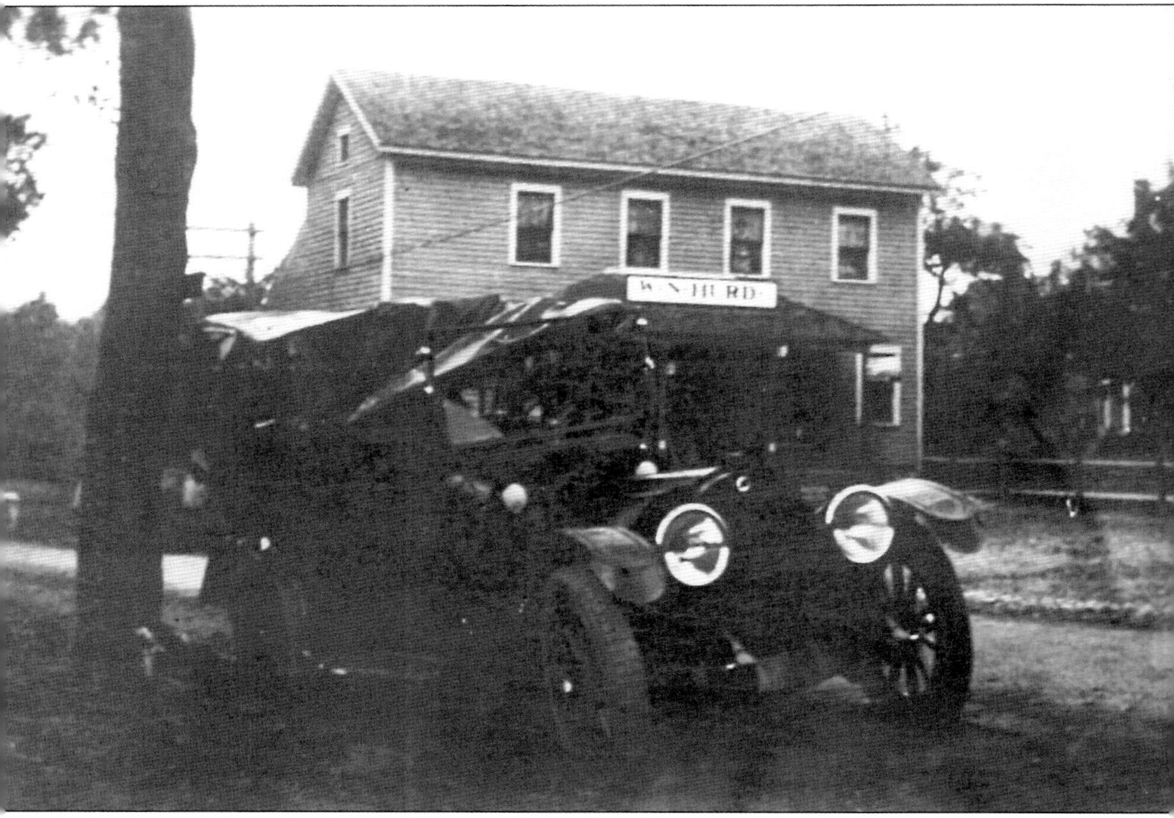


An excerpt from the diary of E. Merrill Beach relates the story of a 1918 carjacking. Mr. Beach wrote that he had walked from his home on Daniels Farm Road to the Burrough's home on Main Street near Church Hill Road to play pinochle. While walking home, he met a man who said he was a jitney (bus) driver. The driver had been held up, and his car taken. They walked up Main Street and found the car smashed near Hurd's Store, but the holdup man was never found.

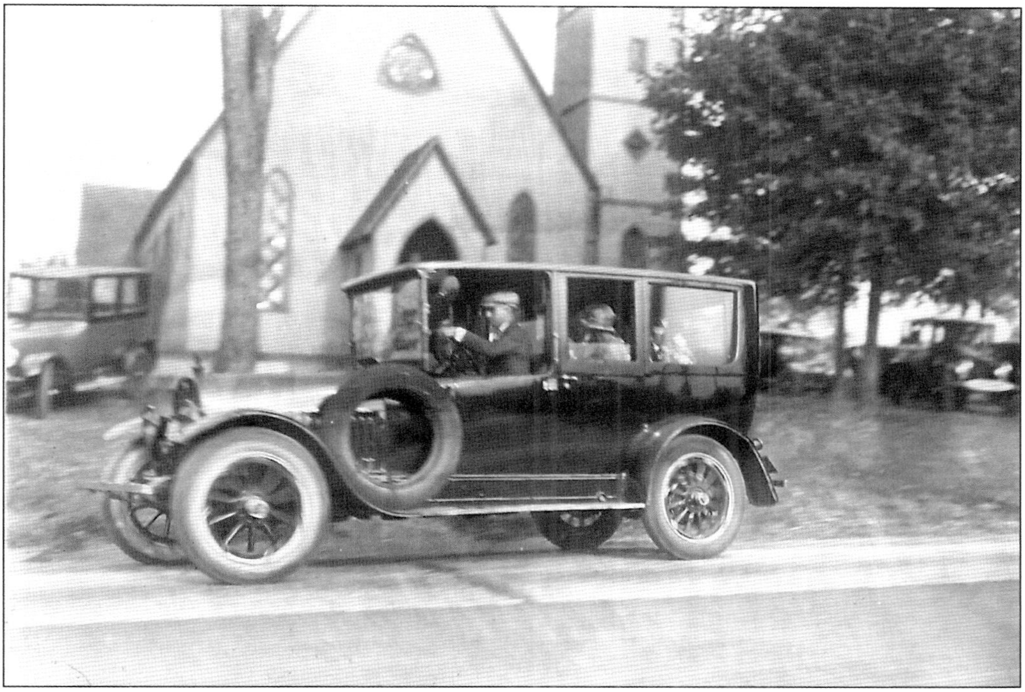

The wedding party arrived in fine style at Grace Episcopal Church in Long Hill on October 13, 1923, in a car hired in Bridgeport for the event. E. Perkins Nichols of Stepney, the groom, wanted to be certain his lovely bride, Helen Hurd of Long Hill, arrived safely at the church. This fine vehicle transported Mr. and Mrs. Nichols to their reception following the ceremony.

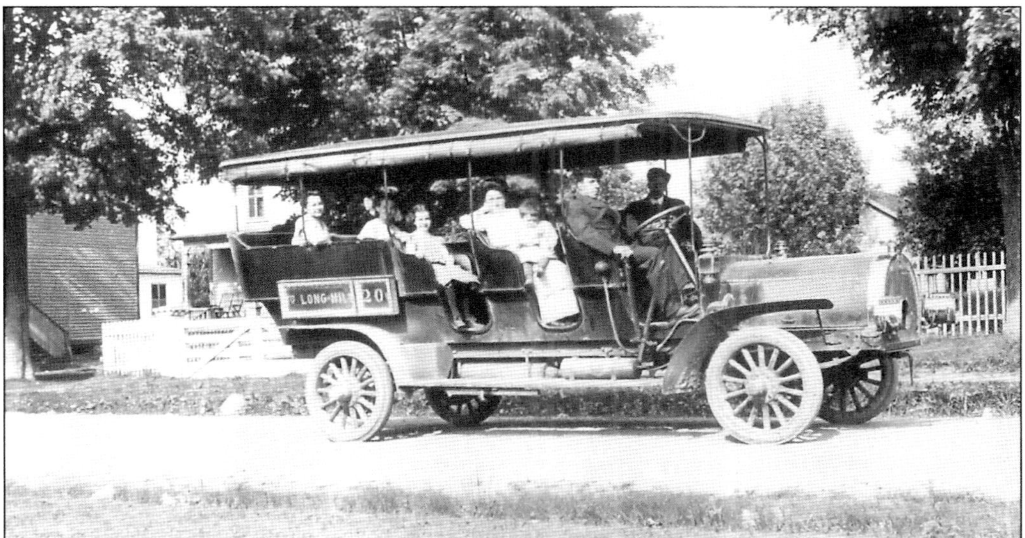


The first Long Hill-to-Bridgeport bus service was started by an enterprising Trumbullite named Campyon Cutter on July 22, 1909. Although the vehicles were built in Bridgeport, they were "right-hand drive." The rolled-up side curtains provided an airy ride in summer and were lowered to protect passengers during inclement weather. The fare from Bridgeport to Long Hill was 20¢.

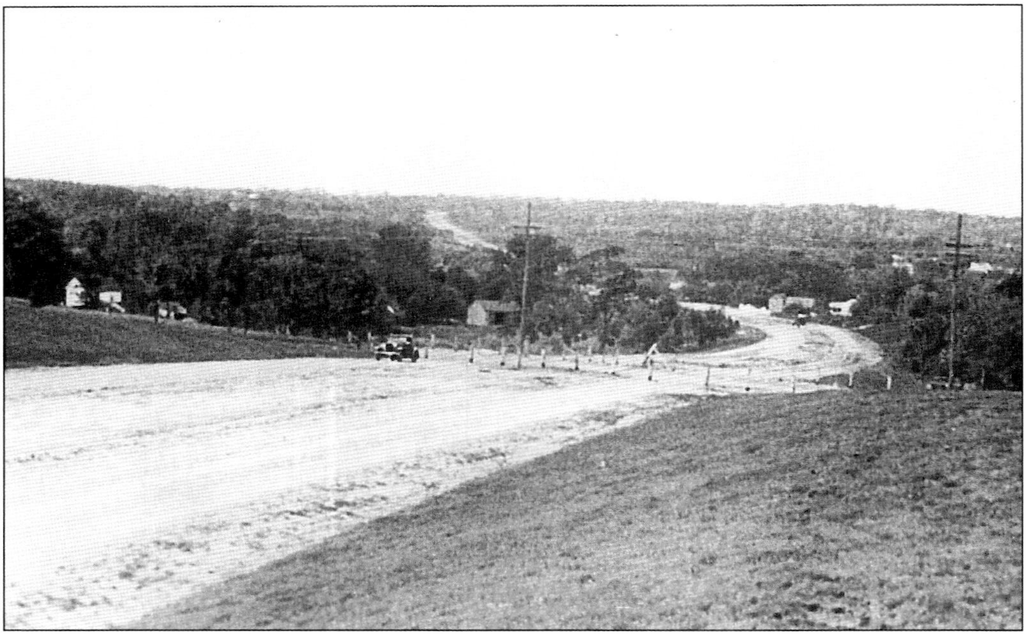

Major changes came to Trumbull in 1940 with the opening of the Merritt Parkway. No longer would Trumbullites traveling north and south have to contend with the Boston Post Road's many traffic lights and its high volume of commercial vehicles. Twenty years of planning and construction culminated in 37.5 miles of parklike highway at a cost of $21.5 million (a bargain by today's standards). Travelers realized they could enjoy the experience of driving without sacrificing speed, efficiency, and safety. In fact, people were so enthralled by its park-like appearance that they thought nothing of parking on the side of the road, putting down a blanket, and having a picnic. Rules had to be enacted. A *Bridgeport Telegram* headline read, "Parking and Sparking Banned on Parkway."

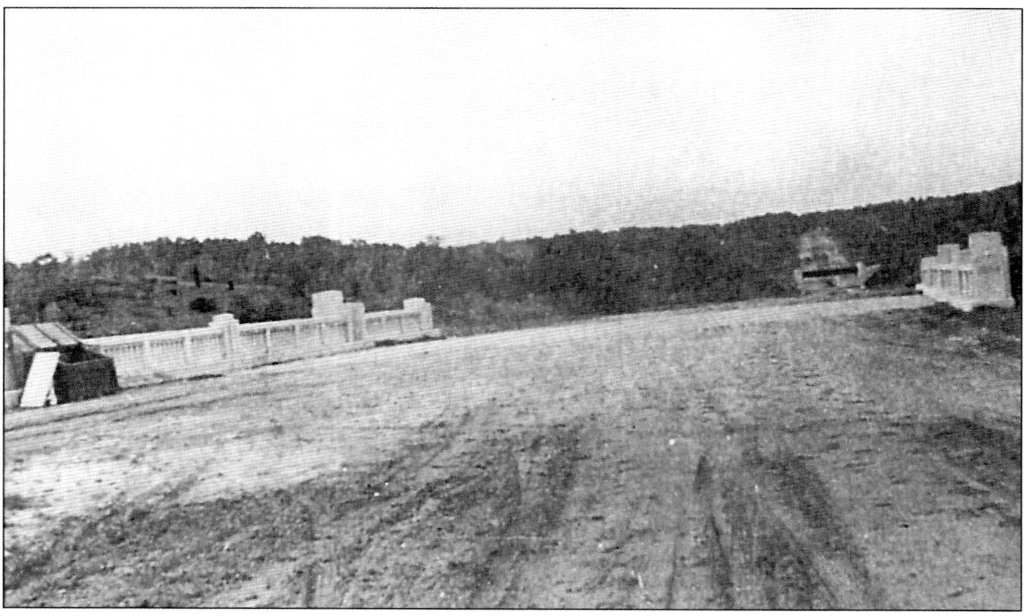

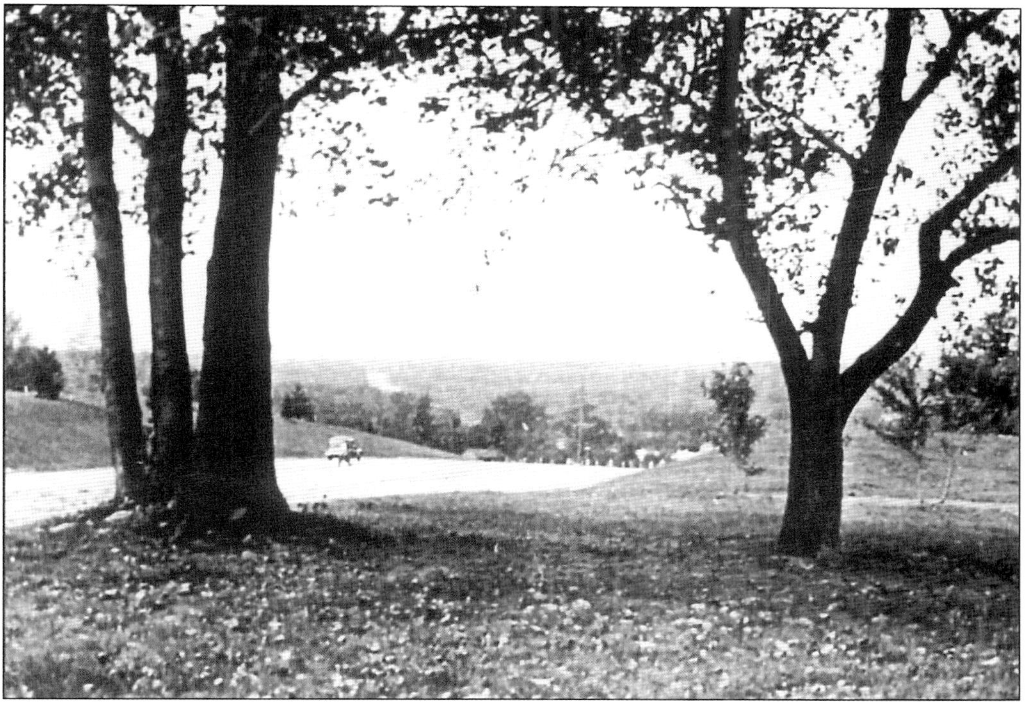

Tolls on the highway were heatedly debated by the lawmakers and it was decided to erect a temporary booth in Greenwich. Later, a permanent booth, done in a rustic log-cabin style, was built. The first month's take was $61,142.90. Considering the toll was 10¢, this represented a large amount of traffic for 1939. This money was earmarked for the construction of the Wilbur Cross Parkway. These photographs, showing the parkway under construction, were taken in 1933 in the area of Unity Road by the Selleck family.

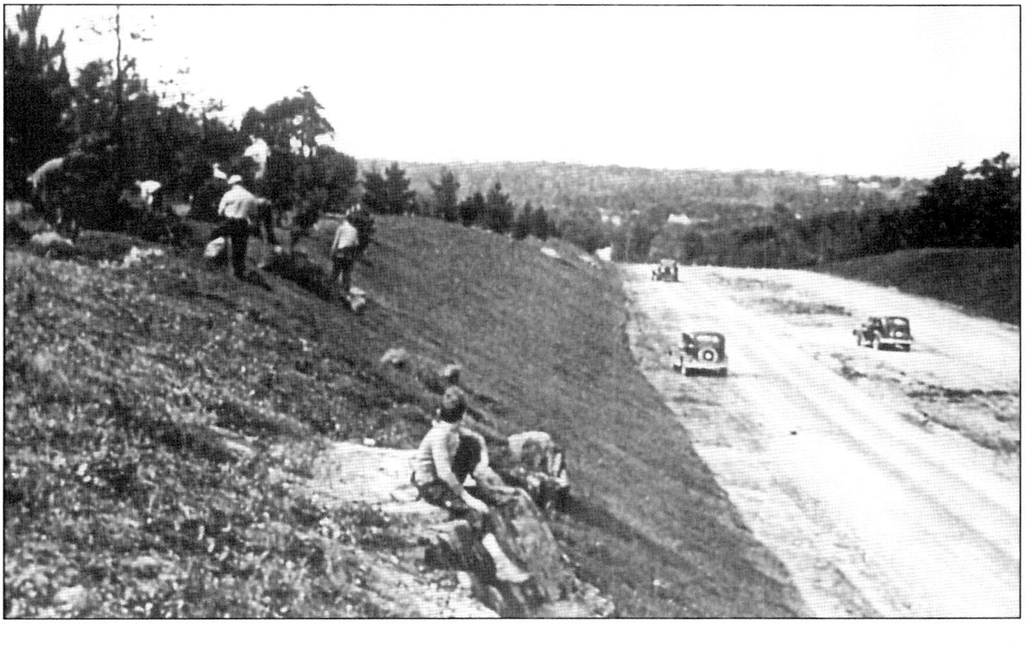

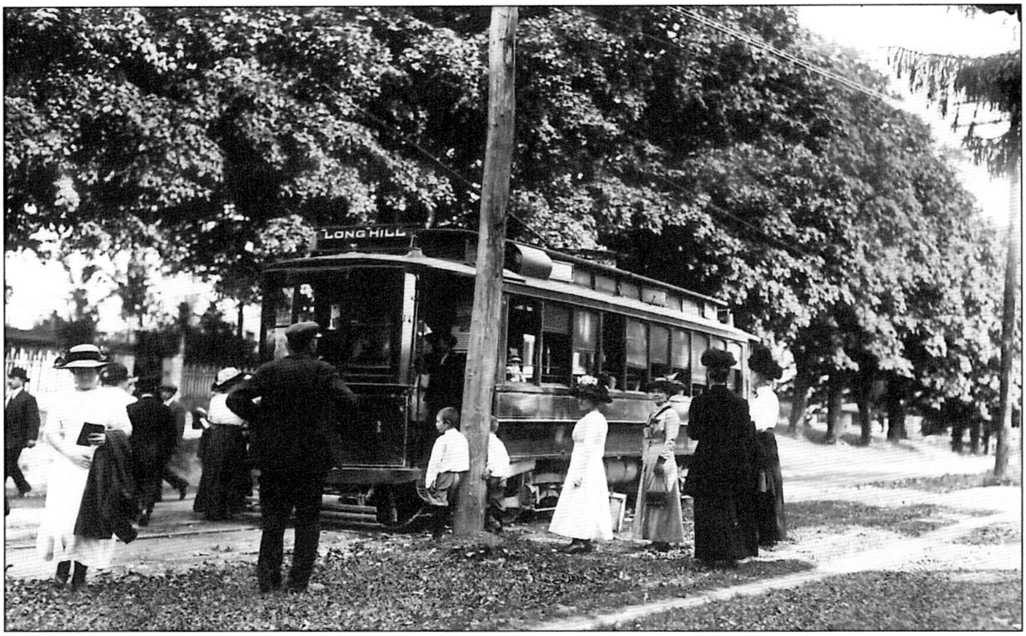


The Long Hill Trolley Company ran through Trumbull along Main Street from Stonehouse Road in Long Hill to Bridgeport. It was in service from May 1913 until February 1919. The fare of 5¢ was collected in three zones. Schoolchildren rode for student rates. The trolley was often referred to as the "Grasshopper," because it was painted green and it pitched and dipped along the tracks. It often jumped the rails at Blackhouse Road, where the tracks crossed Main Street from west to east. During cold weather, space heaters were placed at the rear of the car for warmth, but these efforts were futile. The trolley service ceased operations because of poor service and the increase in bus and automobile competition.

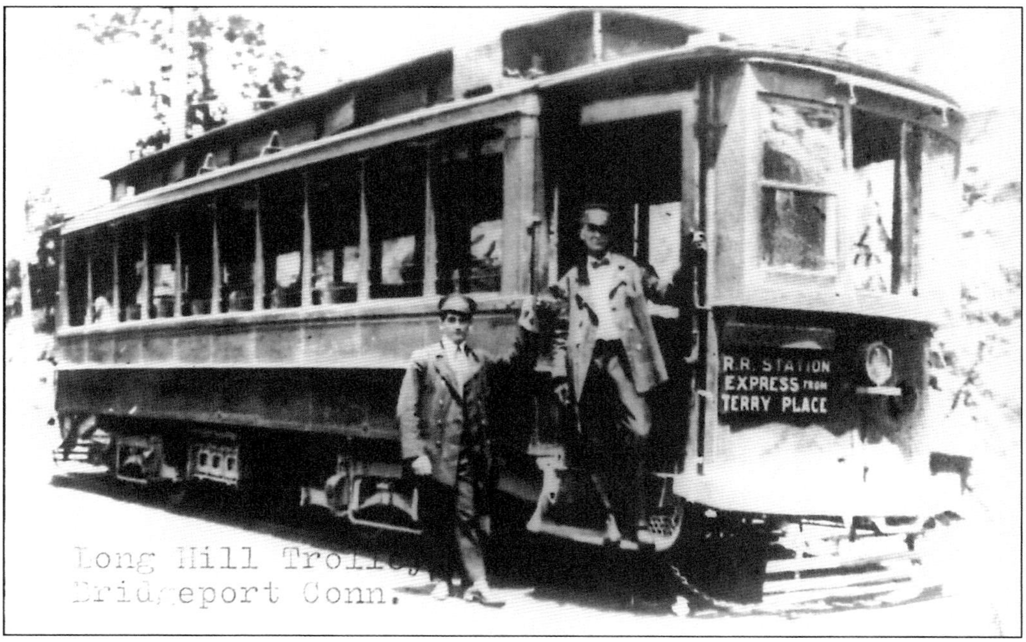

*Six*

# Portraits of the Past

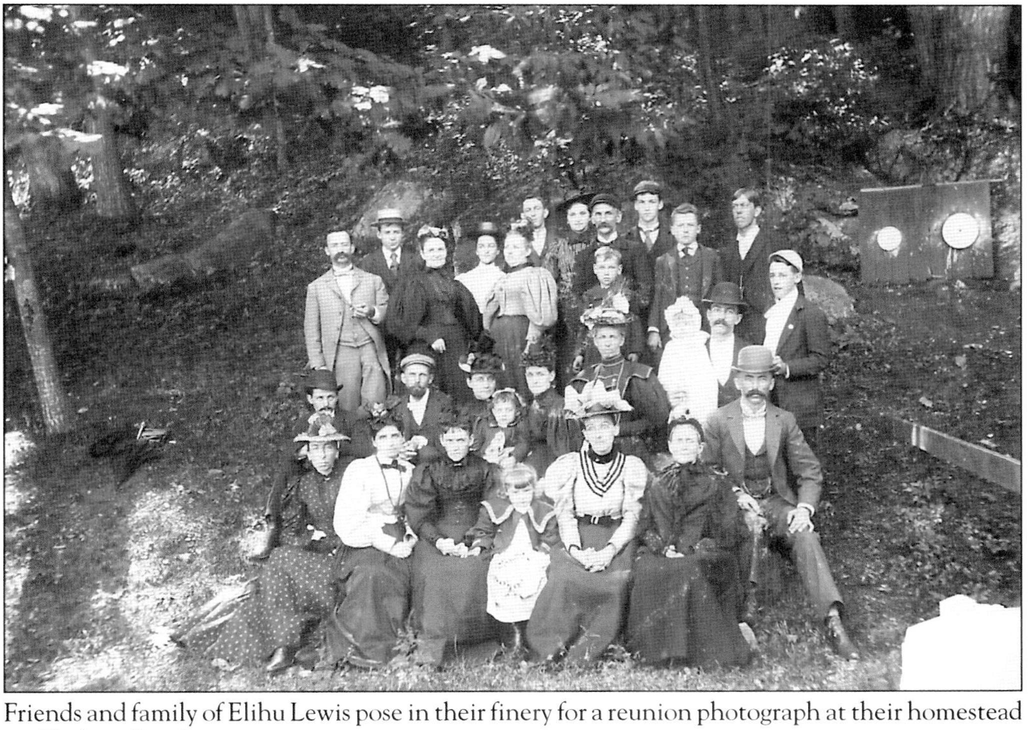

Friends and family of Elihu Lewis pose in their finery for a reunion photograph at their homestead on Shelton Road.

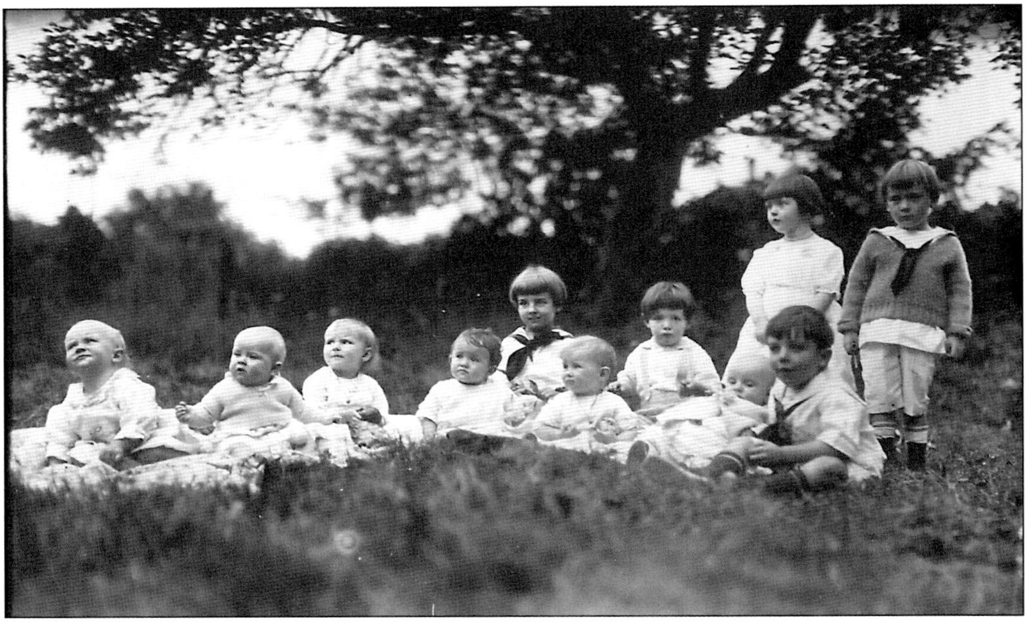

After a happy day of picnicking and partying with family and friends, the younger guests were gathered together for a photograph. Children from the Callahan, Lewis, Lineburg, Silliman, Stern, and Willis families are shown in this *c.* 1920 photograph. Many are still in the area.

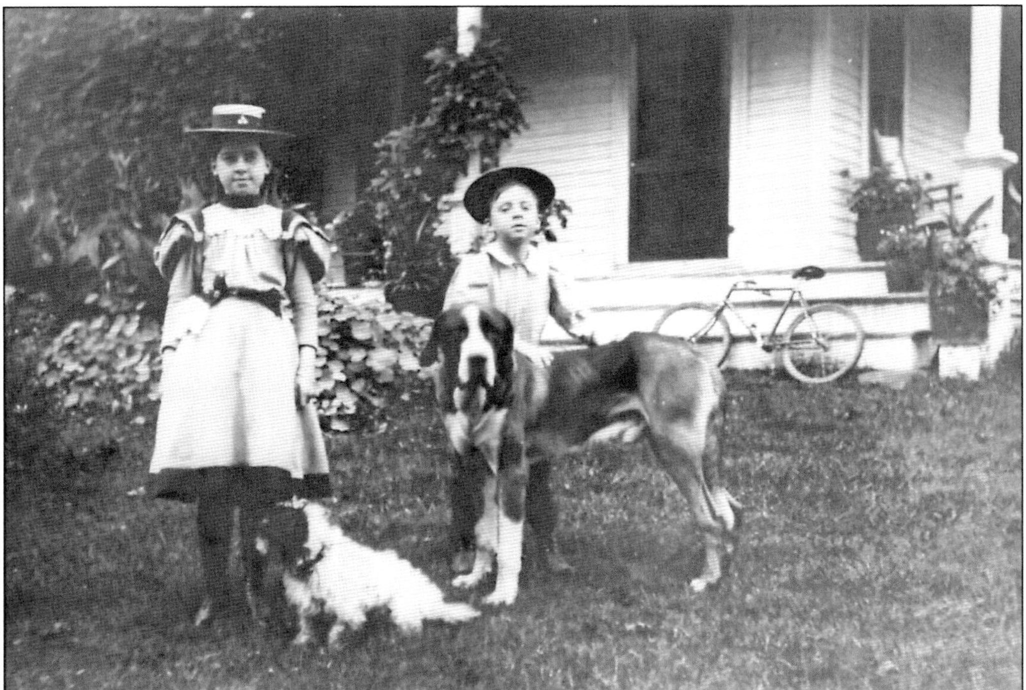

What did Ethel and Clyde Davis need in addition to canine companions and bicycle transportation? This photograph was taken at the corner of Main Street and Middlebrooks Avenue. Perhaps the day was a birthday or holiday—why else would one dress up?

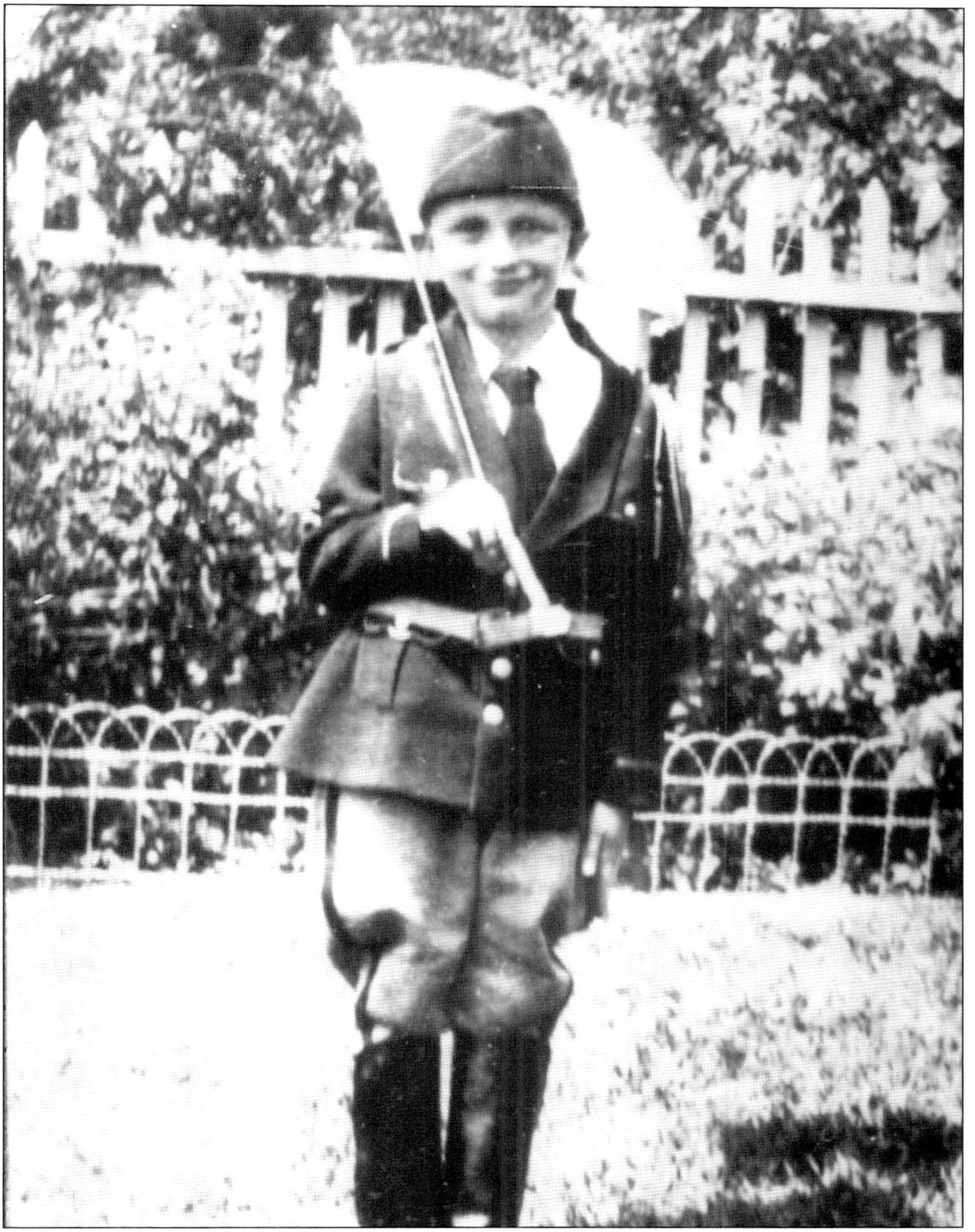

Seven-year-old Robert Greening Beach stands proudly with his flag on Memorial Day 1932. It was in defending that flag that he lost his life in 1944. Stationed in London en route to France, his unit was hit by a German "buzz" bomb. Sixty-three out of the one hundred and forty-three men in his unit were killed, including PFC Beach. In 1946 his parents, Mr. and Mrs. E. Merrill Beach, gave to the town of Trumbull 180 acres "in loving memory of their son and dedicated to the men and women of Trumbull who served in World War II as a living memorial and to be kept as a public park forever."

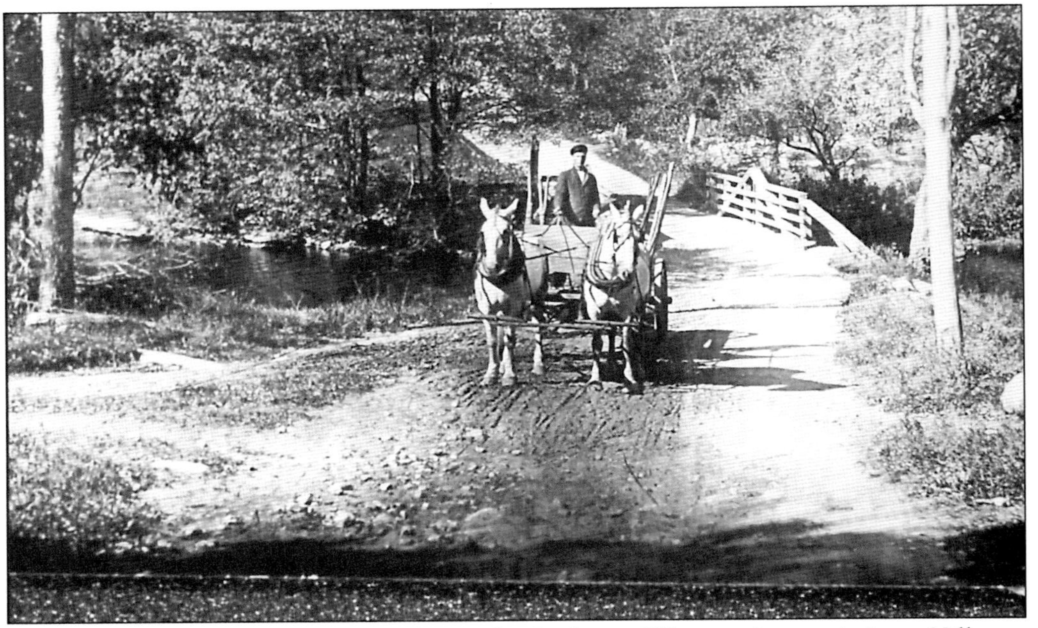

Mr. Wade and his wagon team cross the wooden bridge on Whitney Avenue in Long Hill.

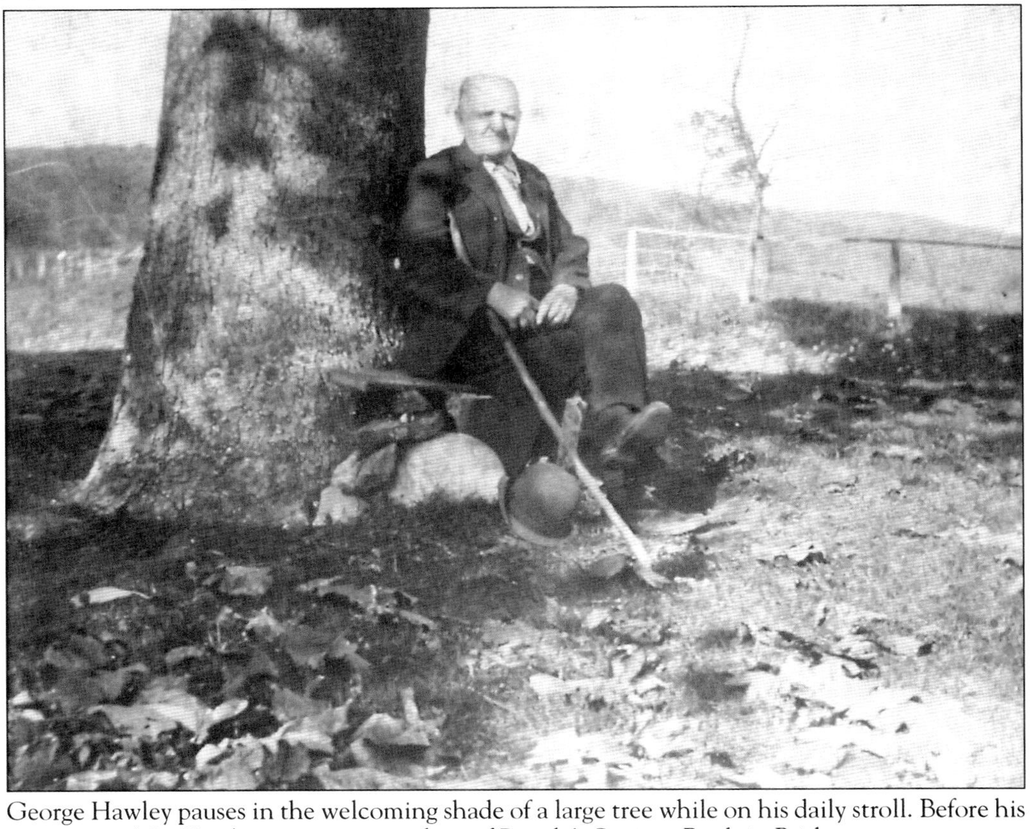

George Hawley pauses in the welcoming shade of a large tree while on his daily stroll. Before his retirement, Mr. Hawley was vice-president of People's Savings Bank in Bridgeport.

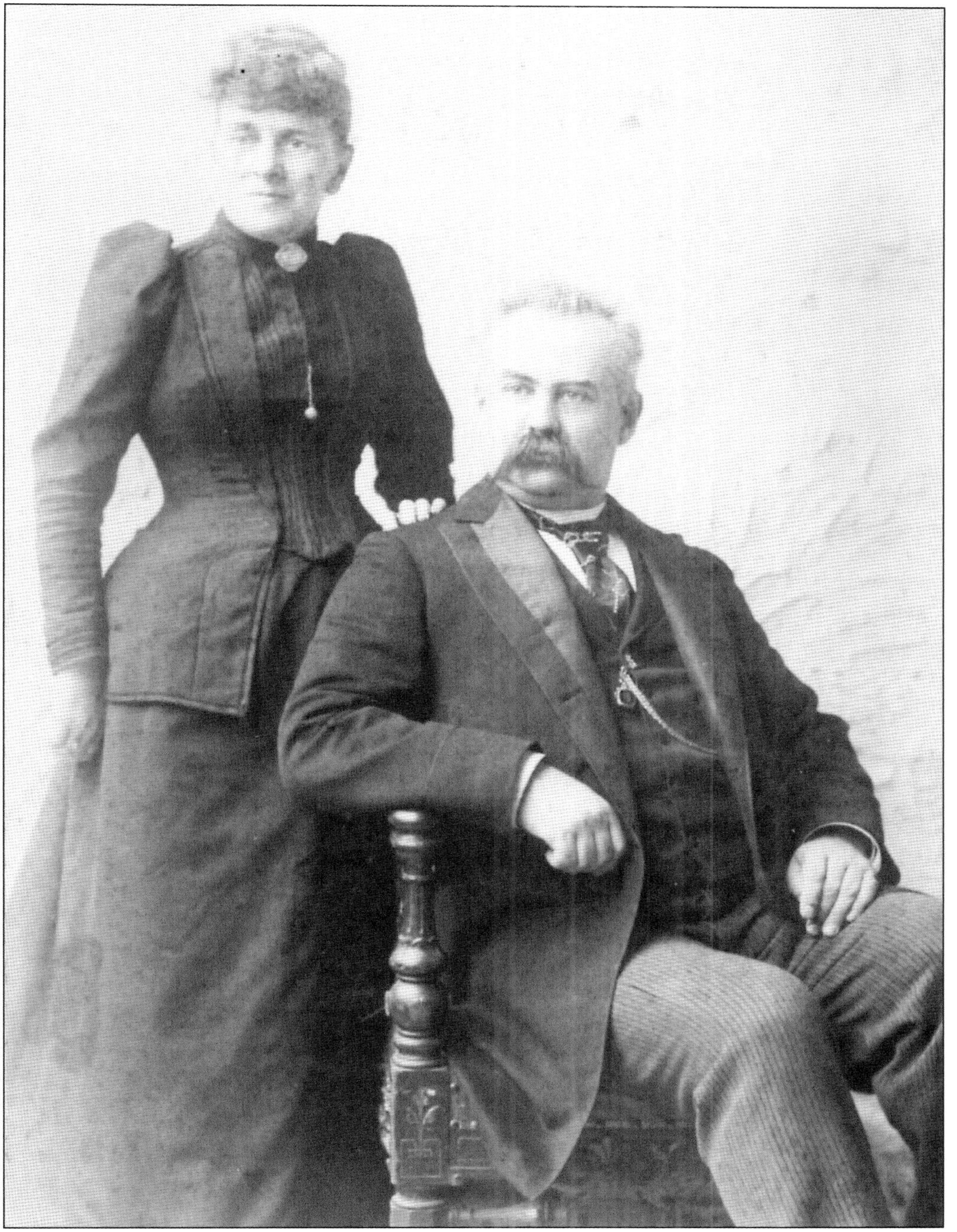

Mr. and Mrs. John B. Peet were prominent citizens of Nichols. Mr. Peet, born in 1849, had a real estate business in New York, but spent his summers in his birthplace of Nichols. Mrs. Peet, née Antoinette Edwards, donated a fountain on the Nichols Green in memory of her husband in 1895. The Nichols landmark stands today on the Nichols Improvement Association property. The Peet Homestead was donated by four cousins of John Peet to Trinity Episcopal Church and today it serves as the parish house and parsonage.

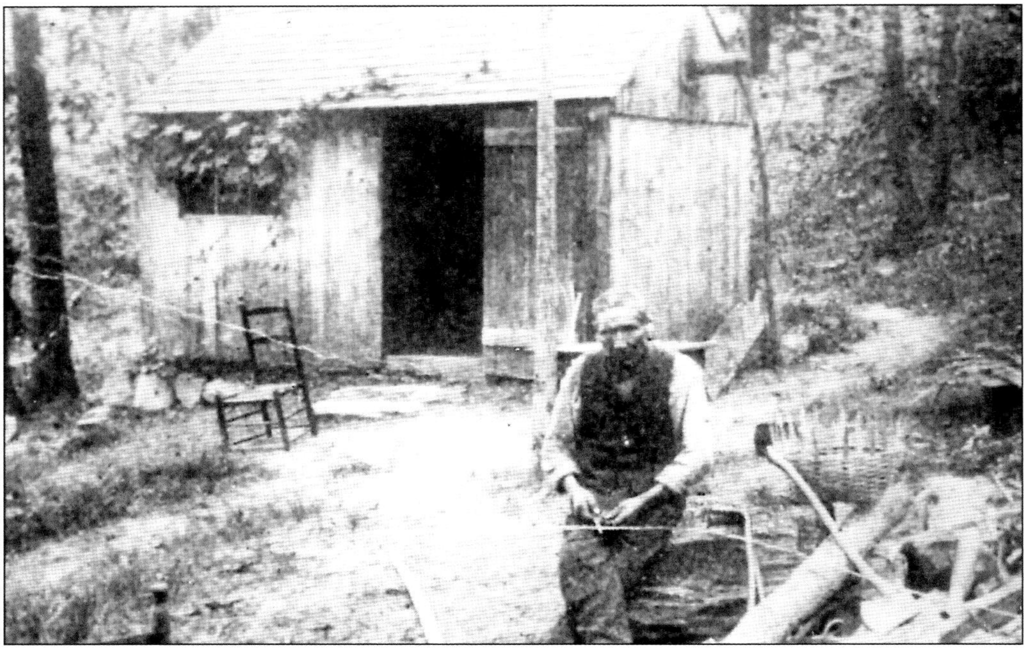

Jack Skickett, the last full-blooded Native American to live in Trumbull, made his home north of Lake Avenue on the east side of Dayton Road. "Jack Indian," crippled by an ox cart accident, made baskets of hickory strips for a living.

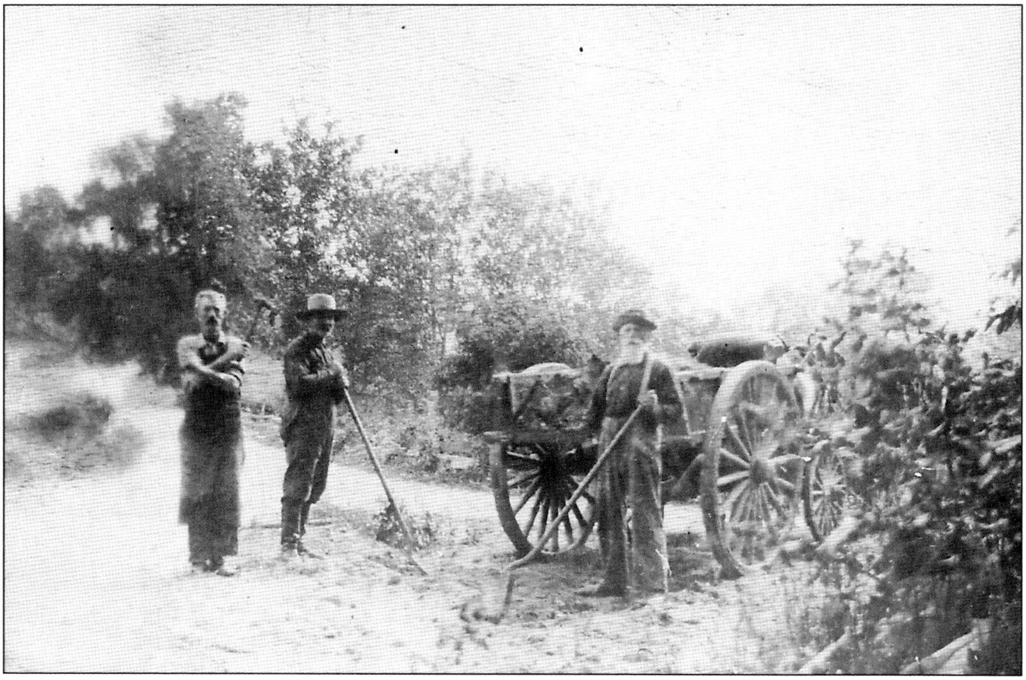

In 1918 work crews of local residents would repair the unpaved roads. This crew of three, Pat Heneghan (a blacksmith) and road workers John Bailey and Leonard Hawley, worked for one and one-half days for $6.37 in pay.

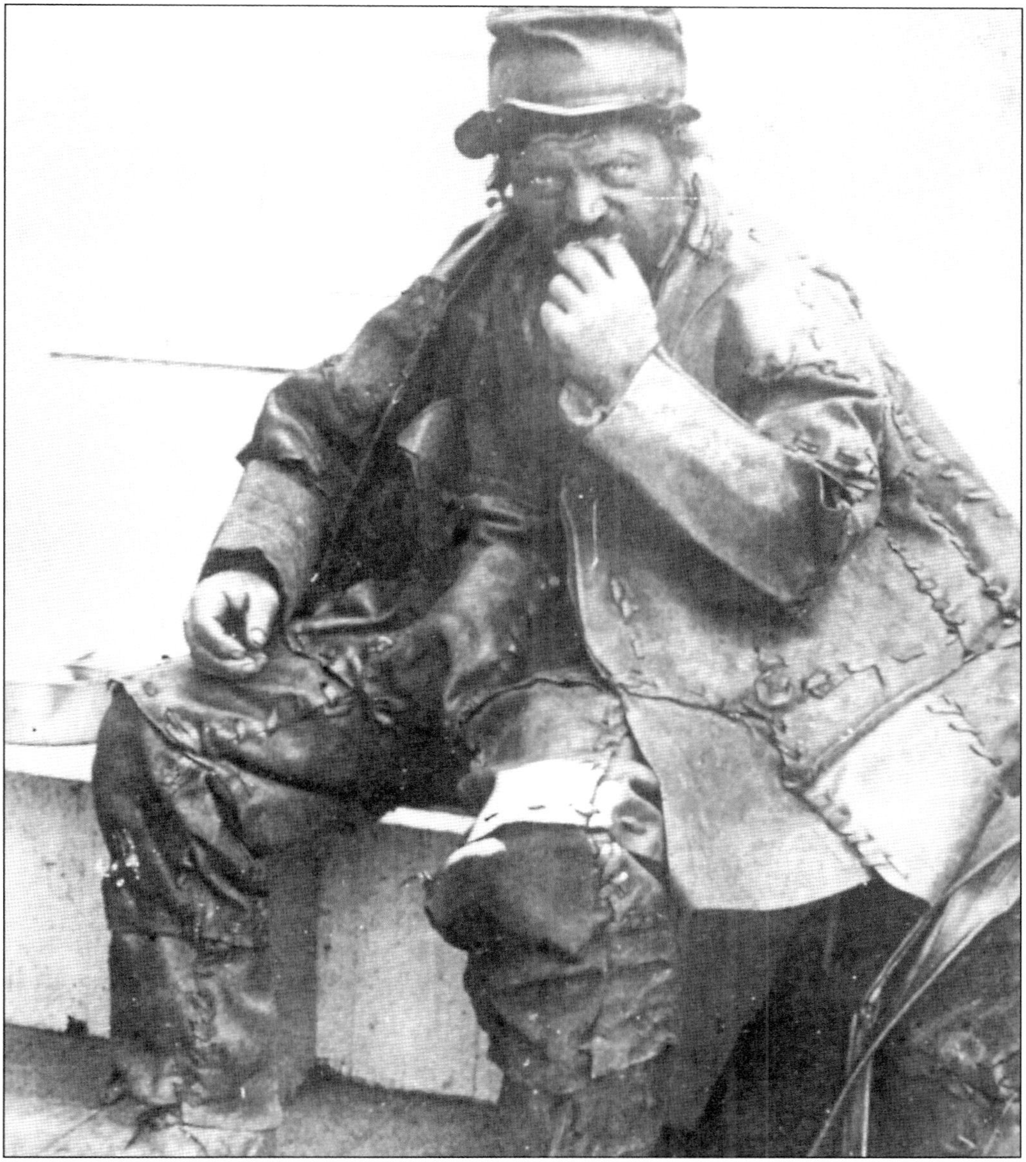

One of the nineteenth century's colorful characters was the "Old Leatherman." He was a solitary Frenchman who wandered throughout Connecticut and eastern New York for thirty years, living in caves along his route. He never spoke and was fed by the people whose homes he passed. His leather suit was made of old leather boot tops fastened together with leather cords and was said to have weighed 60 pounds. His belongings consisted of an 1844 prayer book, a few simple tools, a tin pipe of his own making, and a large leather pouch into which he placed cigar stubs found along the roadway. He appeared often in Trumbull on Huntington Turnpike, Twitchgrass Road, and trudging up White Plains and Church Hill Roads. This photograph was given to the Mahoney family of Main Street in exchange for a meal. In 1889 the body of the Leatherman was found in a cave in Mount Pleasant, New York. Doctors pronounced his death to be of natural causes. His grave in Ossining, New York, is marked by a plaque, as are many of the caves he used for shelter.

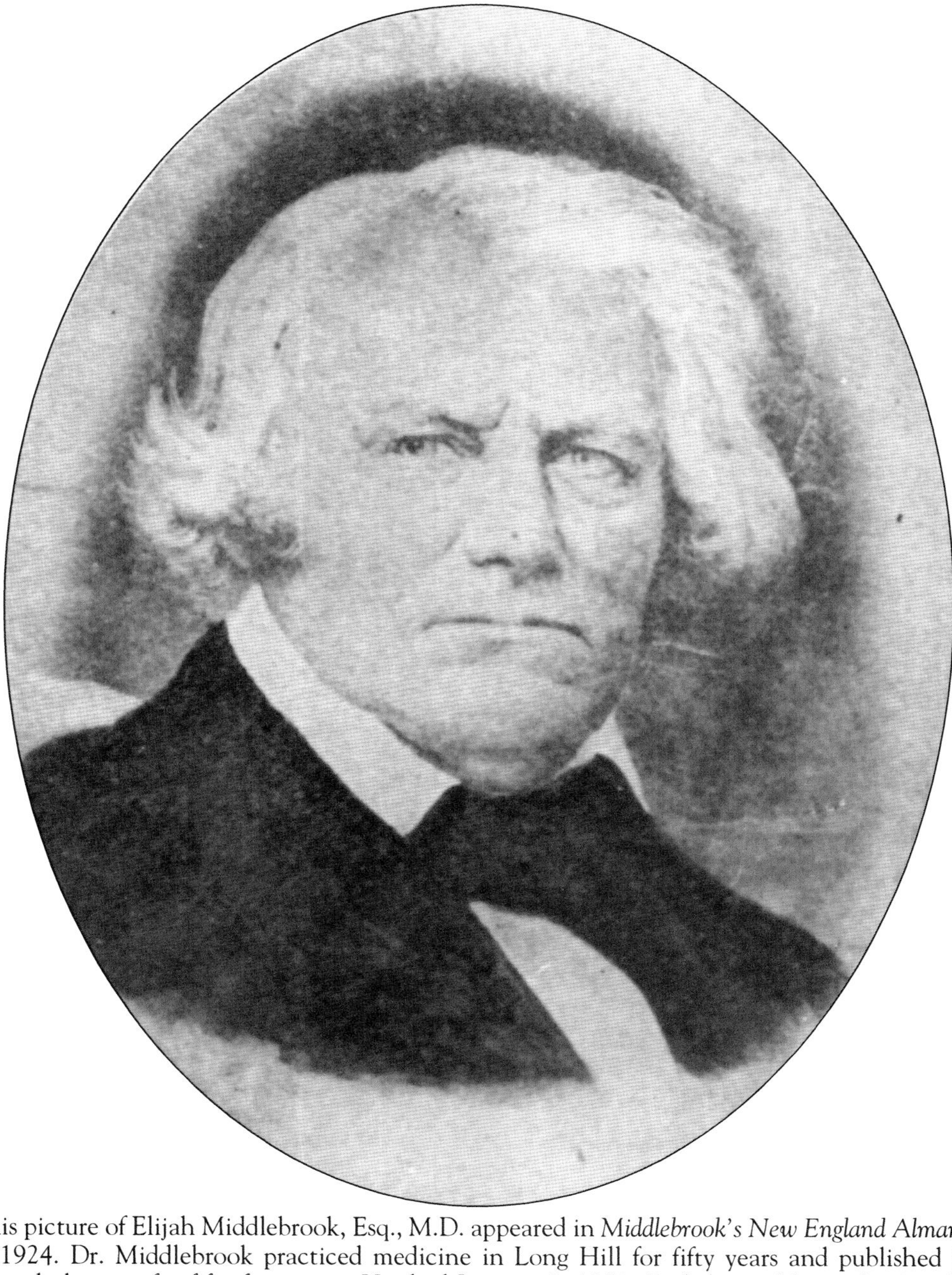

This picture of Elijah Middlebrook, Esq., M.D. appeared in *Middlebrook's New England Almanac* of 1924. Dr. Middlebrook practiced medicine in Long Hill for fifty years and published his annual almanac for fifty-four years. He died January 2, 1859. Both he and his wife, Comfort Burton Hawley, are buried in Long Hill Burial Ground on Middlebrooks Avenue.

Charles Carlos Nichols was the son of David Nichols, who owned the Nichols Carriage Shop on Center Street. Charles was employed there as a bookkeeper. He also served as a private in Company C, 8th Regiment of the National Guard, under Captain Charles Plumb, from August 1865 to August 1871.

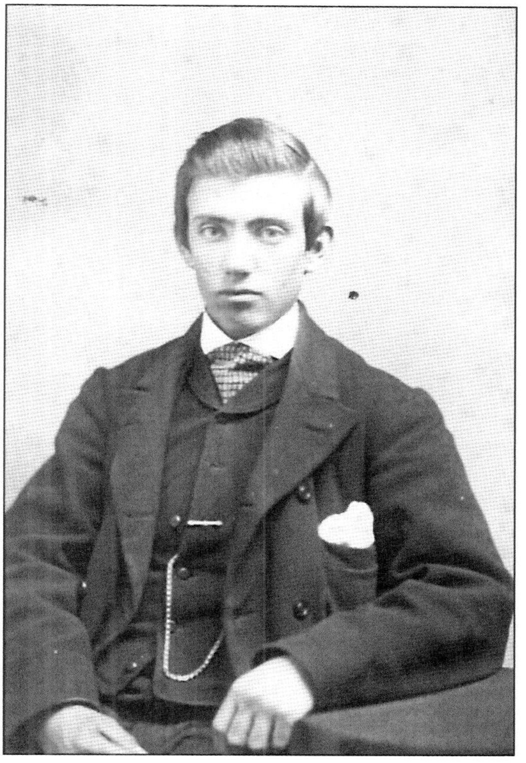

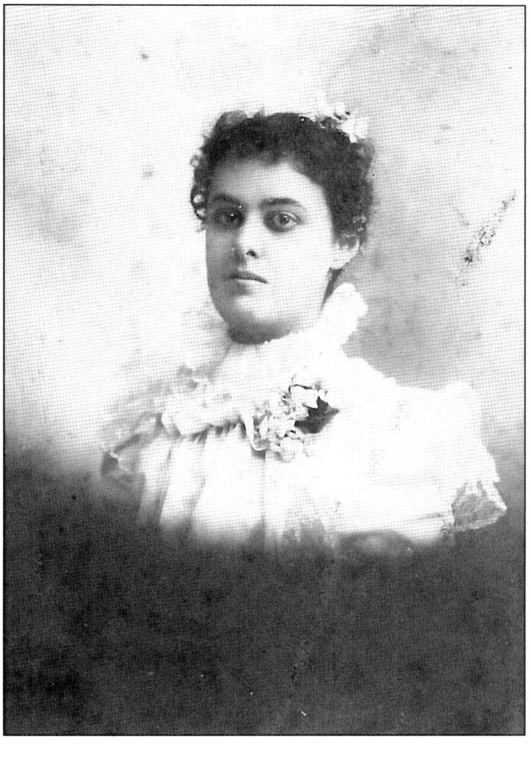

Mrs. Samuel G. Seeley, the former Fannie May Wales, is pictured in her wedding dress on June 15, 1898.

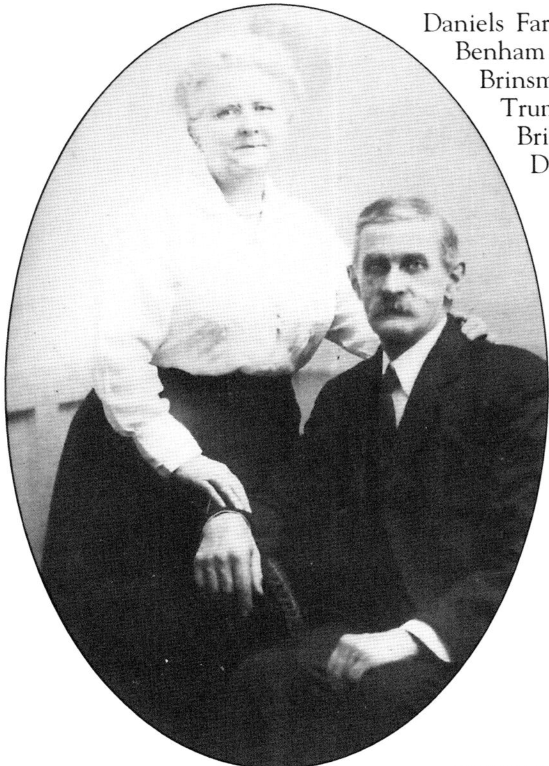

Daniels Farm Road residents H. Stanley and Frances Benham Brinsmade pose for a photograph. The Brinsmade family were early settlers of the Trumbull Center area. An early ancestor, Daniel Brinsmade, owned a large farm from which Daniels Farm Road took its name.

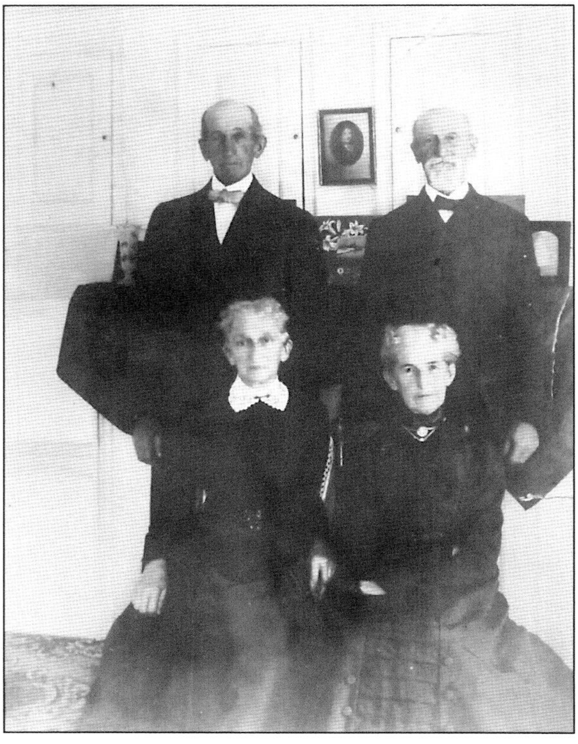

The Hall family poses in the dining room of their home, now on Campbell Road. Standing on the left is Ormel (son); on the right is Dr. Zalmon Hall (father); sitting on the left is Clarissa (daughter); and seated on the right is Mrs. Rhoda Beach Hall (mother).

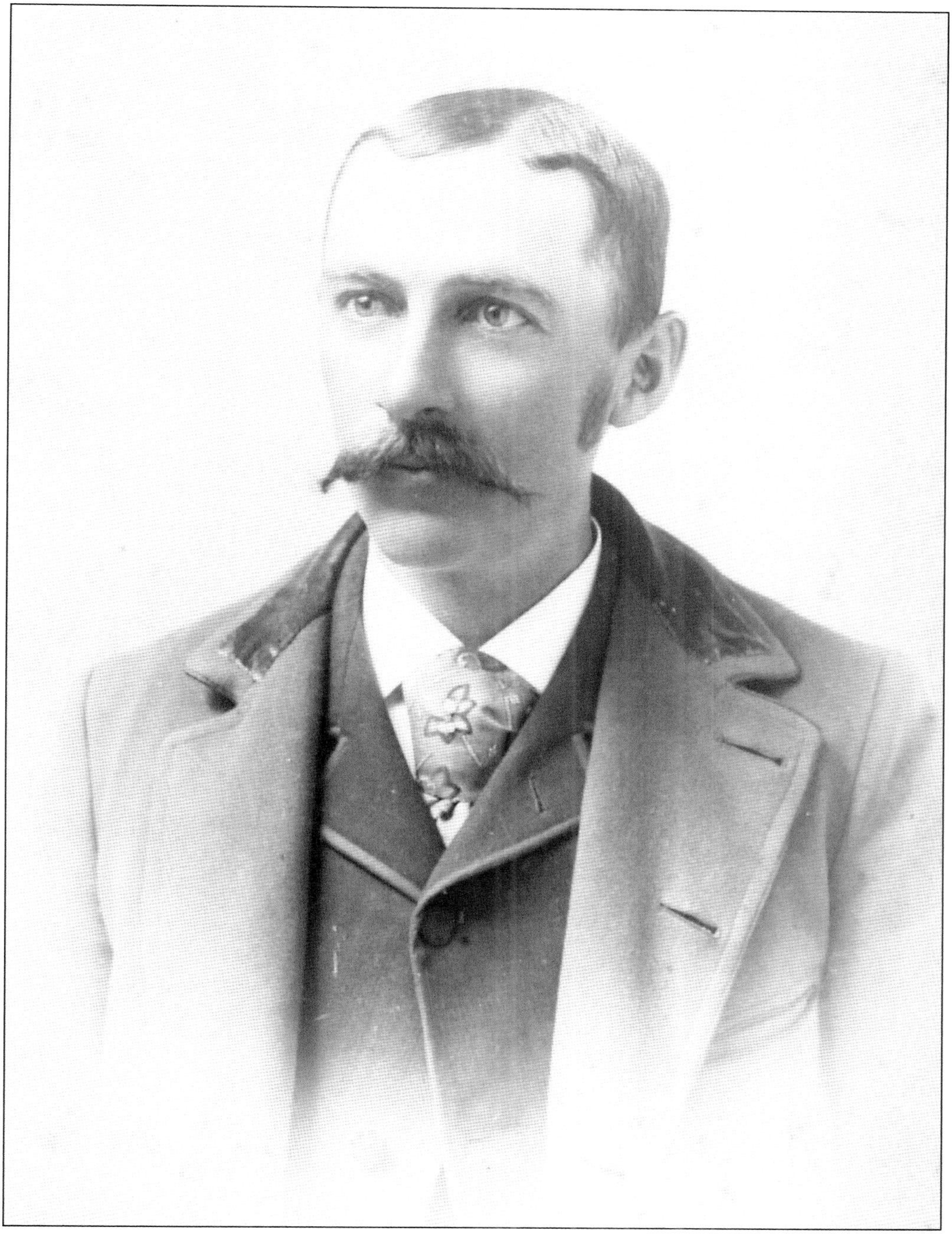

William B. Mallett, a prosperous farmer of Tashua Hill, was the son of William A. Mallett. The Malletts were direct descendants of John Mallett, who was one of the first settlers of Tashua, having left France for America in colonial times. William B. Mallett was married to Minnie Staples from Easton. Mr. and Mrs. Mallett celebrated their golden wedding anniversary in 1933. They had two daughters, Miss Lillian and Miss Maude, who continued to reside in the Mallett Homestead on Madison Avenue until the late 1980s.

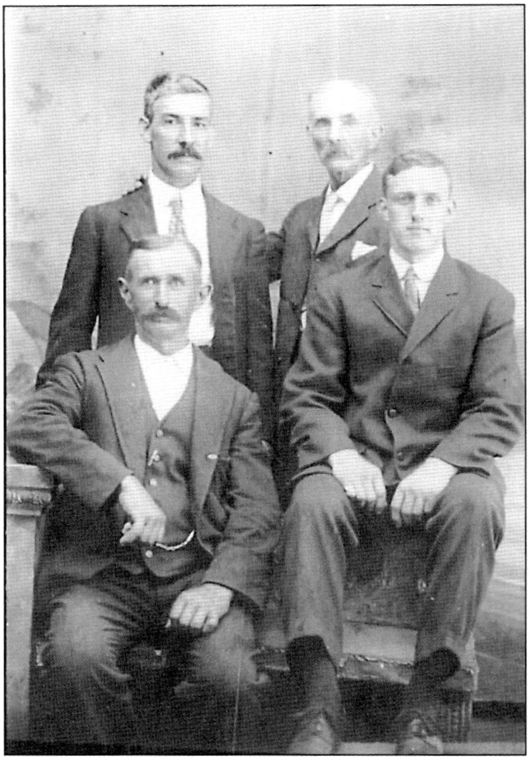

Four influential men posed at a Grange outing in 1911. Pictured from left to right, are: (standing) Albert Linley and Elmer Nichols; (seated) William Brinsmade and Louis Fuller. Mr. Linley lived on the old Plumb Homestead on Church Hill Road and was a dairy farmer. Mr. Nichols lived on White Plains Road and was a farmer. Mr. Brinsmade lived on Unity Road and raised large flocks of sheep. Mr. Fuller lived on Fuller Road and was a dairy farmer who had a milk route.

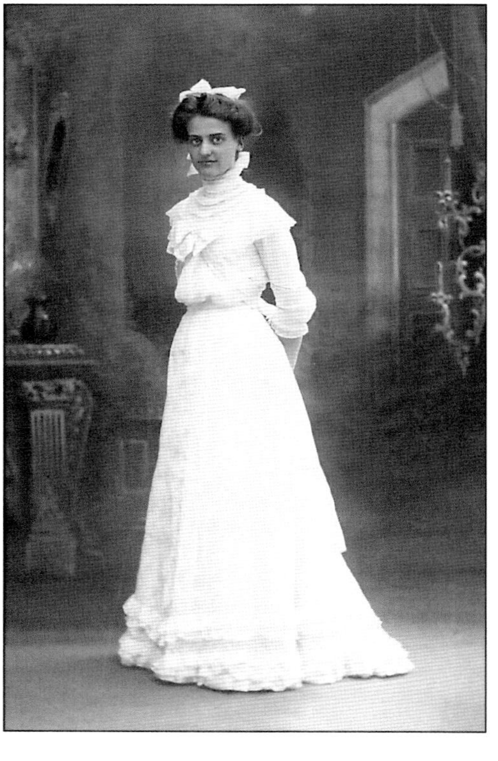

This is an early picture of Mrs. Alice Wellington, one of the most beloved ladies in the Nichols section of town. Mrs. Wellington served many years as librarian at the Fairchild Memorial Library, retiring in 1968 at the age of eighty-two. She had a wonderful rapport and patience with children and helped bring knowledge and happiness to all. Her home on Shelton Road had beautiful gardens and is still a lovely asset to the community.

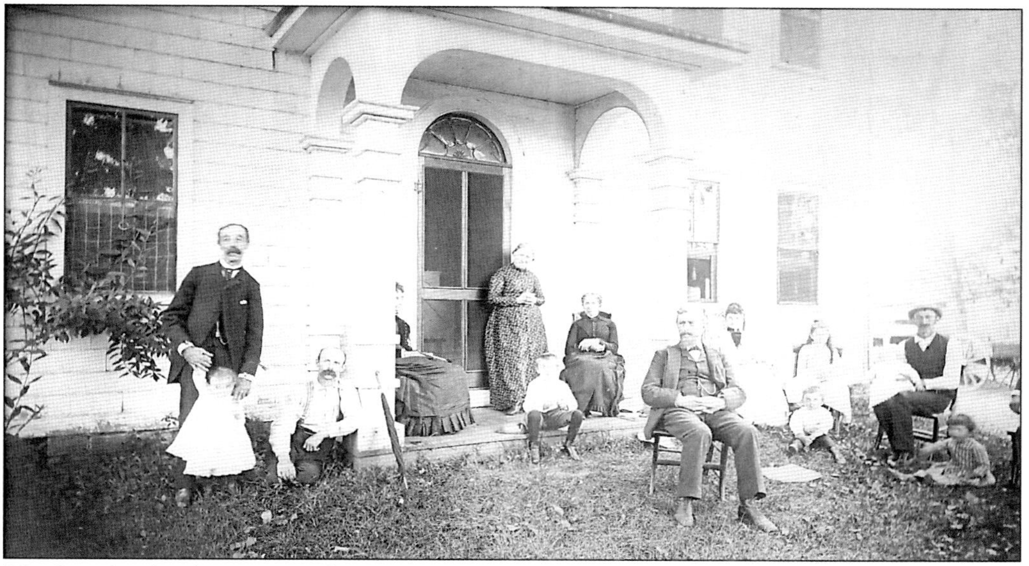

The Joseph Plumb Homestead on Huntington Turnpike (*c.* 1750) was part of a large farm. It passed down through several generations of Plumbs and was later owned by the Cook, Marsh, and Peck families. This photograph pictured the occupants living there *c.* 1890. In 1946, the home was restored approximately to its original internal configuration and outward appearance.

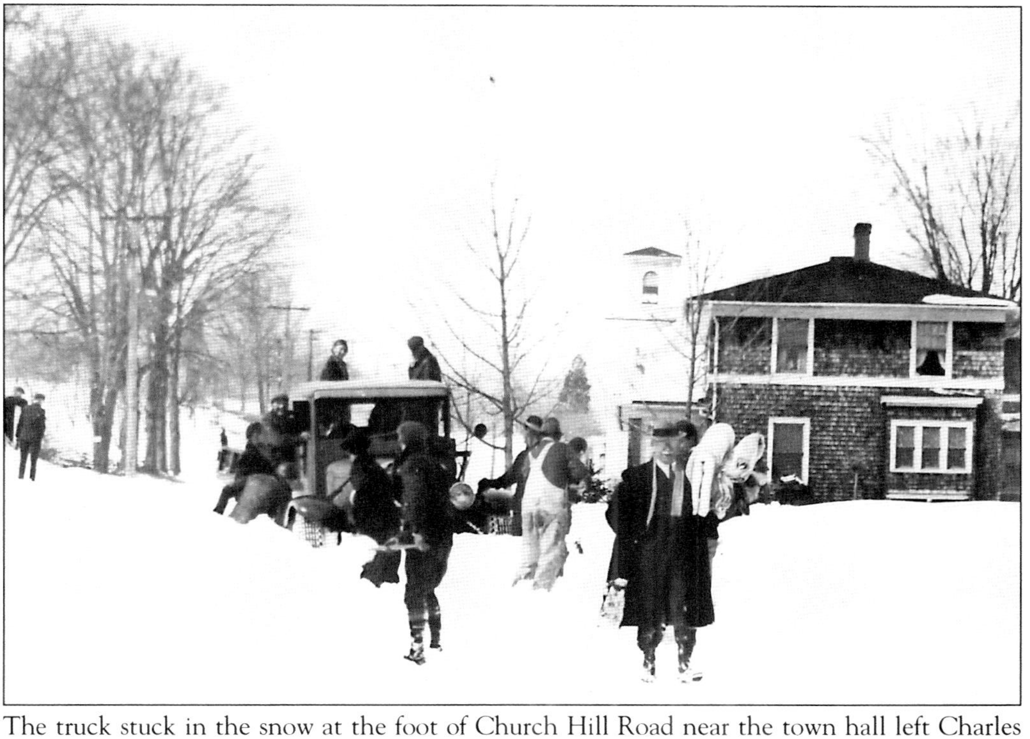

The truck stuck in the snow at the foot of Church Hill Road near the town hall left Charles A. Bradley carrying supplies to the needy during the Depression in 1932. Mr. Bradley was first selectman from 1932 to 1938. He also owned a garage in Long Hill Center. Bradley Hall at Long Hill Methodist Church was named in honor of this well-known philanthropist.

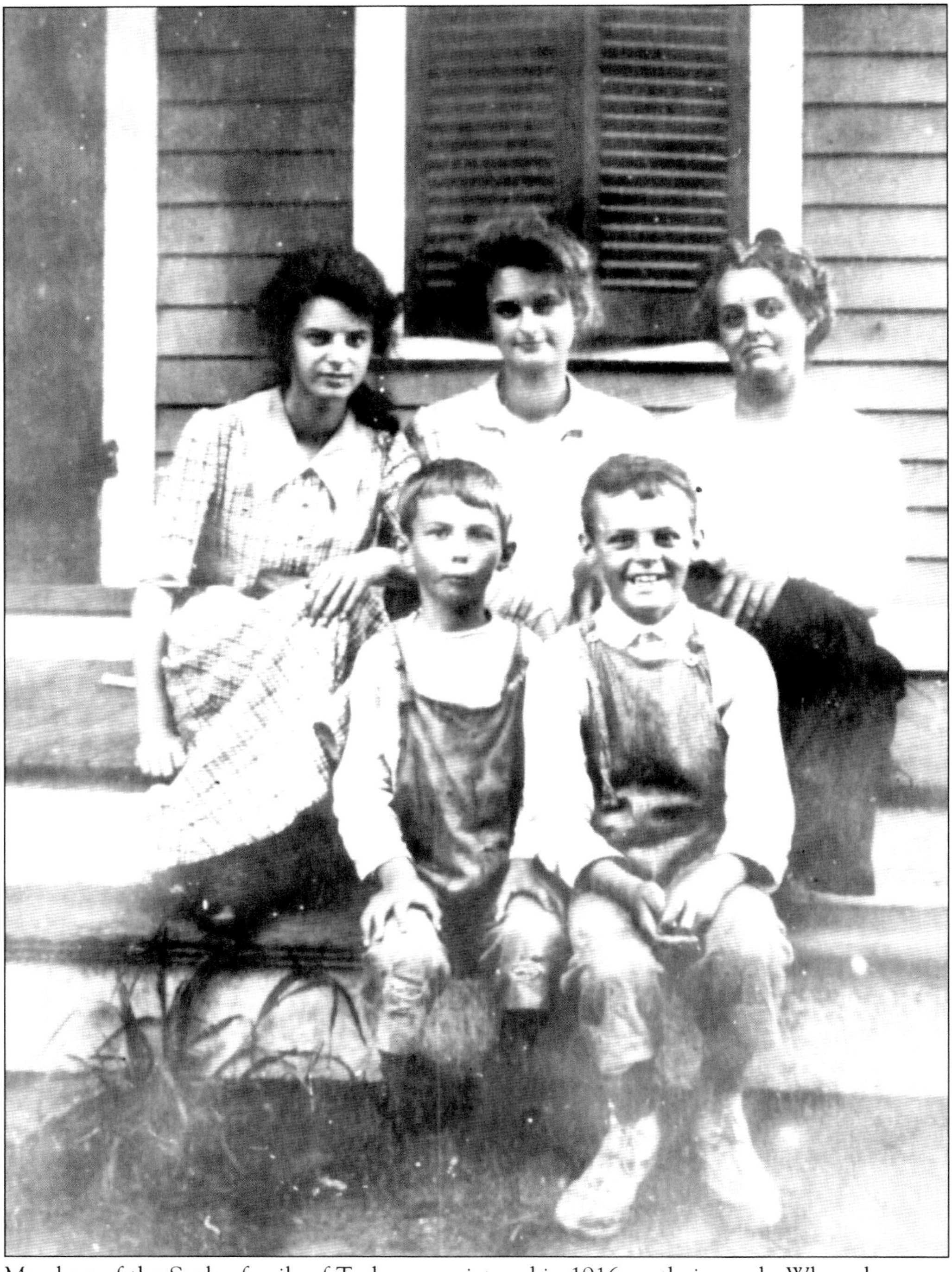

Members of the Seeley family of Tashua are pictured in 1916 on their porch. When she was a child, Dorothy Seeley (top row, left) attended town meetings with her father, and thus was born her intense interest in town history. She was one of the founders of the Trumbull Historical Society. In 1984 she authored the book *Tales of Trumbull's Past* and over the years she gave generously of her time and knowledge to bring alive the history and memories of Trumbull.

# Seven

# Where We Lived

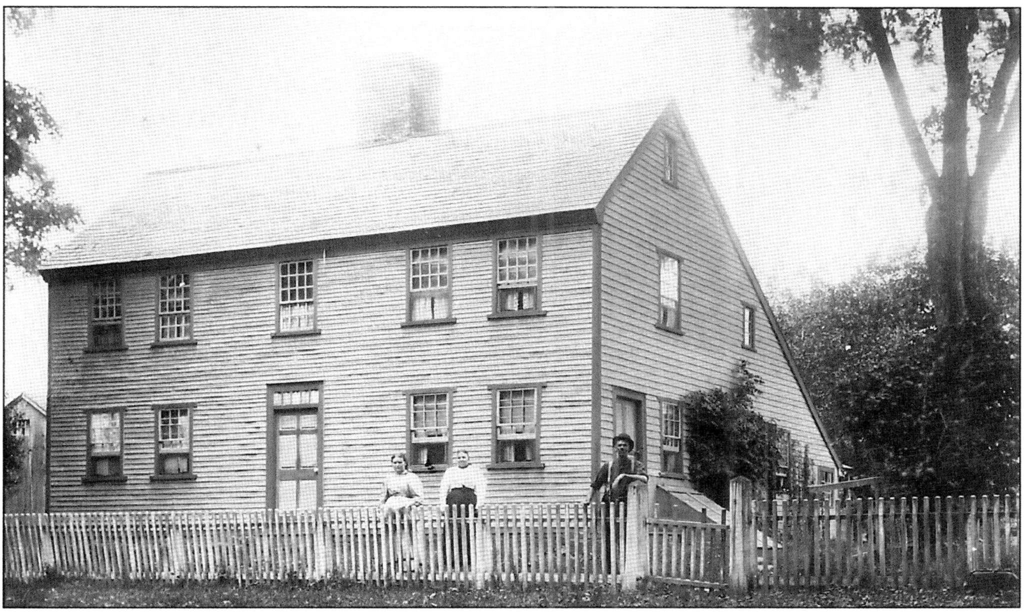

The fine old home of Isaac E. Nichols stands on Huntington Turnpike just south of the Historical Society. A respected farmer in the community, Nichols was the grandson of Isaac Nichols, who in 1671 received the second assignment of land within the present bounds of Trumbull.

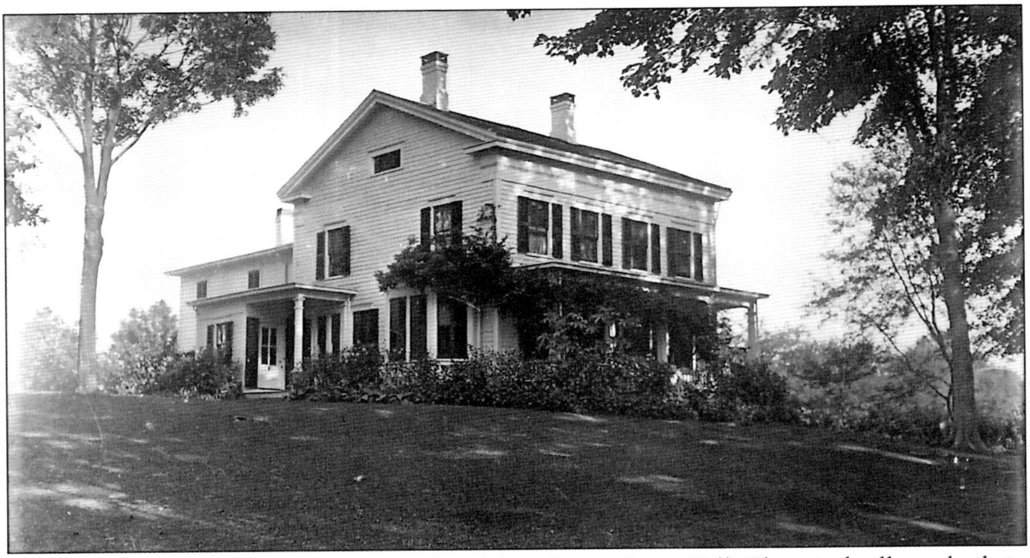

The Harvey Hubbell Estate was located on Main Street, Long Hill. The windmill was built in 1904 and was used for the home and the Hubbell-Hadley Shirt Factory, also located on the grounds. The wind-driven blades, made of steel and wood, reached nearly 100 feet into the sky. The windmill pumped water from the well into a holding tank in the structure. The estate was given to the Bridgeport Roman Catholic Diocese in 1958. The windmill was demolished in April 1976. The house still stands today on the property known as St. Joseph's Manor.

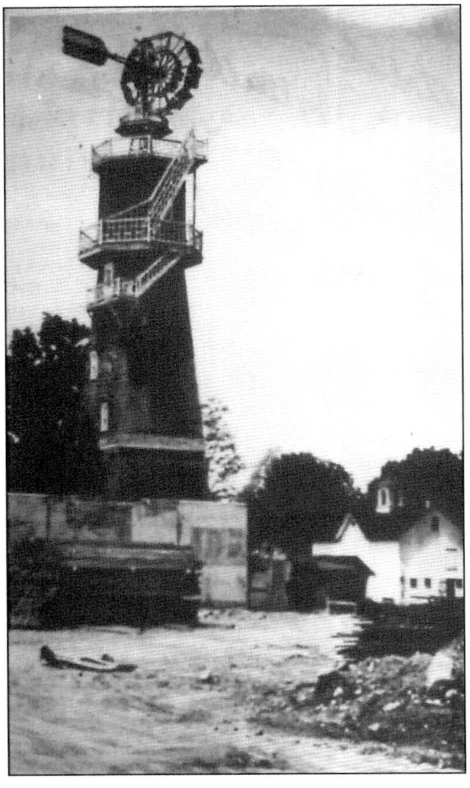

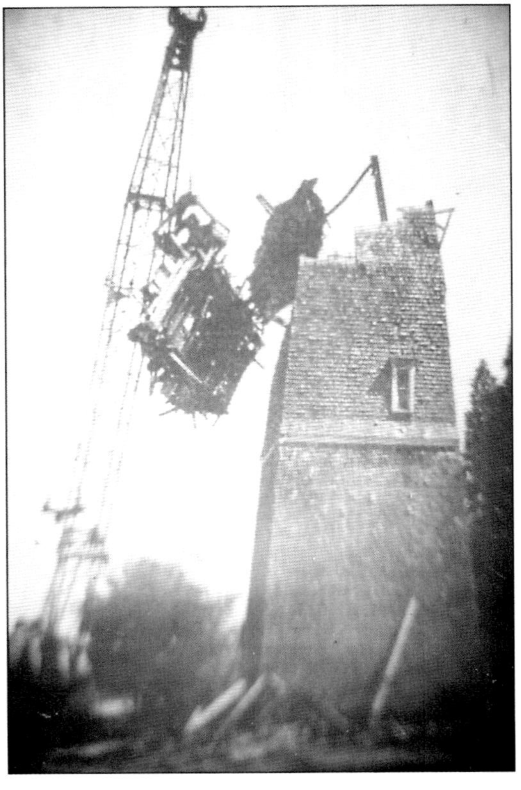

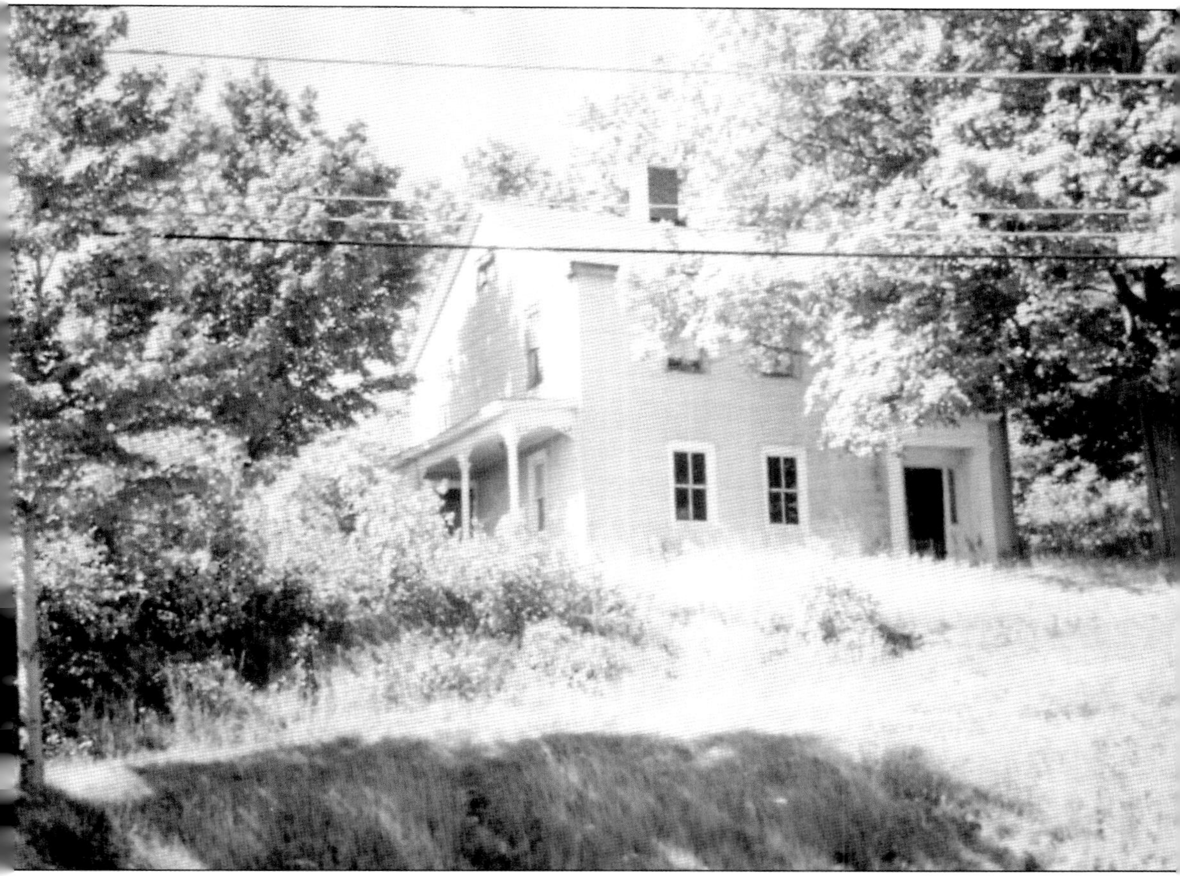

This colonial home stood on Brinsmade Crossing across from the intersection of Church Hill and Daniels Farm Roads. Built in 1787 by Andrew Hawley, it was later purchased by Eliakim Beach who used the home as a post office and tavern. In its day it was a beautiful home with many fine features, one of which was a partition on the upper floor that could be swung by use of a pulley to make one large room where dances were held. Legend has it that Lafayette and possibly Washington slept here during its early existence as a tavern. Sadly, this unique home and property were sold in 1980 to make way for an office building.

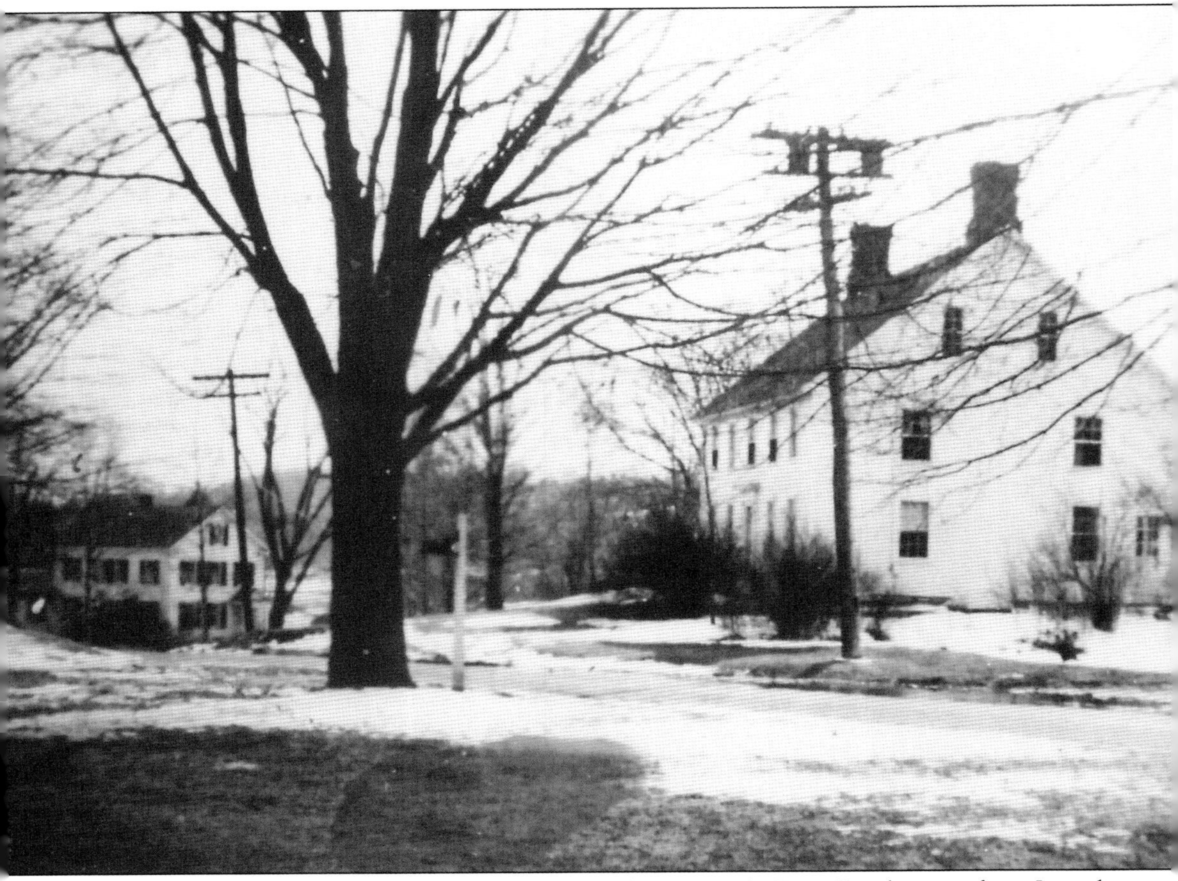

One of Trumbull's lost treasures, this house stood on Daniels Farm Road across from Laurel Street. Built by mill owner Ebanezer Hawley in 1765, it was later owned by Eliakim Beach, Trumbull's first town clerk. During the Revolutionary War, it was often used as a place of refuge for those fleeing the British. It was to this house that Mary Silliman came in 1779. From its upper windows she watched the flames consume her hometown of Fairfield. Two months later, while still at the house, she gave birth to Benjamin Silliman who, in adulthood, became one of America's leading scientists and for whom Silliman College at Yale is named. In 1862 the house was purchased by the Town of Trumbull and it served as town hall for twenty-one years. A succession of owners followed. It was dismantled in 1961 and rebuilt in Darien, where it stands today as a fitting tribute to its proud past. This photograph was taken by Julia Buckley in 1937.

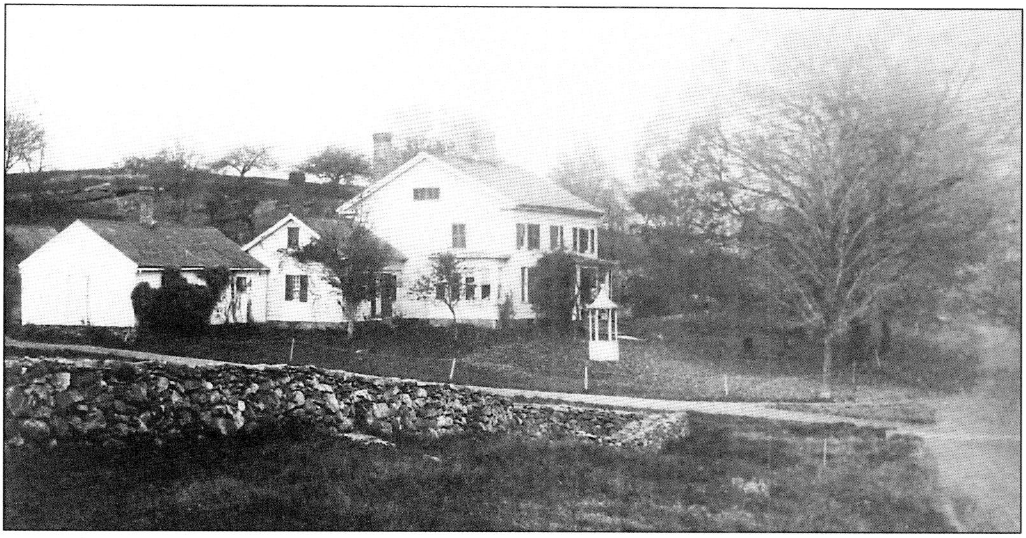

Dr. Seth Hill, who was the only physician in Tashua in the late 1800s, had his office in his home on Tashua Road. He made house calls in a horse-drawn buggy. The charge to deliver a baby was $10, and he prepared medicines from his black bag for a nominal charge. An office visit cost 50¢ and a house call was $1. Patients often bartered for his services with fruits, vegetables, and other local products. He cared for all the people of town, regardless of their ability to pay. The Victorian front parlor of Dr. Hill's home is pictured below. The house still stands today on Tashua Road.

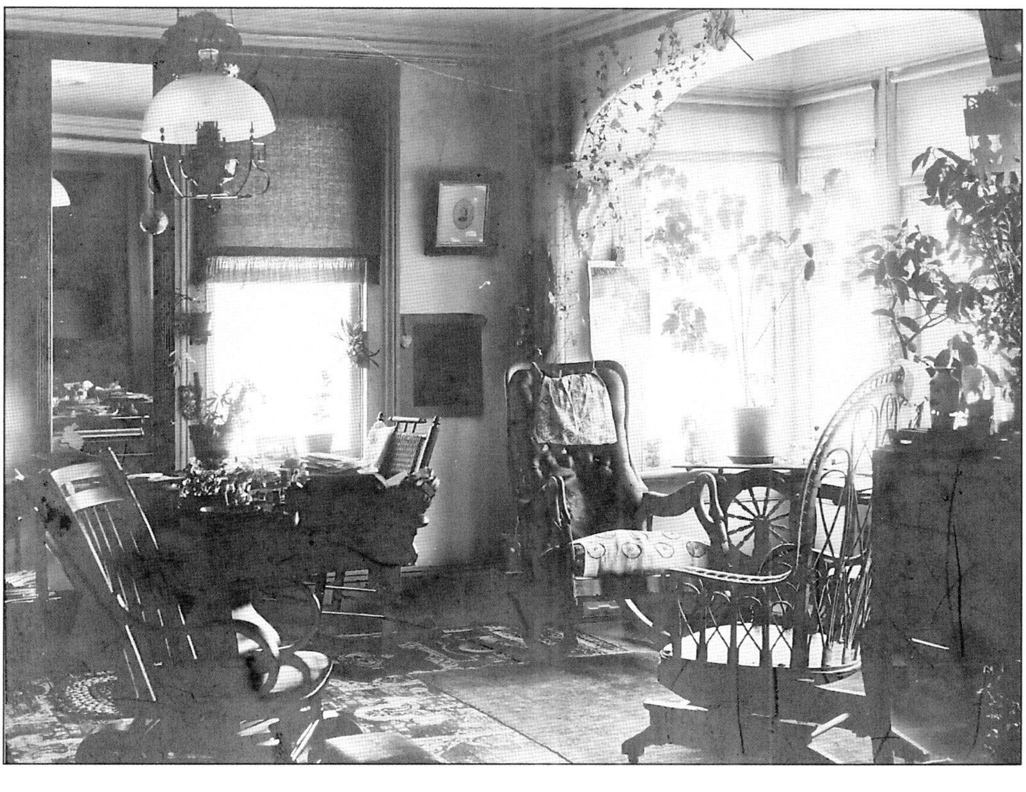

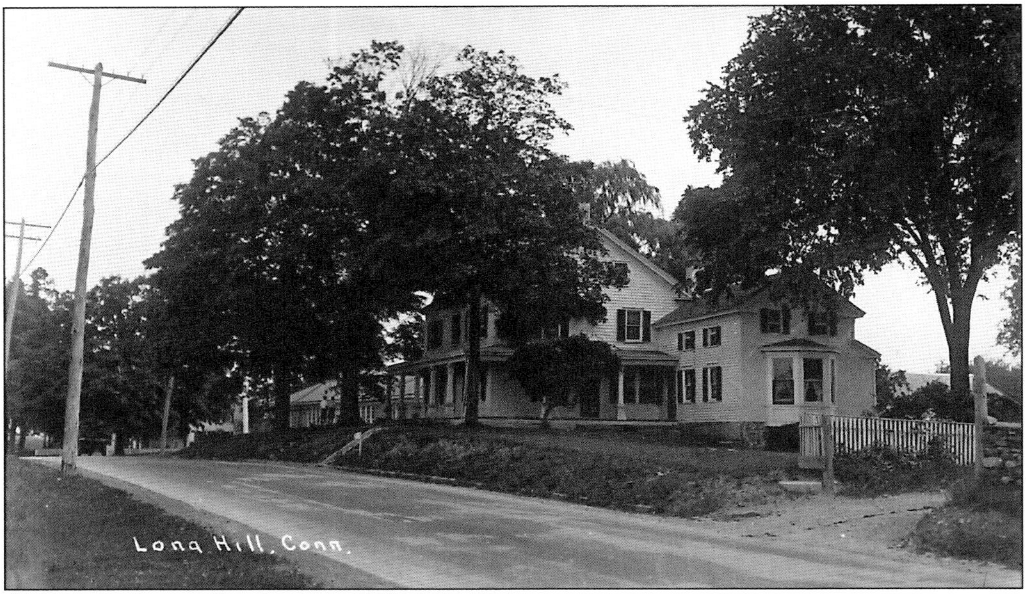


The Beardsley Homestead was known as a popular tavern in the late 1800s. It is still standing on Main Street next to the Board of Education offices.

The Beardsley Homestead's red barn (pictured below) was located across the street from the house. In 1894, Elliot M. Beardsley had a clock manufactured as a gift to the Congregational Church. The church refused to accept the clock because it had been purchased with profits from Mr. Beardsley's tavern. Instead, Mr. Beardsley had the clock installed on the barn, where it remained for many years until the barn was to be demolished for a housing development. The barn was moved to the Charles A. Edward's estate on Madison Avenue. In 1964, Mr. Edwards donated the clock to the Trumbull Historical Society.

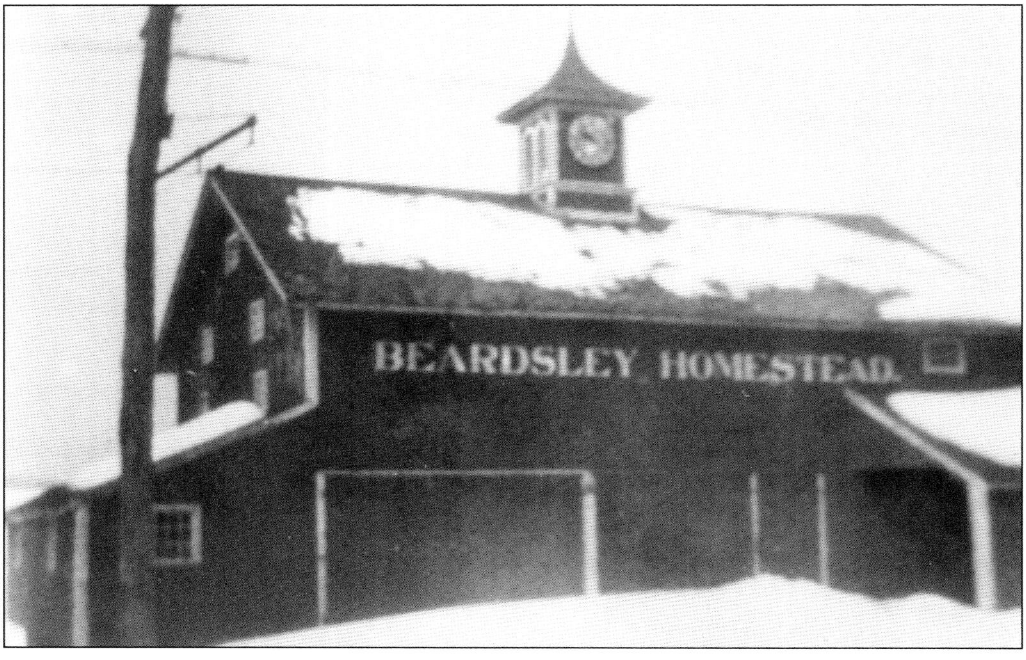

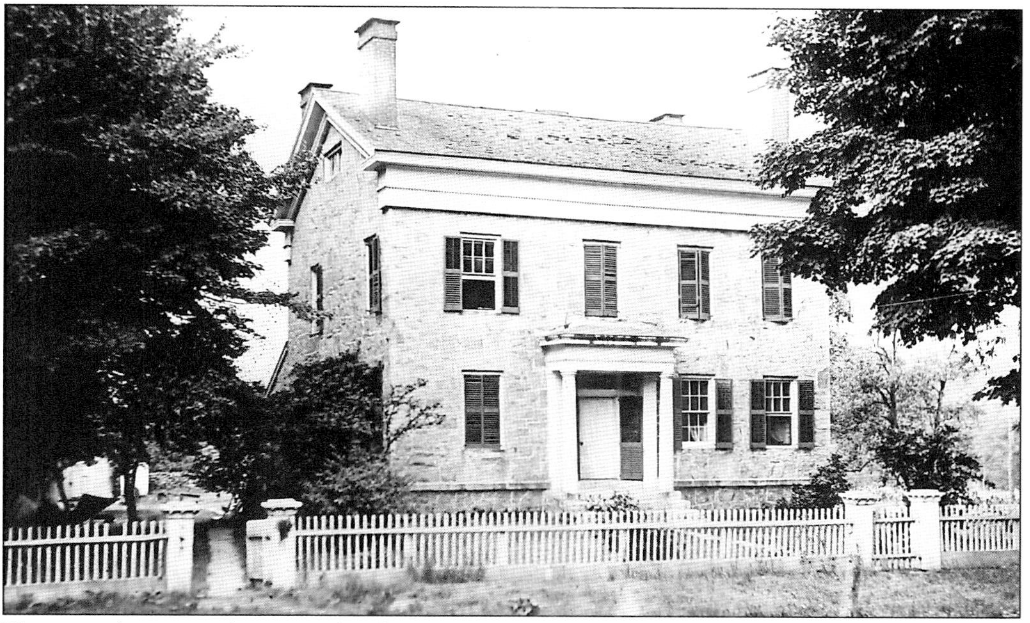

The stone house on the west side of Main Street was the Morrissey family home for many years. Stonehouse Road takes it name from the house that is still standing today.

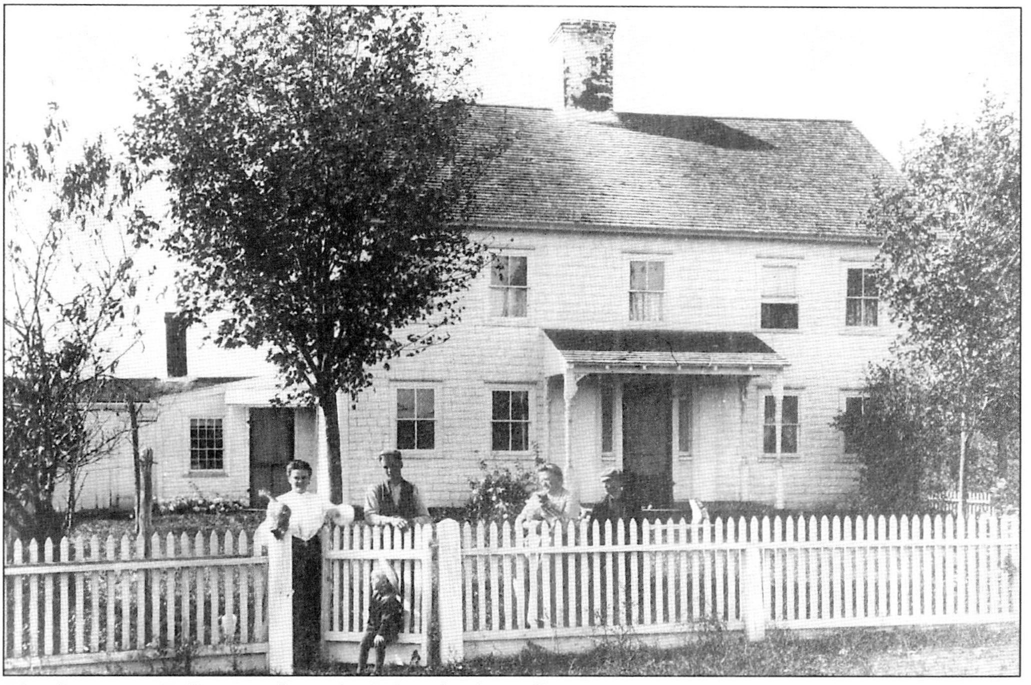

This home on Fuller Road was built by Elijah Mallett in 1798. Originally a saltbox-style home, two rooms were added upstairs to give it the square look it has today. In 1904 it was purchased by the Fuller family, who operated Fuller's Dairy and for whom the road was named. Before the 1930s, when Bridgeport Hydraulic dammed up the Mill River, Fuller Road extended into the town of Easton.

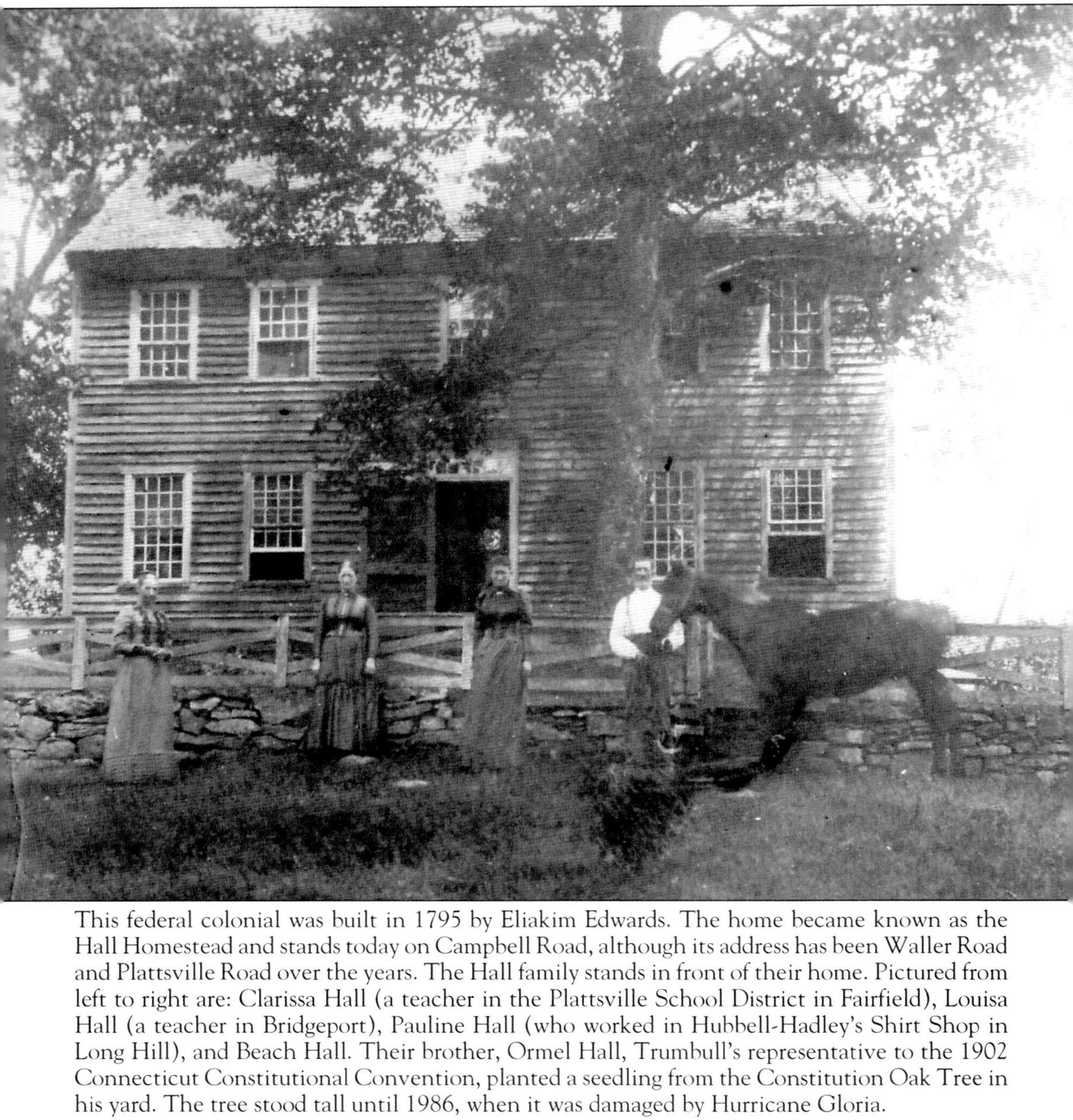

This federal colonial was built in 1795 by Eliakim Edwards. The home became known as the Hall Homestead and stands today on Campbell Road, although its address has been Waller Road and Plattsville Road over the years. The Hall family stands in front of their home. Pictured from left to right are: Clarissa Hall (a teacher in the Plattsville School District in Fairfield), Louisa Hall (a teacher in Bridgeport), Pauline Hall (who worked in Hubbell-Hadley's Shirt Shop in Long Hill), and Beach Hall. Their brother, Ormel Hall, Trumbull's representative to the 1902 Connecticut Constitutional Convention, planted a seedling from the Constitution Oak Tree in his yard. The tree stood tall until 1986, when it was damaged by Hurricane Gloria.

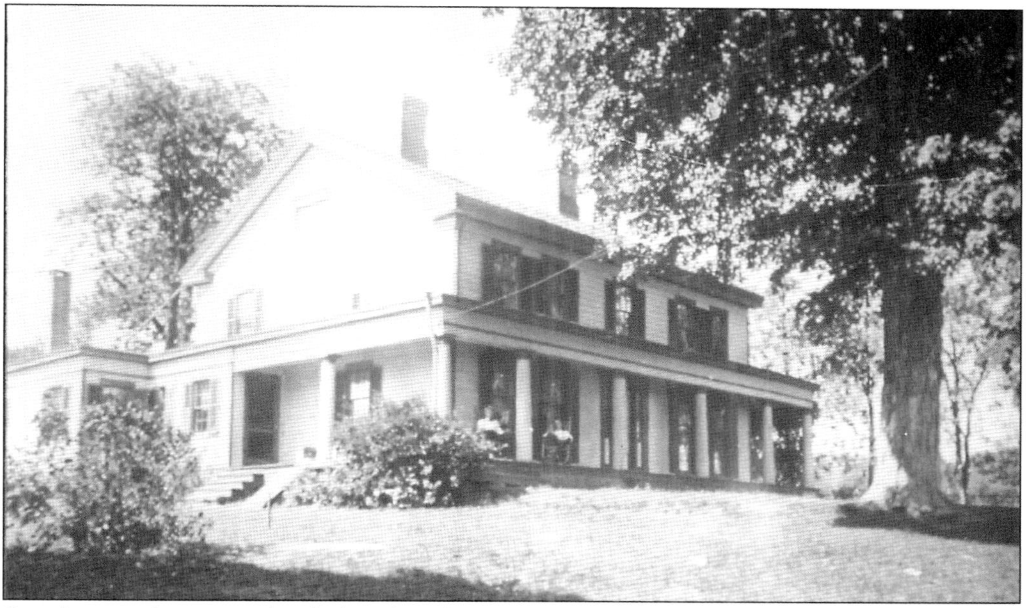

Standing on the west side of Church Hill Road, this stately home was known to many as the "Linley Farm," which is understandable because the Linleys owned it for over fifty years. No longer sporting the wraparound porch seen here, it still has its five fireplaces. Built in 1785 by Solamon Booth, its special significance to the historical society is that it was the birthplace of Helen E. Plumb.

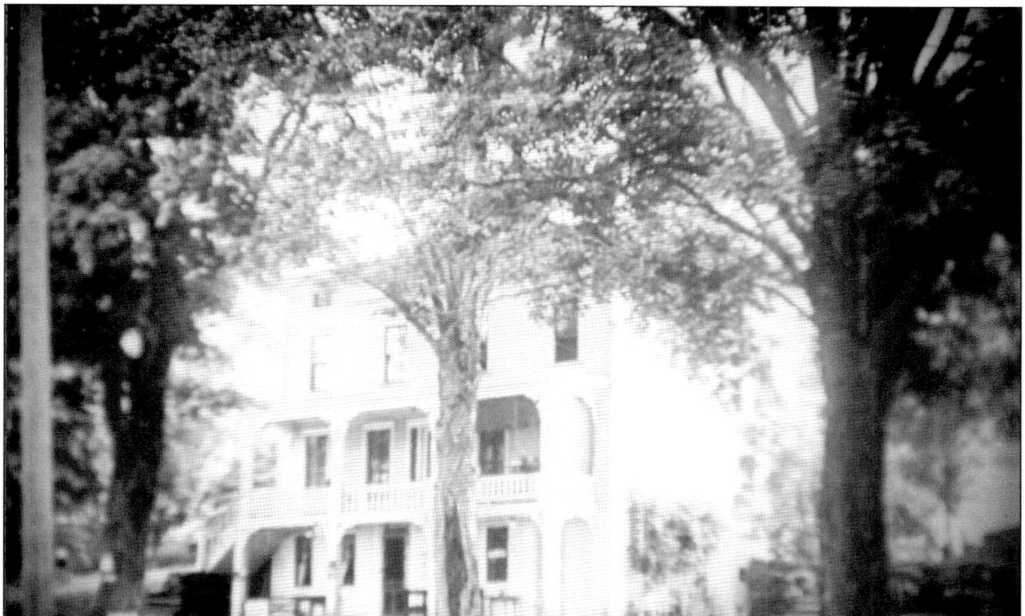

This home at Main and Elizabeth Streets has changed very little since this picture was taken in the 1940s. It once had front stairs that led to the second-floor porch. It was owned by the Zamary family, who operated a grocery store on the ground floor. It is now the Corner Deli.

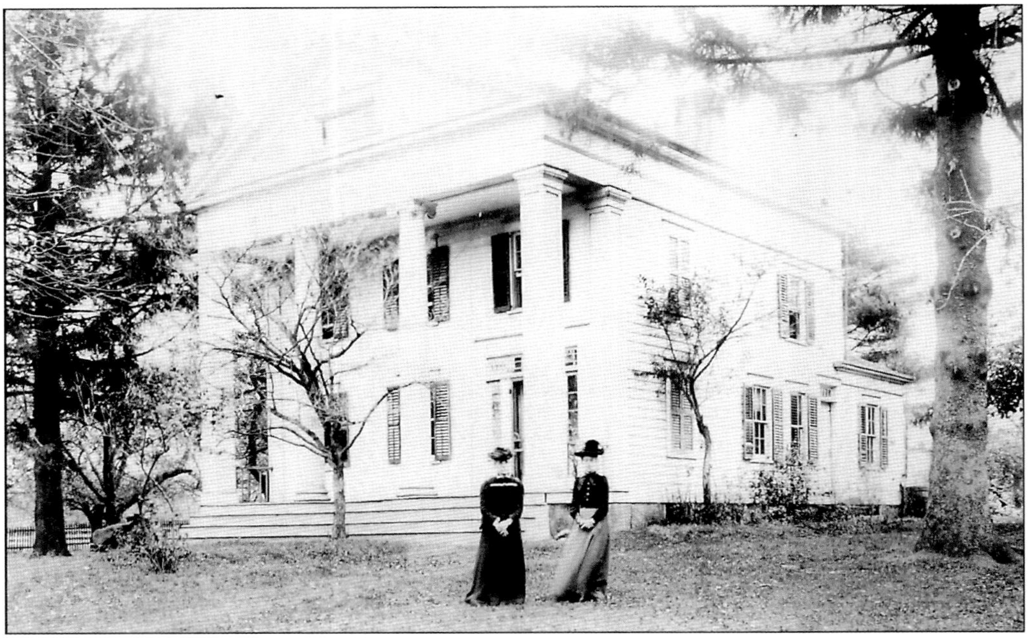

The Burroughs Homestead stood at 5924 Main Street, *c.* 1805. It was a dignified Greek Revival-style house with chestnut floor boards, hand-cut posts and beams, and four fireplaces. The home's front columns were an interesting feature, combining both Ionic and Doric styles. Two former occupants claimed to have seen a ghost here, but we can only see two elegantly garbed ladies strolling while, to the left, a cow grazes on the front lawn. This majestic home was sold in 1996 and dismantled to be rebuilt at a new location.

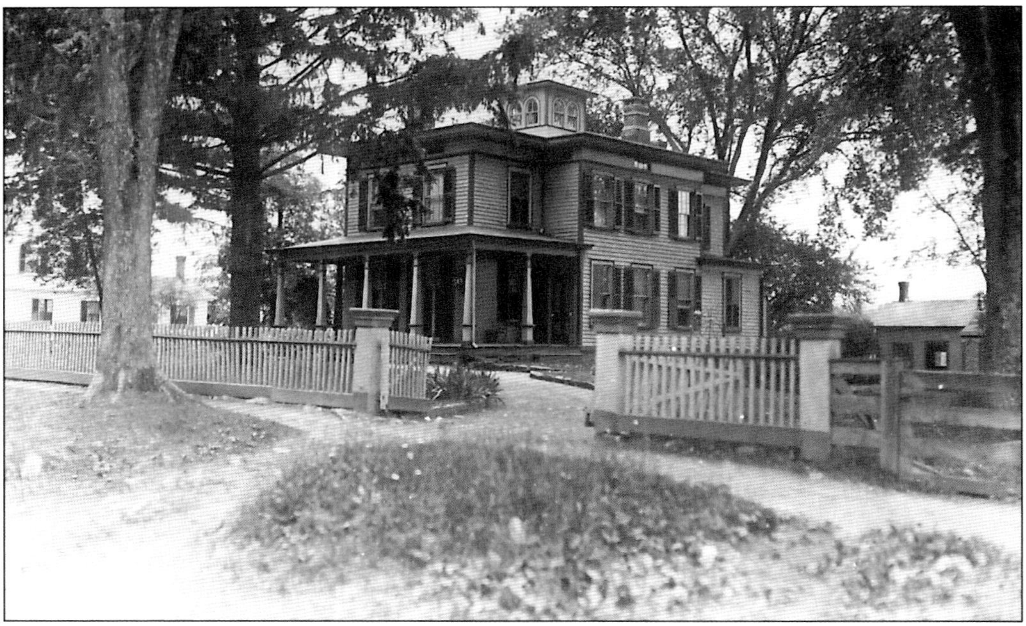

This homestead on the west side of Main Street, near Long Hill Green, was built by Samuel Hoyt in 1862. Mr. Hoyt owned a carriage shop that occupied a large box-like building on the green.

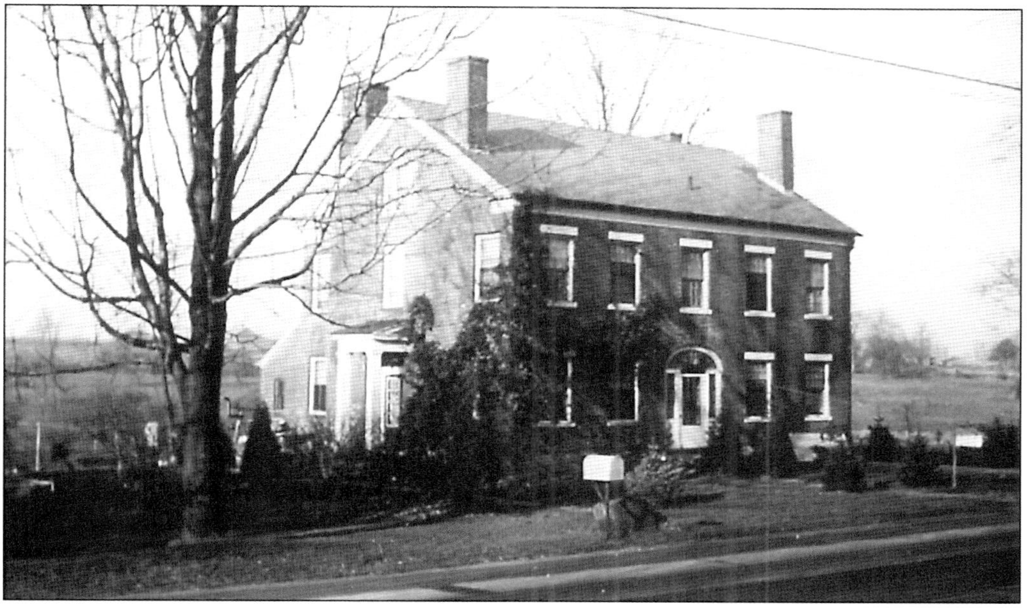

Stepping Stones, the home of Elijah Middlebrook, Esq., M.D. and his wife, Comfort, was a red brick mansion built in 1824. The clay for the bricks came from the banks of a stream that ran through the property. The house still stands today on Main Street. The fields in the background are now filled with houses.

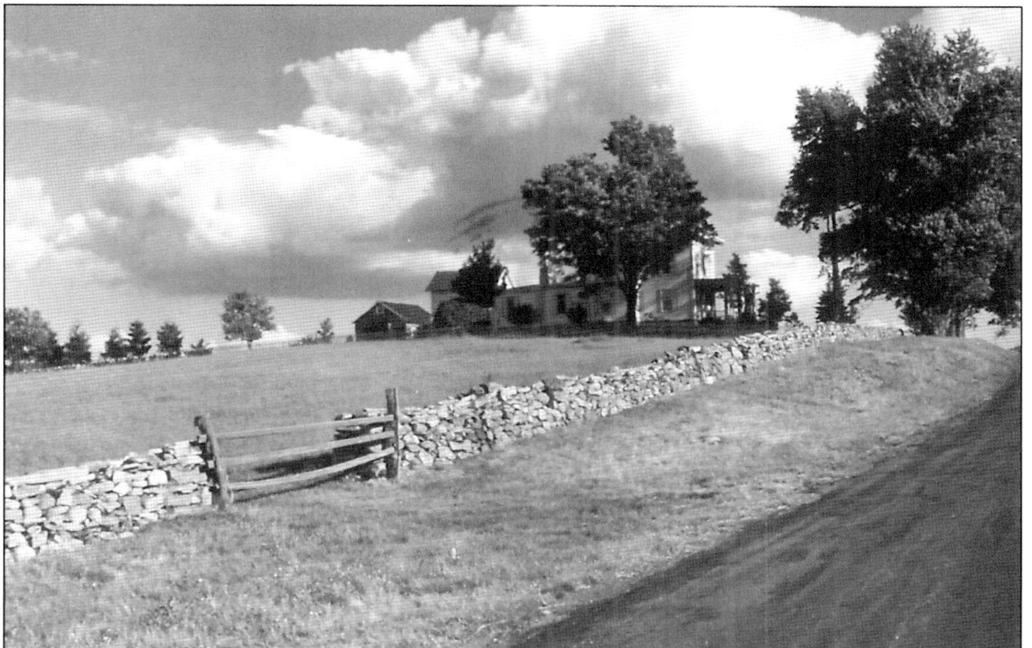

This house on Madison Avenue was built by William A. Mallett in 1860 and is an excellent example of the Italianate style. Much of the acreage of the Mallett farm is now Tashua Knolls Golf Course. The house is now still perched on the peak of the hill, surrounded by a cluster of colonial-style homes.

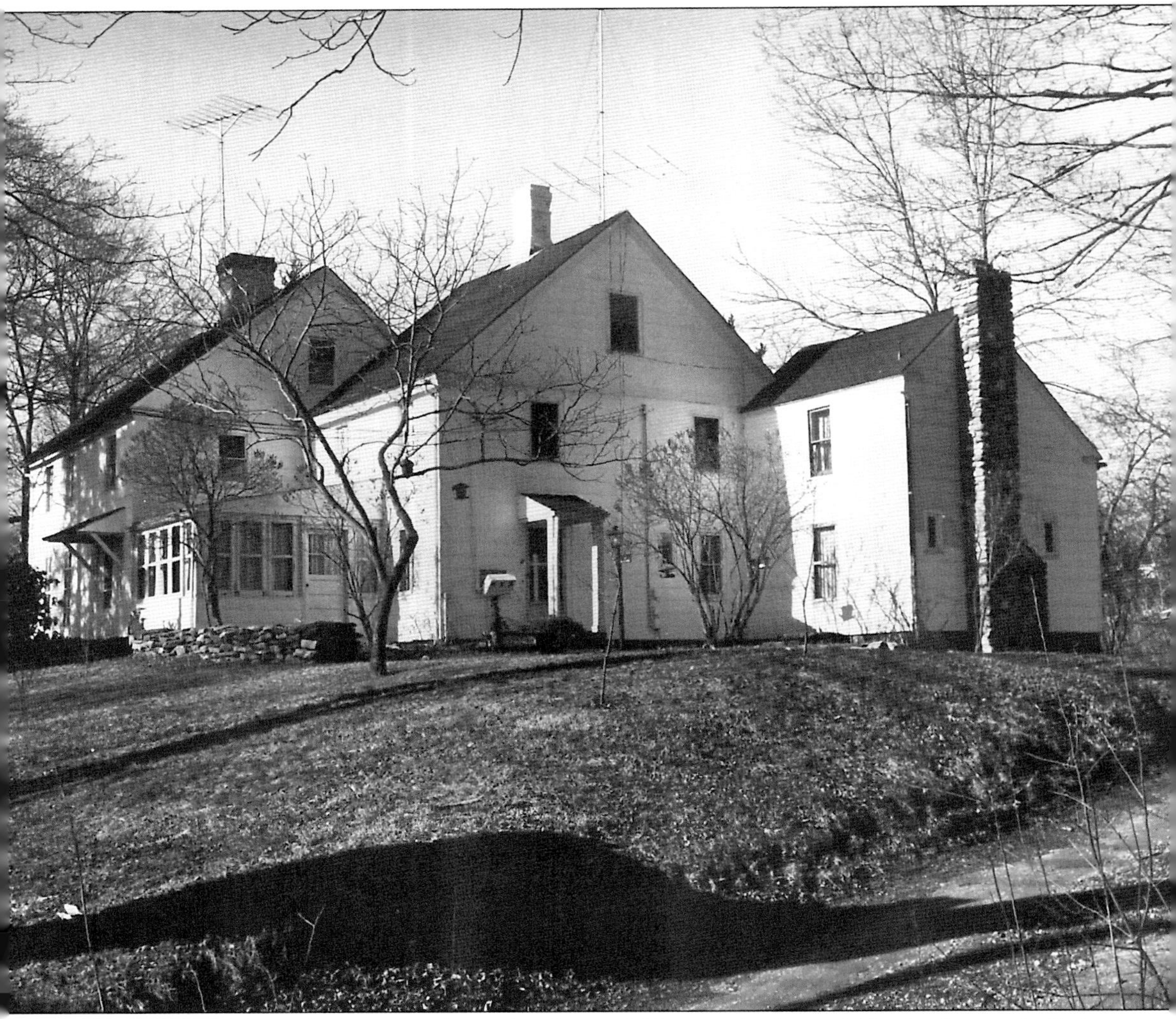

At the foot of Daniels Farm Road stands a beautiful home, the Daniel Hawley house, built in 1756. Daniel Hawley, a wealthy landowner, was the owner of negro slave Nero Hawley, who fought in the Revolutionary War and afterwards was granted his freedom. It was in the spring of 1968, in the early hours of the morning, when the lady of the house was startled to see a ghostlike black man in a grayish blue uniform standing in the doorway. He said to her, "Have no fear, I will do no harm." Frightened, she called her husband, but the ghost disappeared and was never seen again. Although she had never heard of Nero, all evidence would indicate it was his ghost. His burial place at Riverside Cemetery was only 500 feet away.

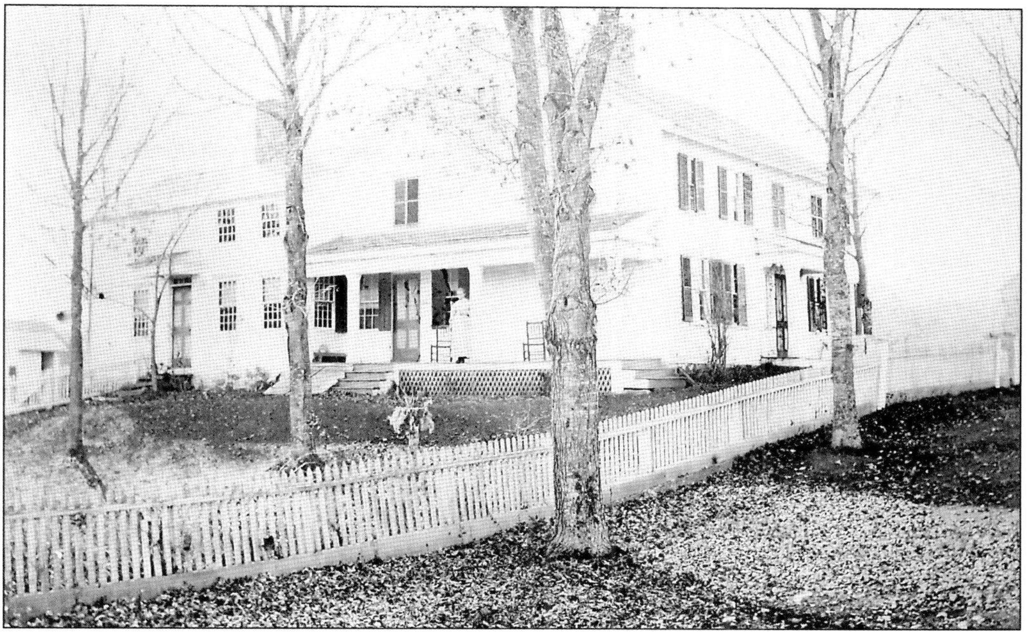

This beautiful house on White Plains Road has changed very little since the picture was taken in 1890. Occupied for many years by generations of the Booth family, it is believed to have been built by Isaac Booth in 1780.

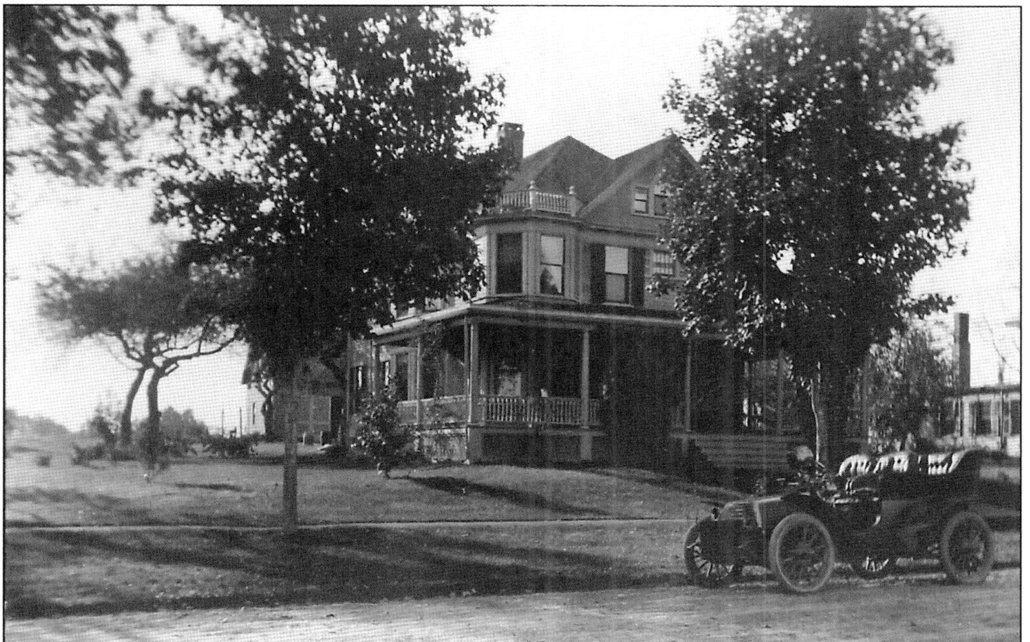

During the early 1900s, the Nathan Curtiss house on Huntington Turnpike was occupied by Frank Lalley and family. Mr. Lalley was an automobile dealer. The auto pictured in the front of the home was one of his current models. The house was destroyed by fire in the 1930s and replaced by a modern colonial home.

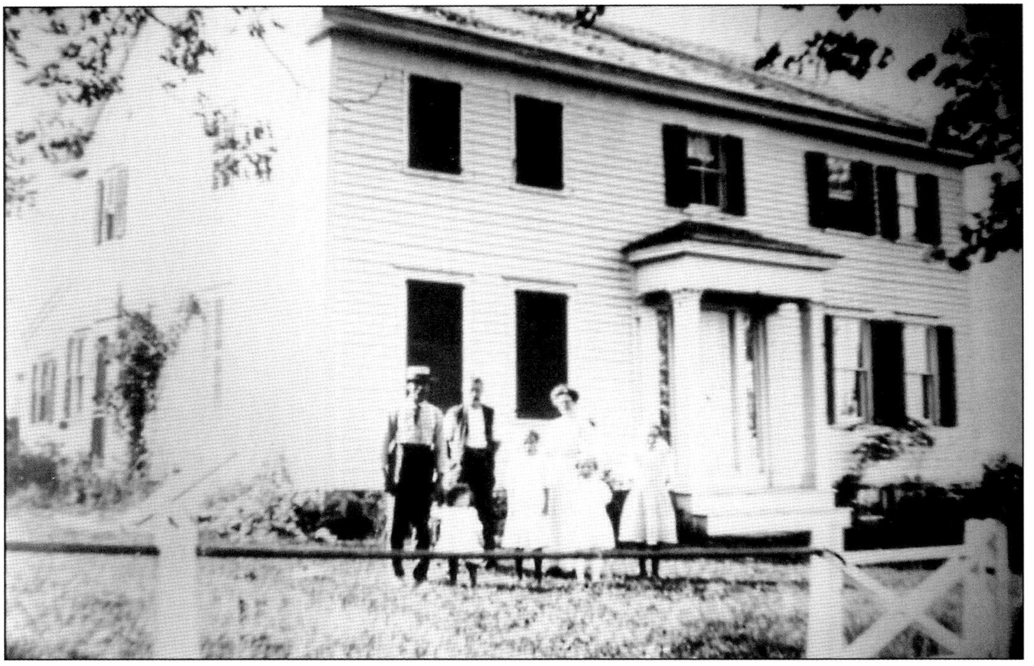

The Stephen Sterling Homestead, built in 1757, still stands on the north side of Edison Road. From the 1700s to the late 1800s, the Sterling family owned all the land on both sides of Edison Road from Williams Road to Church Hill Road. The folks in the photograph could be the Sterlings or the Malletts, who purchased the house in 1914.

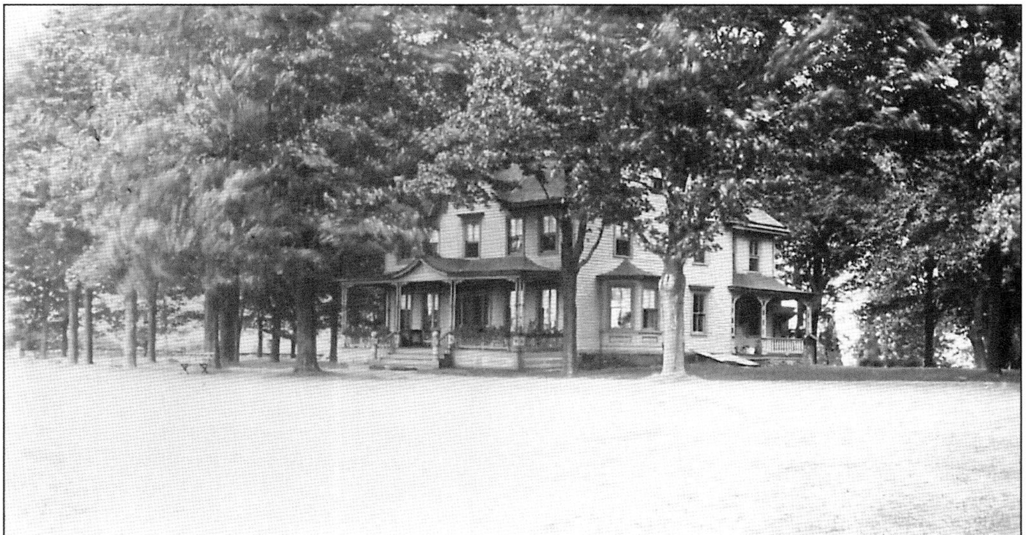

The Aaron Sherwood Homestead was built in 1880 on the southeast corner of Main Street and Church Hill Road. It was the home of Dr. Clarence Atkins, a dentist, and later the Hillcrest Hygienic Lodge, a convalescent home. It is now the site of Trumbull Town Hall.

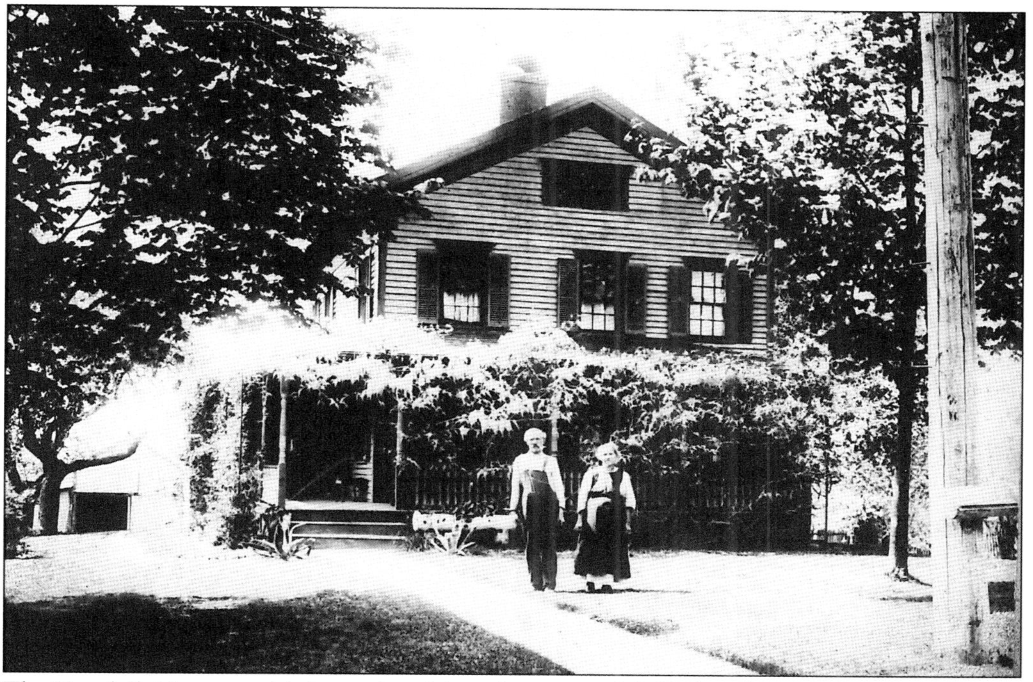

The Hauslaib Homestead is located on Main Street near Middlebrooks Avenue. Milk and eggs from the farm were taken to Bridgeport to be sold. Fresh vegetables, especially corn, were sold at a roadside stand along with strawberries, raspberries, and blackberries.

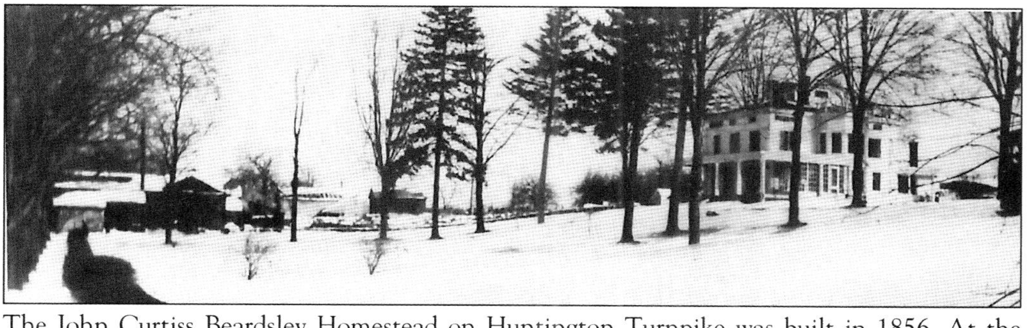

The John Curtiss Beardsley Homestead on Huntington Turnpike was built in 1856. At the time of this photograph in 1900, the house was owned by Erwin Fairchild. His store and cider mill can be seen near the road to the north of the house. Erwin Street now enters Huntington Turnpike where the store and cider mill once stood.

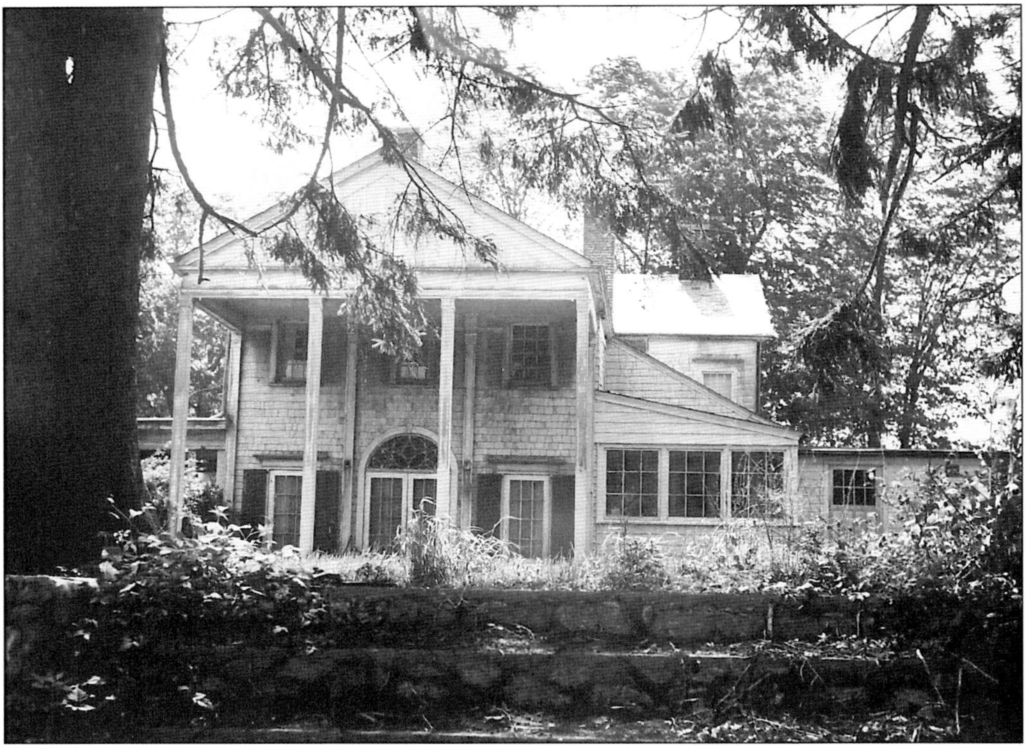

Located on 6 acres of beautifully landscaped grounds on White Plains Road north of Beardsley Parkway, many will have vague memories of this home known as Crystal Gardens. For many years, the Mundre family operated a small roadside farm stand where the locals could buy fruits and vegetables. The house was demolished in 1972. The land is now owned by a developer.

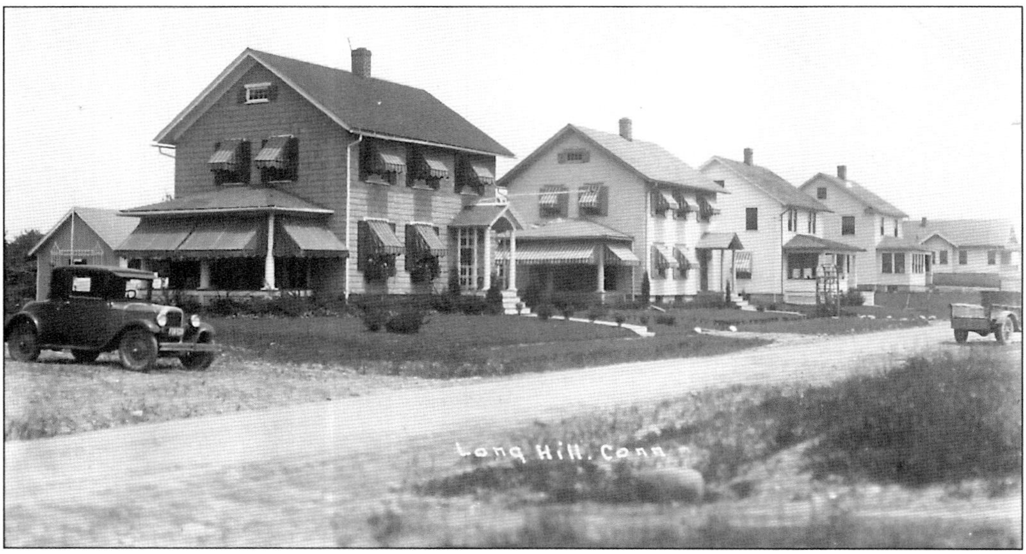


These new homes on John Street, pictured in 1928, were part of one of Trumbull's earliest housing developments. As use of the automobile increased, suburban living became a popular option for people living in Bridgeport.

*Eight*

# Spare Moments

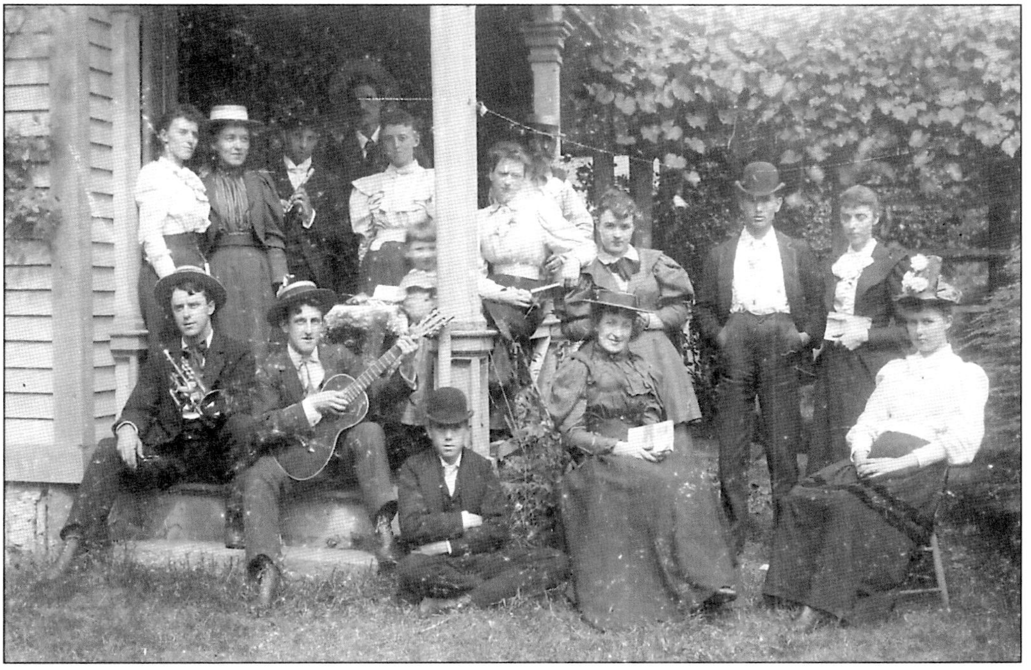

A group of Long Hill friends gather at the Walker Homestead for an afternoon of music and poetry reading. Dressed in their Sunday best are members of the Radcliffe, Middlebrook, Freer, and Walker families. Many of their descendants still live in Trumbull today.

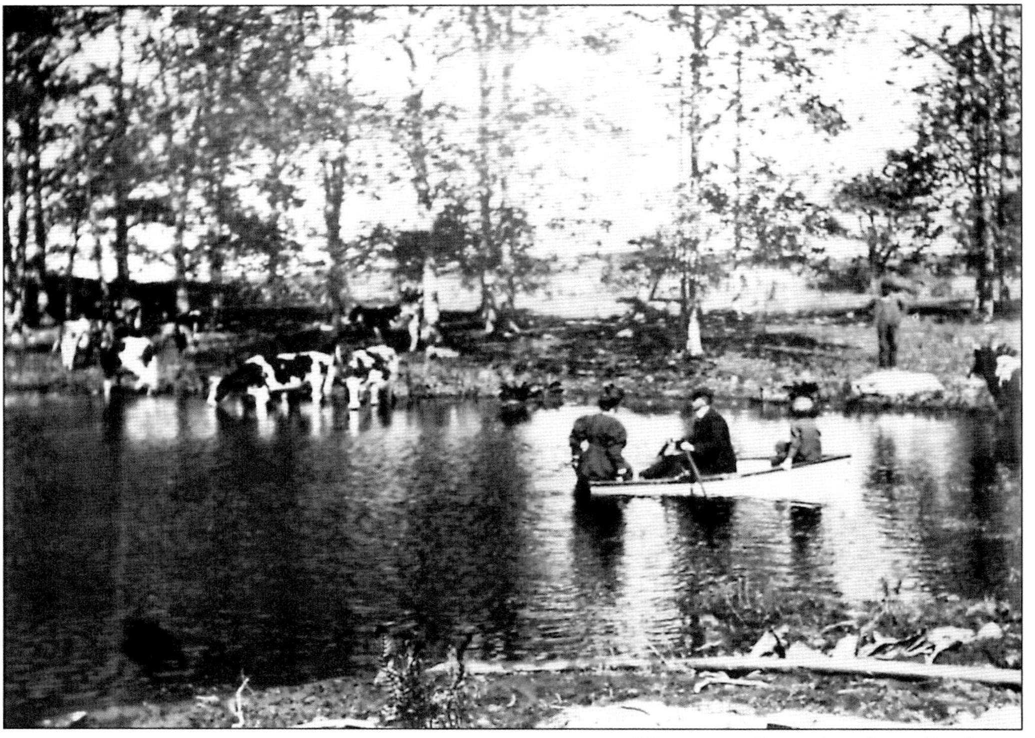

Three people rowing share Buck Hill Pond with thirsty cows on Agur Beach's Farm on Plattsville Road, c. 1906.

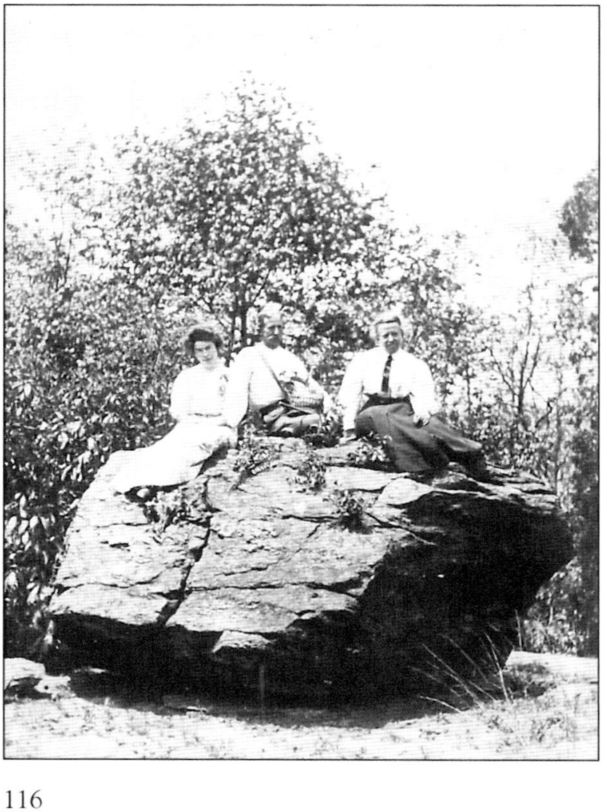

Ormel Hall and friends relax at Parlor Rock. Mr. Hall, a distinguished Trumbull resident, was a teacher at Lower Long Hill School in Trumbull as well as in Oregon, Missouri, and New York. He was Trumbull's representative in the Connecticut General Assembly in the 1850s. While serving as the town's first selectman (from 1896 through 1898), he received a salary of $74 per annum.

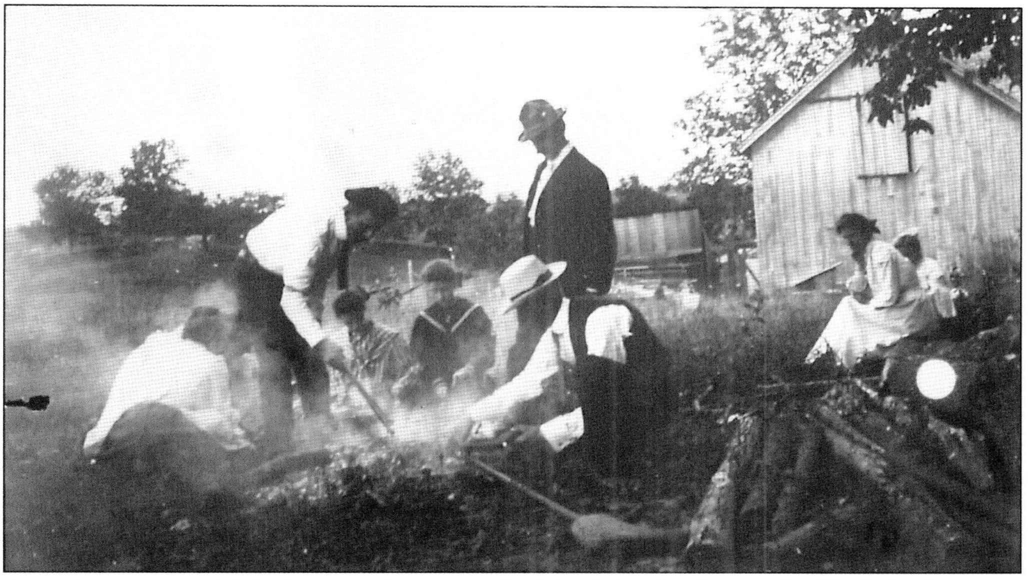

An early-morning visit by horse and wagon to St. Mary's-by-the-Sea, in the Black Rock section of Bridgeport, brought an eager group to the shore. Half the fun of a clambake was digging in the moist sand and wading along the water's edge looking for clams and filling pails for the feast. Here the "cooks" are busy preparing for the clambake to be held at the Beach Farm on Plattsville Road in 1905.

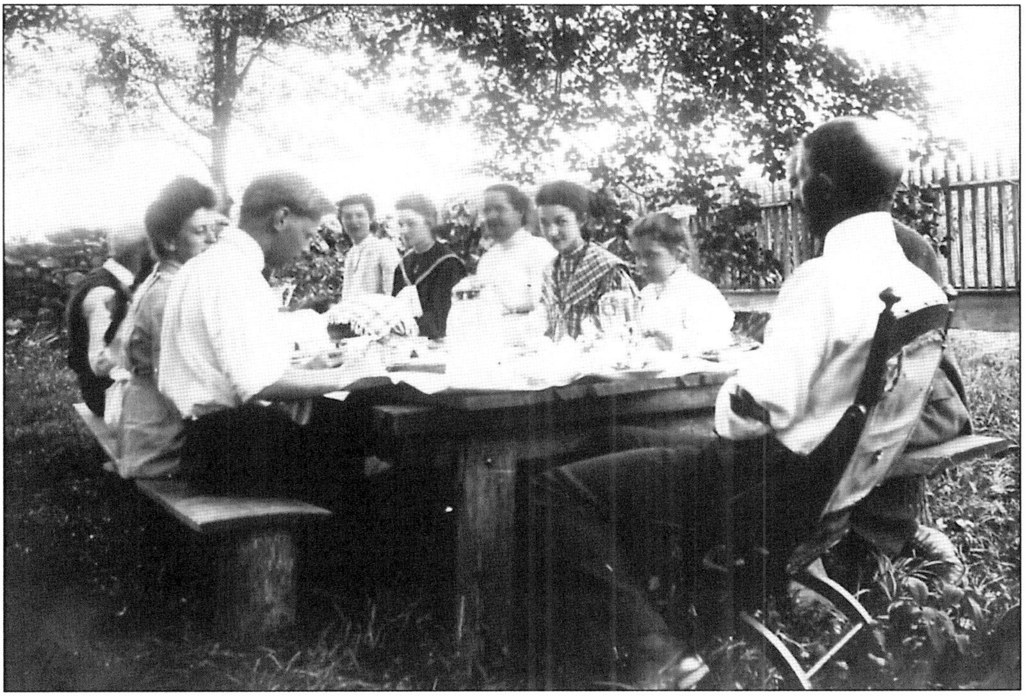

The family and friends of Agur Beach sit down to enjoy a reunion picnic. The food was so special: steamed and roasted clams, homemade bread and butter, clambroth, vegetables, and fruits. A perfect day made picnic fun for all.

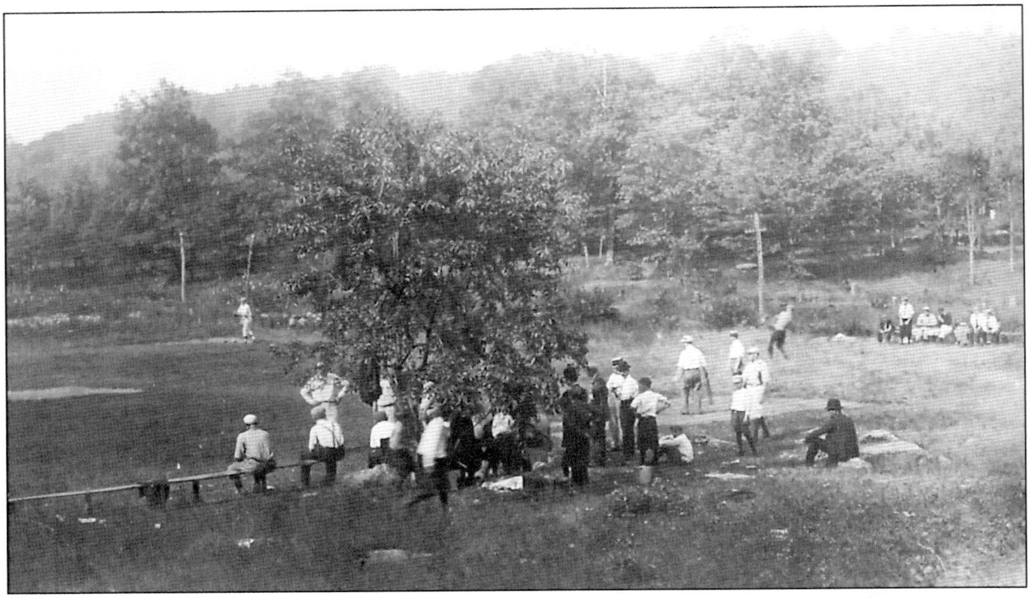

A true "Yankee Stadium," Trumbull-style, existed in the early 1900s across the Housatonic Railroad tracks to the west of Parlor Rock Amusement Park. Many exciting games were enjoyed here, a start perhaps for major-league players of the future.

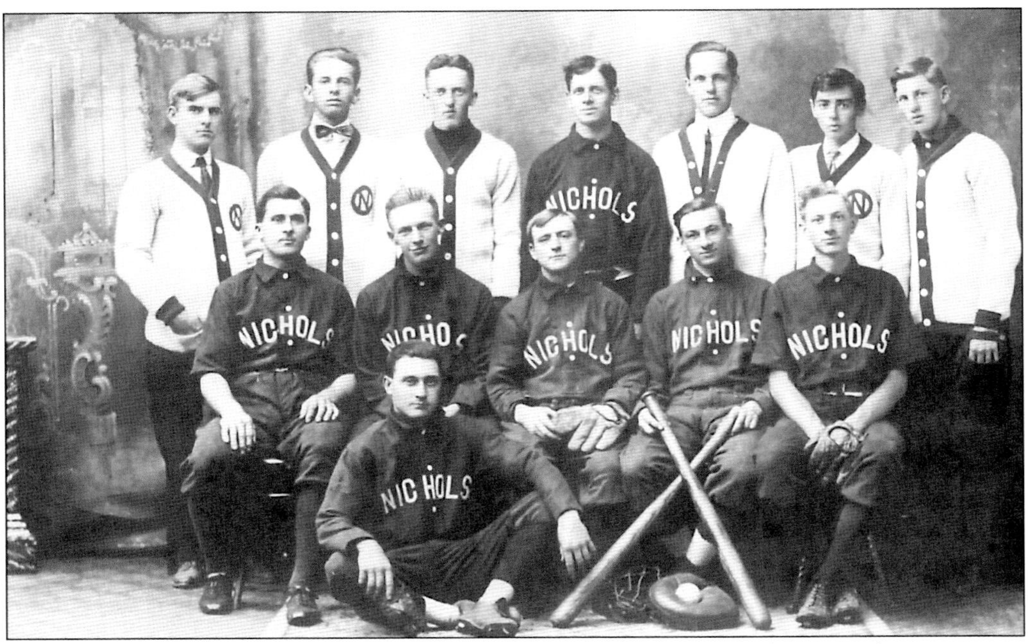


The Nichols Baseball Team is shown in this 1916 picture. Among those on the team were Lester Nothnagle Sr., Horace Wellington, Elliot P. Curtiss, and Clarence Cooper.

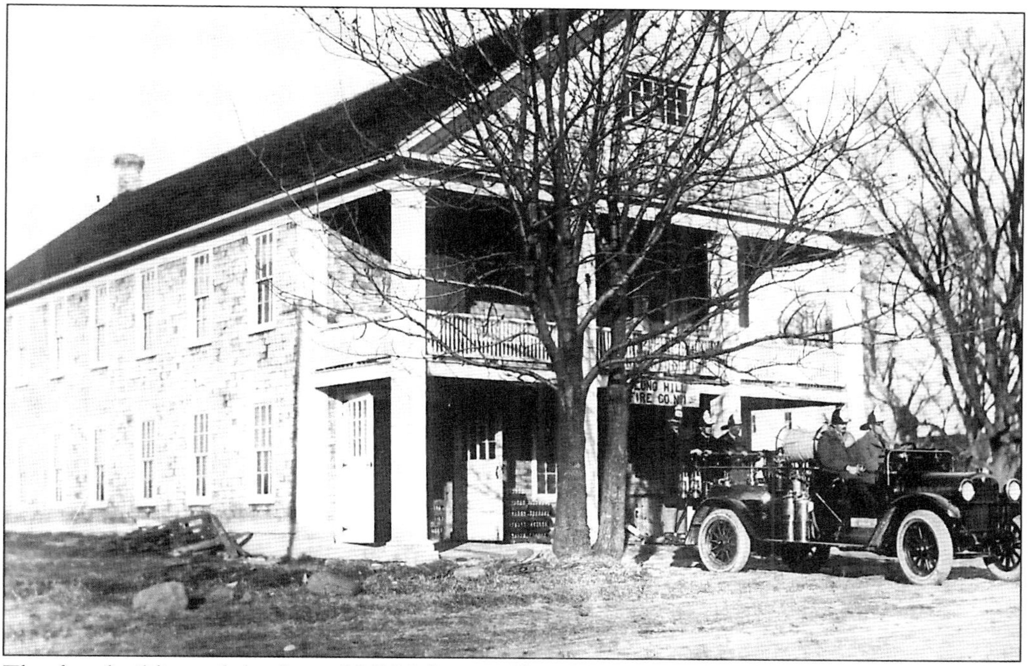

The first building of the Long Hill Volunteer Fire Company, No. 1 was erected on Meadow Road in 1922. Volunteers are ready to roll on the first piece of fire apparatus, a 1924 chemical engine purchased from Peter Pirsch and Sons Co. As the town grew in population, the station became outdated. A new firehouse was constructed in 1964 at the corner of Main Street and Clemens Avenue.

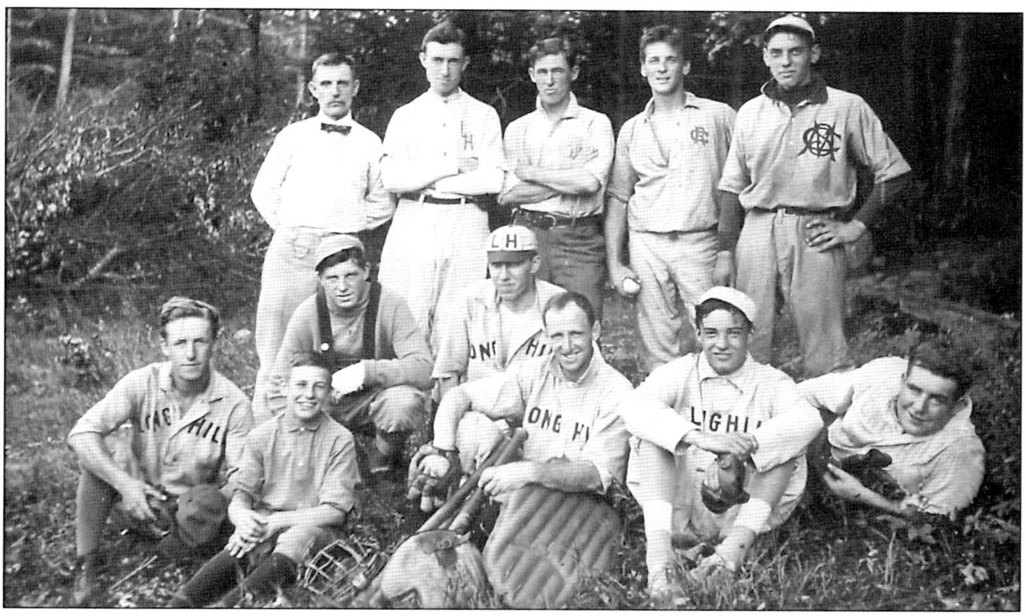

Although the fire departments were organized to protect the residents, they also provided a chance for the men to meet and socialize. This picture shows the Long Hill Fire Department baseball team with uniforms and equipment.

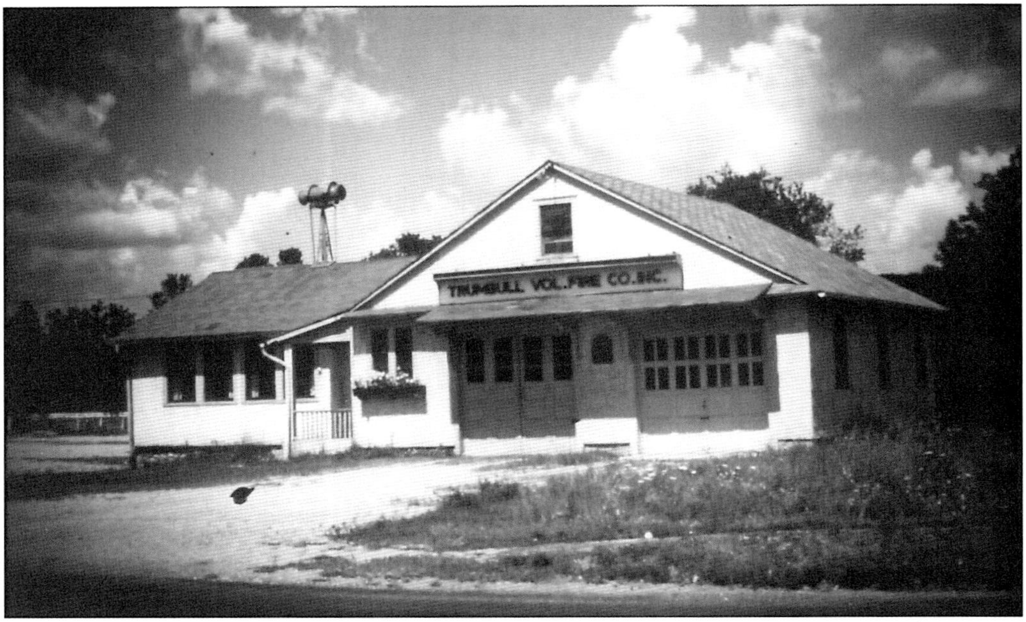


The Trumbull Volunteer Fire Company, No. 1, was formed in 1923. This view of the station in 1945 shows the addition of truck bays to the original firehouse, which earlier had been the annex of the old White Plains School. In its place today, at the intersection of White Plains Road and Reservoir Avenue, stands a modern brick firehouse that was erected in 1976.

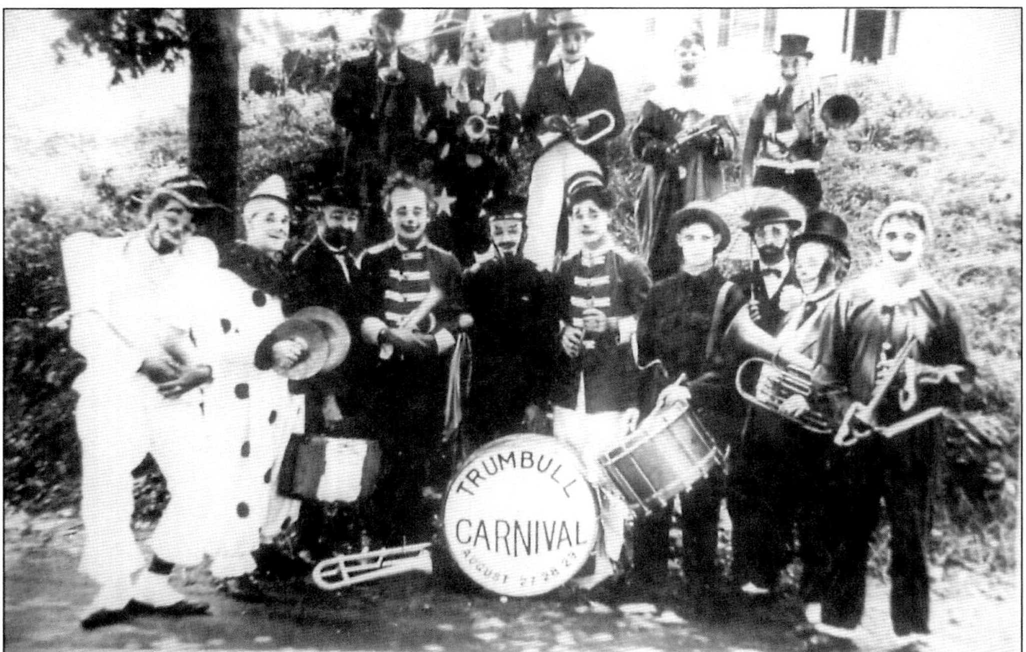


The clown band added jollity to the second annual carnival of the Trumbull Fire Department Company, No. 1. The event was held during August 1925 in celebration of the fire company's incorporation.

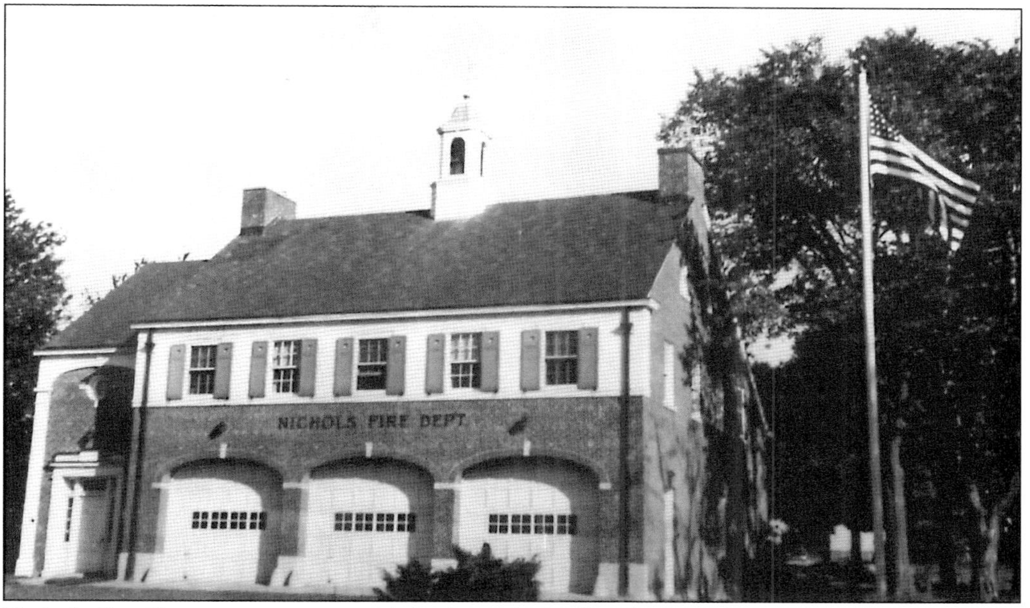


Nichols Fire Department was established in 1916. They had no fire truck and relied on the Nichols Methodist Church bell to signal fire calls. In 1919 they purchased a second-hand Model T for $350 and equipped it with two 50-gallon chemical tanks for their first fire engine. After using the abandoned schoolhouse on Shelton Road for a number of years, the building pictured was erected in 1938.

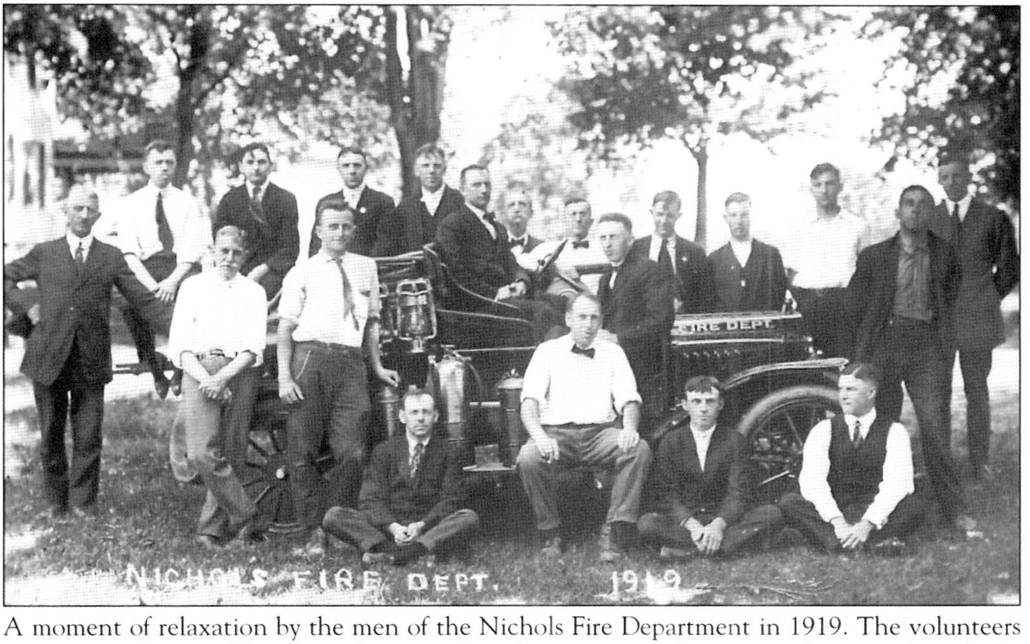


A moment of relaxation by the men of the Nichols Fire Department in 1919. The volunteers spent many hours of their time keeping their fire engine in shining condition and ready for emergencies. Junior volunteer firemen from Trumbull's three departments joined together to learn how to fight fires at "smoke-eaters school."

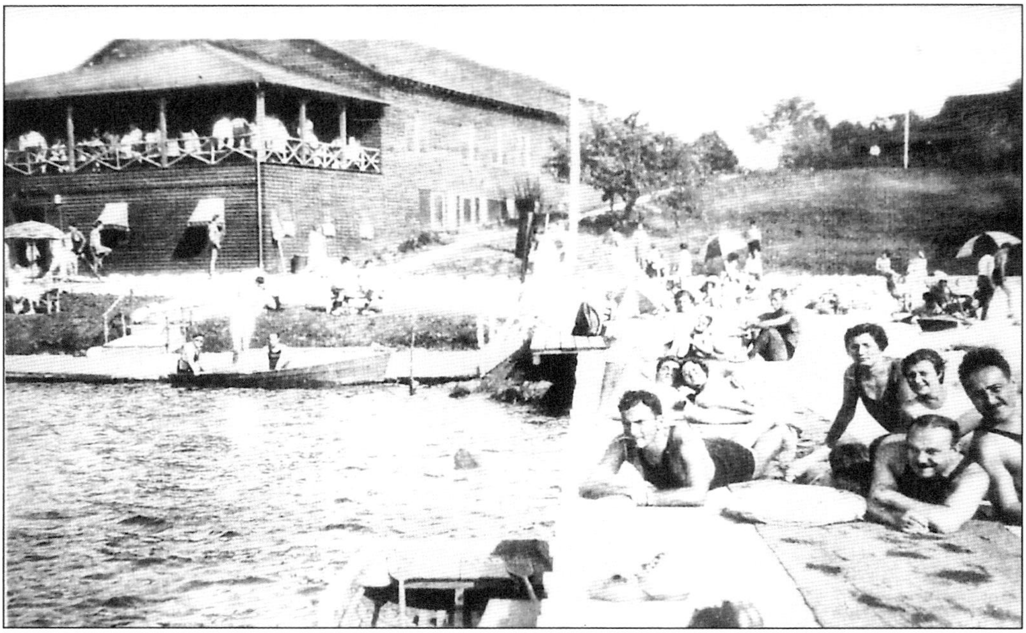

Pine Brook Country Club was incorporated in 1930. Built by Benjamin Plotkin, it was comprised of forty cabins and had an auditorium with a novel revolving stage. The grounds included areas for different sports as well as private places for contemplation in the country. Active members served and volleyed at the tennis courts. Some members found themselves resting by the lakeside at the sanitary crib.

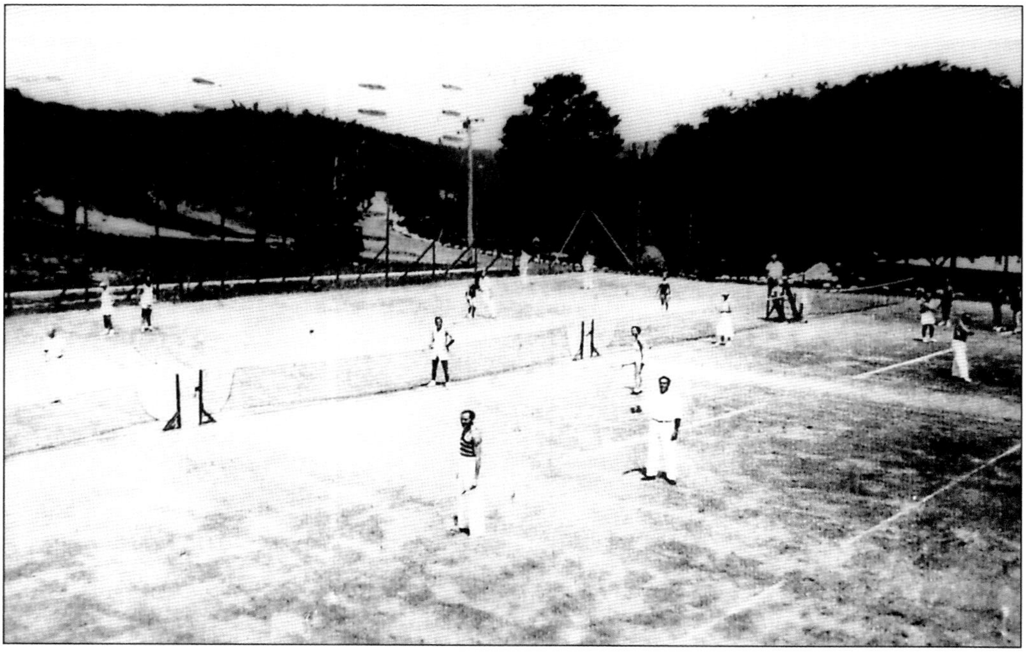

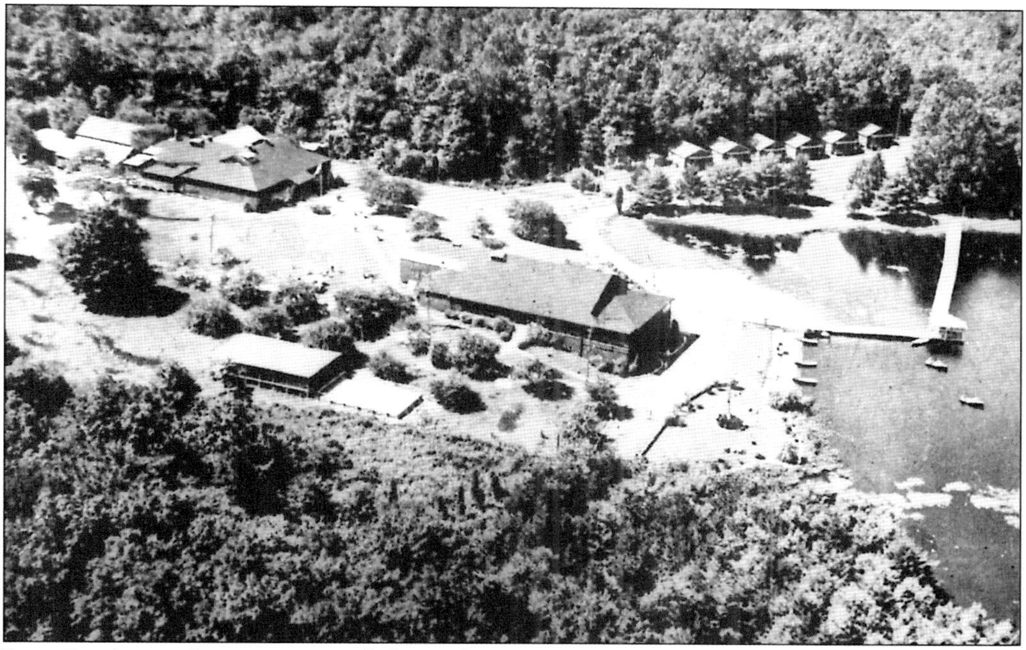

Pine Brook was the summer workplace of many New York actors and directors in the early 1930s. As many as twenty-six actors of the New York City-based Group Theater lived, studied, and acted together here including Lee Strasberg, Cheryl Crawford, Harold Clurman, and others who became celebrated contributors to the American theater. In 1944, the Pine Brook Country Club was sold, reorganized, and chartered as the Pinewood Lake Association.

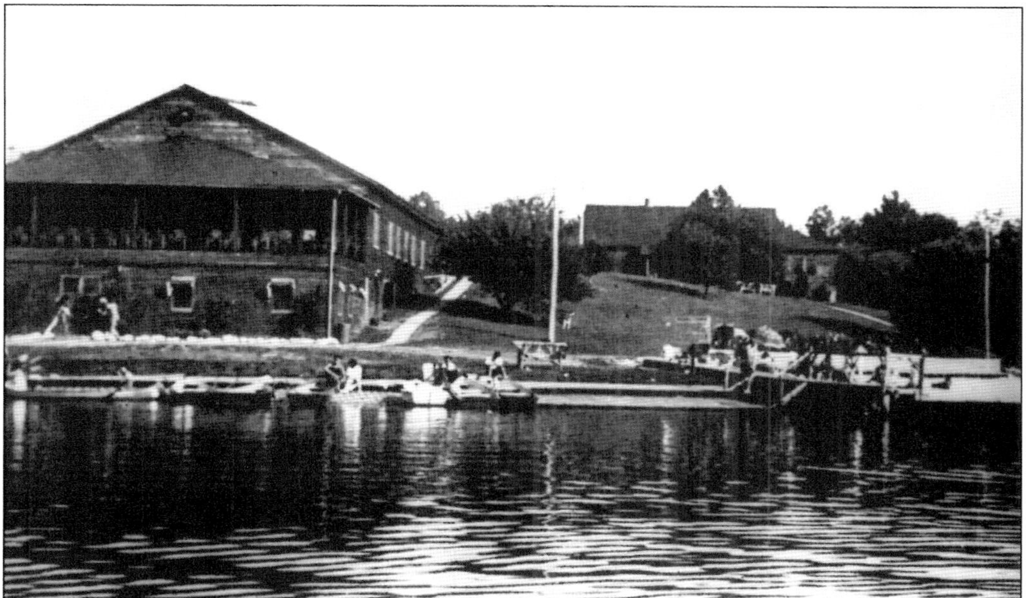

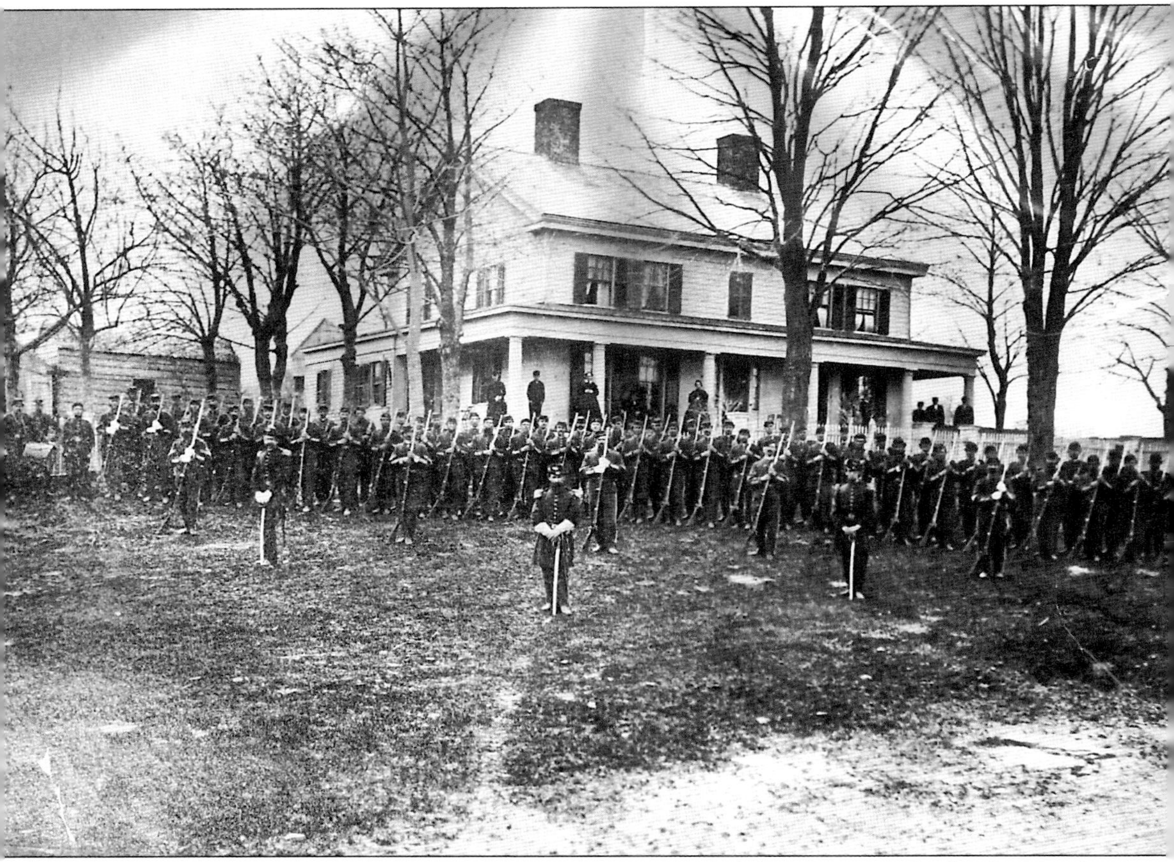

National Guard, Company C, 8th Regiment, commanded by Captain Charles E. Plumb, stands in full military regalia in 1868 in front of the Plumb Homestead on Church Hill Road. Authorized by General Headquarters in 1866, Captain Plumb built an armory for the company east of the Pequonnock River north of Daniels Farm Road. The company disbanded in 1871. The armory continued to be used as a community hall until it was purchased by S.J. Parks, moved across the river, and added to the south side of his grocery store.

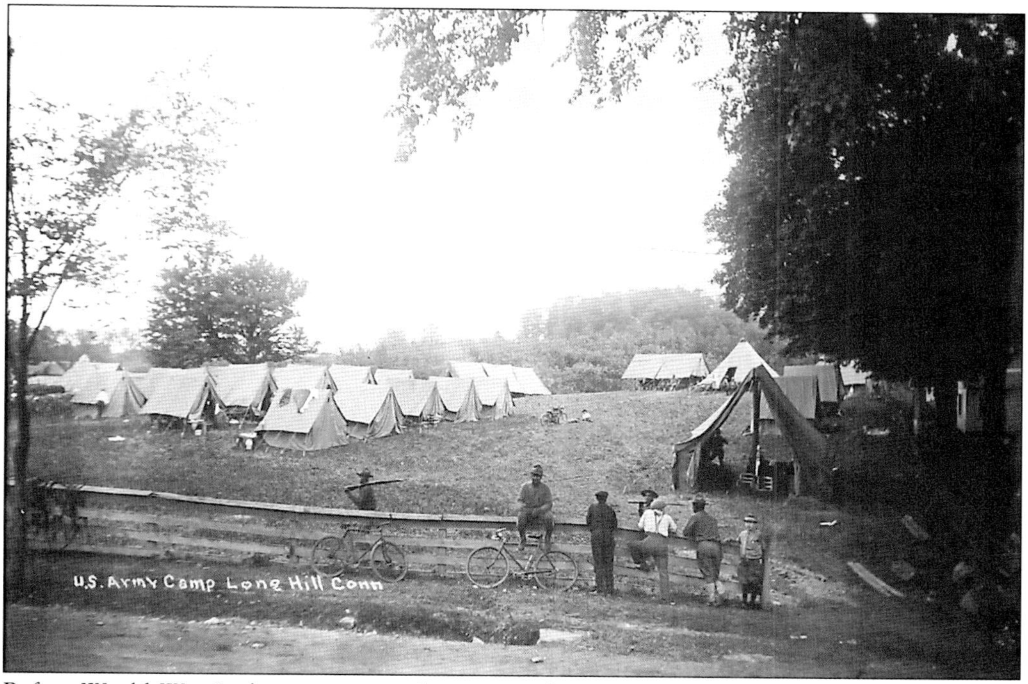


Before World War I, the troops were kept in readiness and mock battles were held at Camp Miles. It was located on the west side of Main Street at the north end of Long Hill Green.

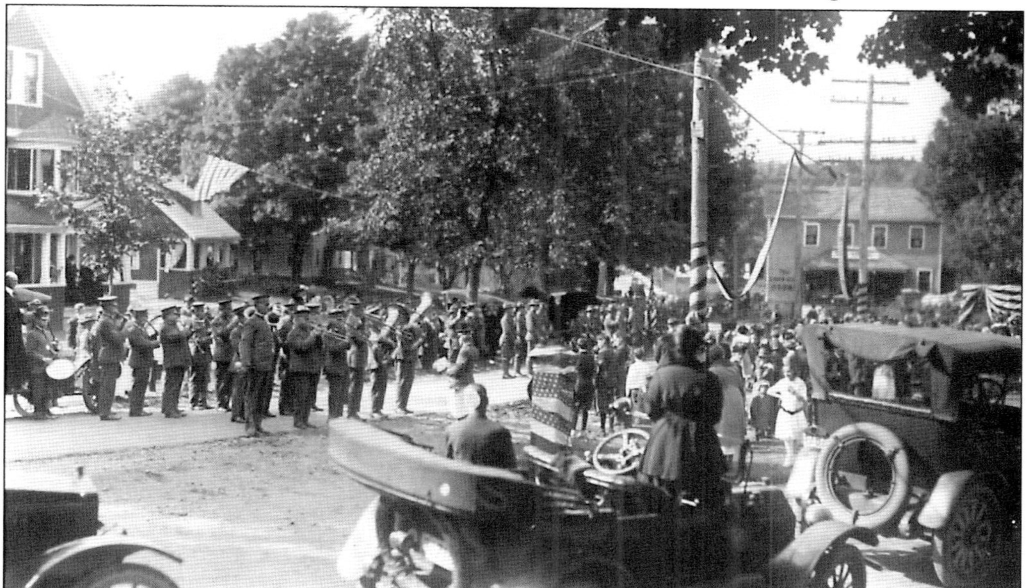

The Harvey Hubbell band provided the music at the 1919 dedication of the World War I Memorial on the Long Hill Green. In 1926 the wooden Honor Roll was replaced by a bronze plaque set in stone at a cost of $300. It reads: "In grateful recognition of the valor and devotion of the young men of this community who served in the World War for Liberty and Justice. 1914–1919." The Honor Roll lists the names of thirty-six Long Hill men.

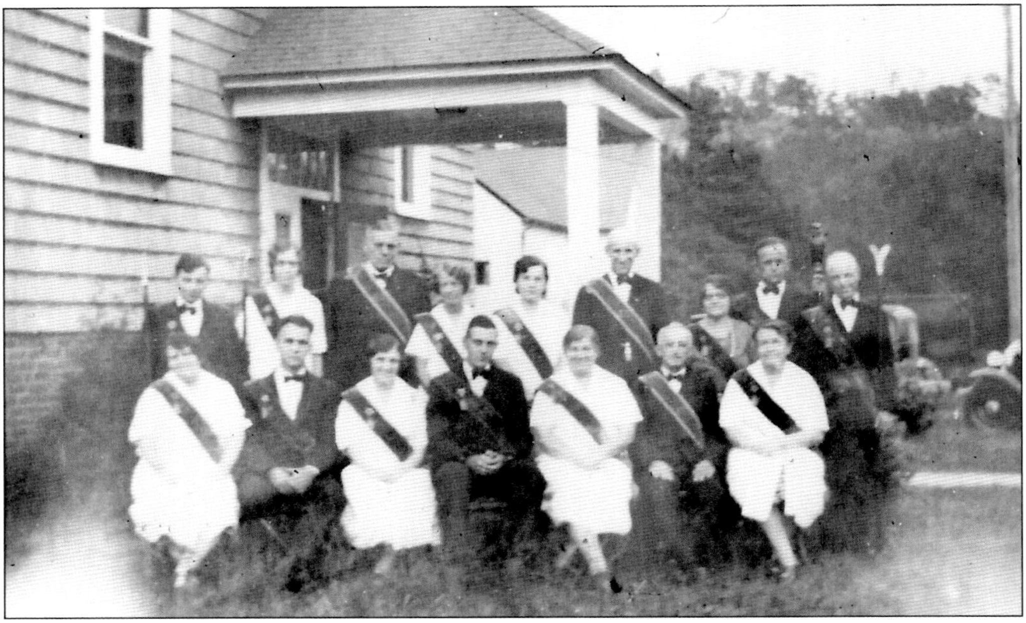

Members of the Trumbull Grange No. 134 Patrons of Husbandry, Inc. pose for a group photograph outside their meeting place in 1931. The Grange Hall was located on Pequonnock Street. The property was acquired in 1971 by the State of Connecticut for the new Route 25.

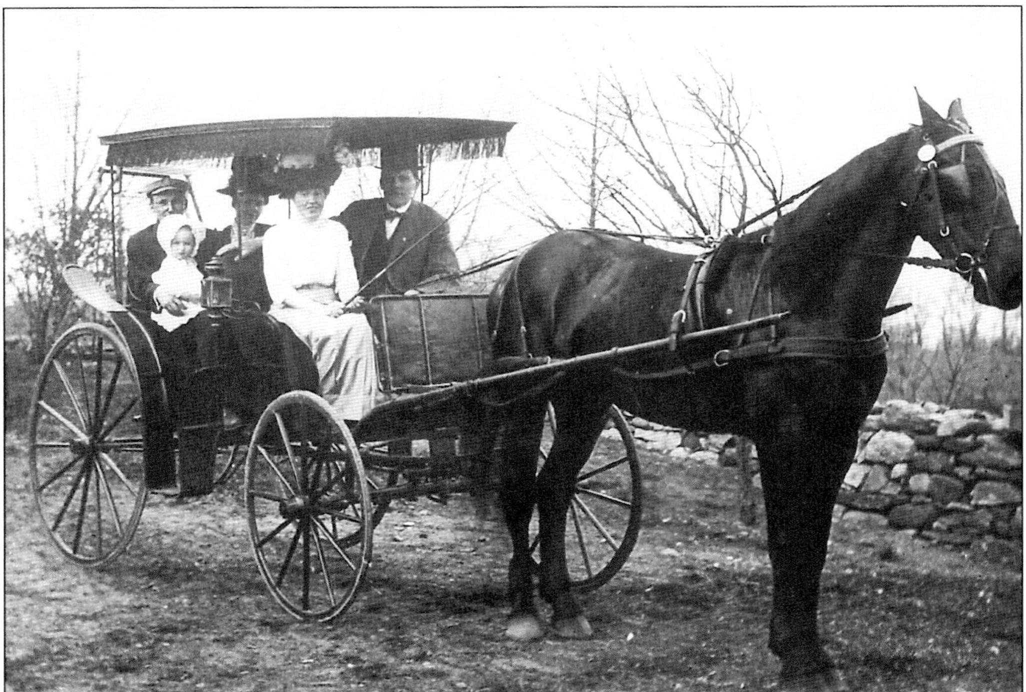

A group of Trumbull residents is out for a Sunday drive in their new surrey in 1910 on Pork Lane, known today as Park Lane. Mr. and Mrs. Gustave Anderson are in the front seat. The back-seat passengers are Mr. and Mrs. Axel Morin, and their daughter Lillian.

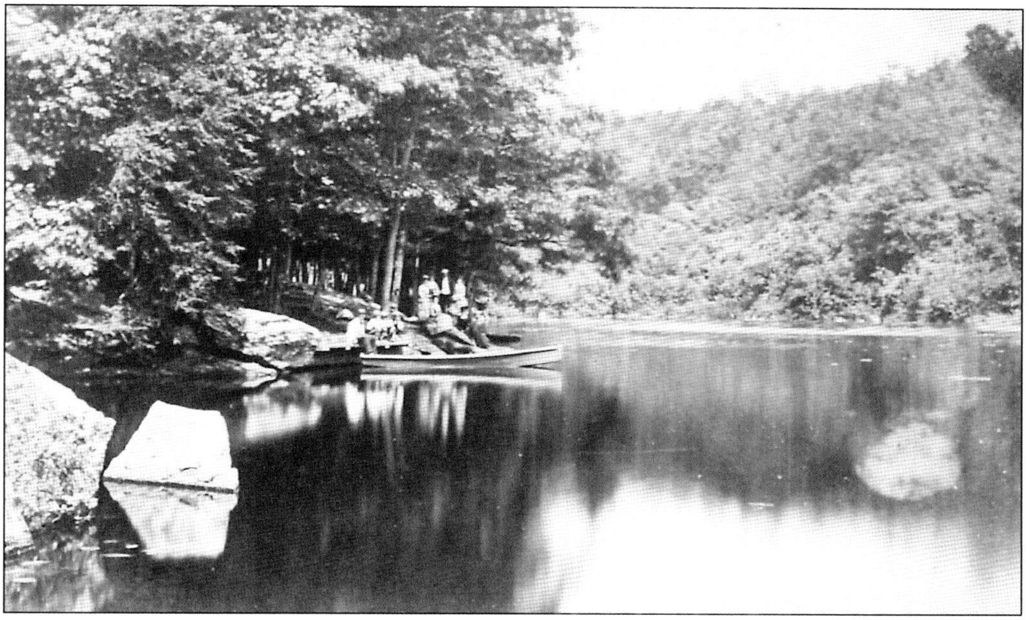

Parlor Rock was a haven for picnickers, who came from as far away as New Jersey and Massachusetts. The park had facilities for boating, a dance hall, a roller skating rink, a merry-go-round, croquet grounds, and a photo gallery. There were picnic shelters and refreshment stands serving peanuts, watermelon, ice cream, and soda.

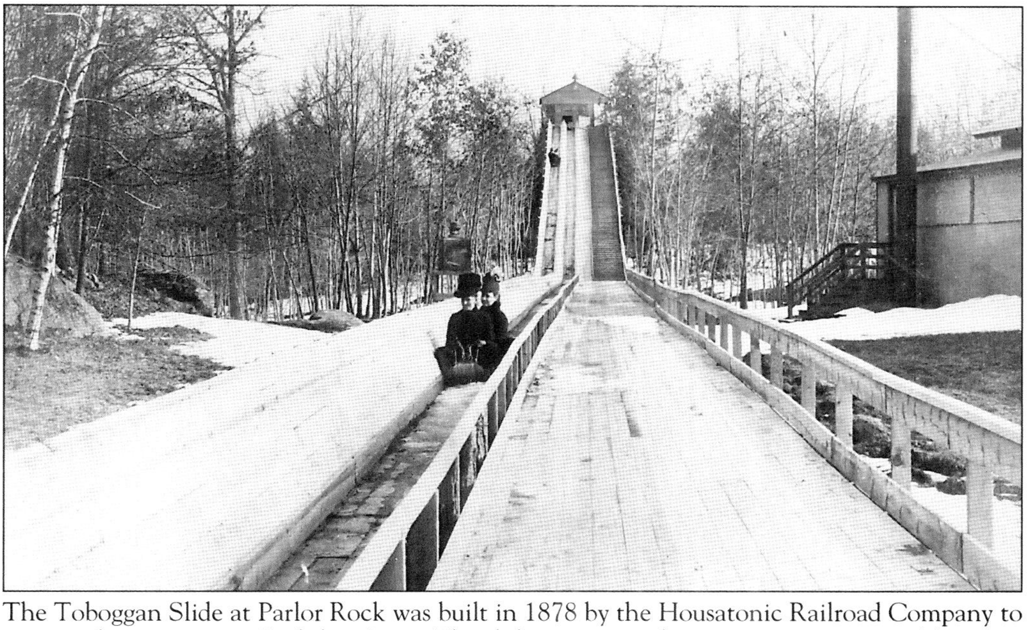

The Toboggan Slide at Parlor Rock was built in 1878 by the Housatonic Railroad Company to increase business on its Berkshire Line. The slide was a popular winter amusement. After they climbed the steep stairs on the right, a toboggan would propel the riders down the ice-packed slide onto the frozen lake.

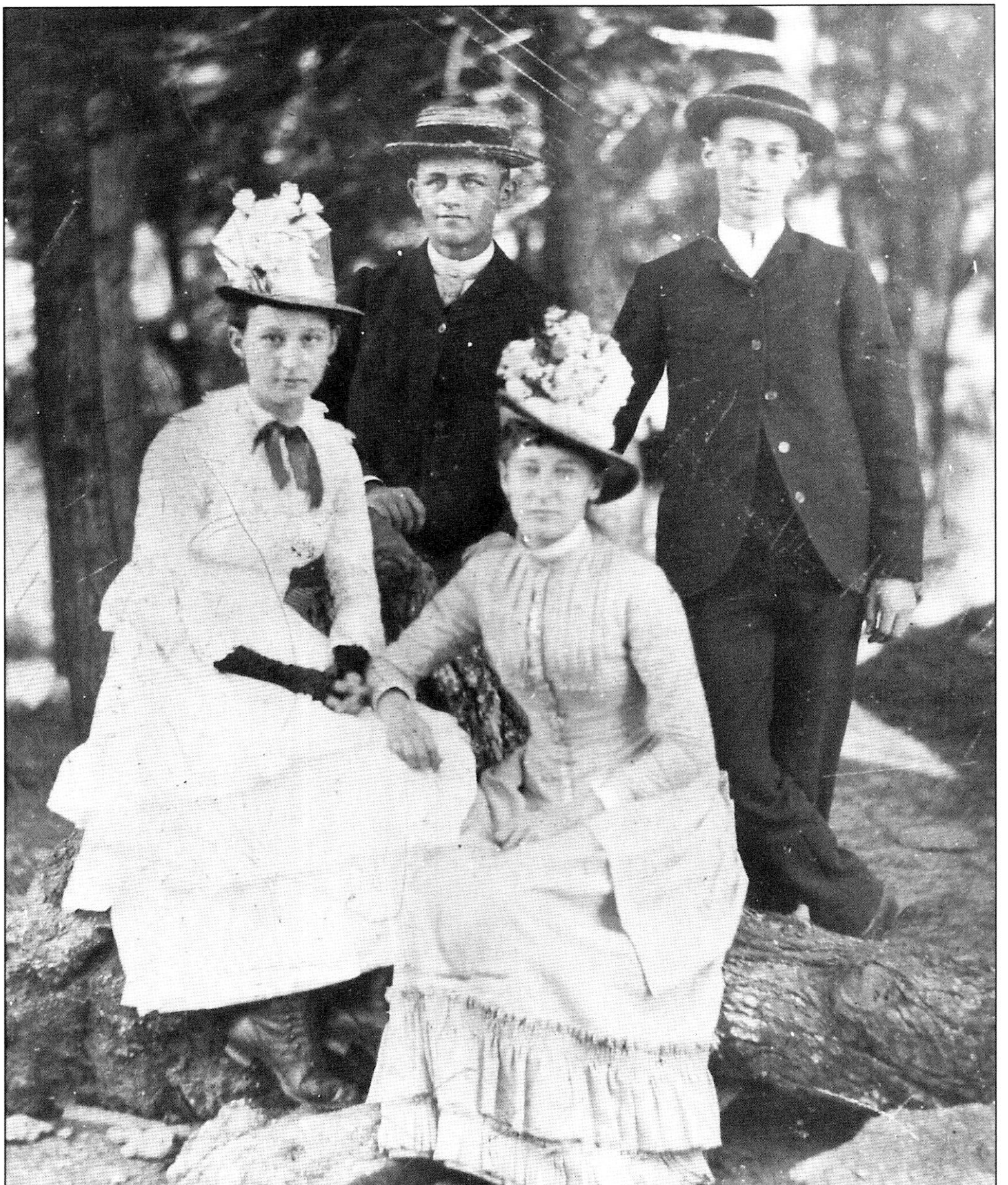

Sam and Dasie Seeley (brother and sister) and their friends pose in 1896 at Parlor Rock.